Taunton's

BUILD LIKE A PRO™
Expert Advice from Start to Finish

WINDOWS *and* DOORS

BUILD LIKE A PRO™

Expert Advice from Start to Finish

WINDOWS *and* DOORS

SCOTT McBRIDE

The Taunton Press

The Taunton Press

Inspiration for hands-on living™

The Taunton Press, Inc., 63 South Main Street, PO Box 5506, Newtown, CT 06470-5506

e-mail: tp@taunton.com

Taunton's Build Like a Pro™ is a trademark of The Taunton Press, Inc., registered in the U.S. Patent and Trademark Office.

DESIGNER: Lori Wendin

LAYOUT: Potter Publishing Studio

ILLUSTRATOR: Ron Carboni

COVER PHOTOGRAPHERS: Frank and Esther Schmidt (front cover, top left, and back cover, top and center); Charles Miller ©The Taunton Press, Inc. (front cover, bottom left); Scott Gibson ©The Taunton Press, Inc. (front cover, right); Jefferson Kolle ©The Taunton Press, Inc. (back cover, bottom)

Library of Congress Cataloging-in-Publication Data:

McBride, Scott.

    Windows and doors : expert advice from start to finish / Scott McBride.

      p. cm. -- (Build like a pro)

    Includes index.

    ISBN 1-56158-483-5

    1. Windows. 2. Doors. I. Title. II. Series.

TH2270 .M37 2002

690'.1822--dc21   2001054012

Printed in the United States of America

10 9 8 7 6 5 4 3

About Your Safety: Homebuilding is inherently dangerous. From accidents with power tools or hand tools to fall from ladders, scaffolds, and roofs, builders and homeowners risk serious injury and even death. We try to promote safe work practices throughout this book, but what is safe for one builder or homeowner under certain circumstances may not be safe for you under different circumstances. So don't try anything you learn about here (or elsewhere) unless you're certain that it's safe for you. If something doesn't feel right, don't do it. Look for another way. Please keep safety foremost in your mind whenever you're working.

For Alexander McBride, my Dad

Acknowledgments

FIRST I WISH TO THANK my friend and colleague, Andrew Wormer. As the authors of the "Build Like a Pro" series have struggled to give birth to a new format, Andy has been the able midwife. In my case, his skillful editing has been invaluable in fitting fifty pounds of subject matter into a five-pound bag. Thanks also to Steve Culpepper, for bringing me on board, and to Carol Kasper, Meredith DeSousa, Wendi Mijal, and all the others at Taunton, who have shepherded this project through to completion.

A major debt is owed to carpenter/author Gary Katz. Many of the insights and photographs in this book were gleaned from Gary's ground-breaking treatise *The Doorhanger's Handbook*. Readers wishing to delve deeper into this exacting craft will find no better authority.

I extend a warm thank you to Frank and Esther Schmidt for their crystal-clear photography. This husband-and-wife team is better known for their fine architectural portraiture, but they crossed over into the workaday world of how-to photography with cheerfulness and aplomb.

I received much assistance from the gang over at *Fine Homebuilding* magazine. Roe Osborn and Andy Engel helped in all sorts of ways, but I'm especially grateful for their advice on the scope of this book. Without it I would have wandered off in unfruitful directions. Mike Guertin gladly photographed several of his building projects and shared his experience in areas where my knowledge was deficient.

I'm grateful to the following persons for help in acquiring product photography: Nicole Welu at Marvin Windows, John Gillstrom at Andersen Windows, Tom Martucci at Roto, Joseph Johansen at Velux, Mark Hayes at Sun-Tek skylights, and June Eng at Larson Storm Doors.

Thanks to my friends John and Brenda Van Ness for letting us use their home-in-progress as a set for photography, along with John's trusty apprentice, Josh Axelrod.

Finally, I'm grateful to my wife Nancy for her patience with a project that eclipsed almost everything else, and seemed as though it would never end.

Contents

(continued)

Introduction

WHEN I STARTED out as a young building contractor twenty-five years ago, I found that there were many things I could figure out on my own. There's a wonderful commonsense accessibility to carpentry that we first experience as kids playing with wooden blocks: "First you build the floor, then the walls ..." It was different, however, when it came to millwork, the collective term builders use to denote all prefabricated woodwork, especially windows and doors. That's where things got really complicated, so I needed help.

I was fortunate to have a millwork maven at my local lumberyard. Jim Schlicting was a gentleman of vast experience in the business of getting the right window into the hands of a builder or homeowner. He probably couldn't hammer a nail, but he knew millwork from A to Z, and he was a good teacher. "The width comes first, kid, then the height. Door swing is taken from the outside, facing the door. Draw a little diagram if there's any doubt," he told me. As the years passed, Jim guided me through the arcane world of in-swing casements, extended sill horns, and reversible prehung doors.

I had teachers in the field as well. Frank Kelly was a burly Irishman who could open a six-foot folding rule to its full length in one graceful flourish. He laughed when he saw me taking measurements for the leg casings of a door. Tucking his pencil behind his ear, he deftly mitered one end of the trim, stood it upside down against the previously installed head casing, and ticked off a cut mark. "Don't measure unless ya hafta," he instructed. Frank was a door hanger of the old school; most carpenters today shoot for a ⅛-in. gap between the door and the jamb, but Frank's standard was the thickness of a dime.

In this book, I'll share the gist of what I've learned about this complex, sometimes tedious, but always critical aspect of building and remodeling. Such a book cannot hope to be comprehensive, especially considering the explosion of new options and materials in today's rapidly changing millwork industry. But with such a valuable commodity at stake, a primer on millwork seems eminently worthwhile. Pound for pound, doors and windows are the most costly architectural components in a home, with the possible exception of cabinetry. A little knowledge will go a long way when you peruse the Andersen catalog or Home Depot delivers your new patio door. Hopefully, this book will shed some light on a difficult subject. The rest is up to you.

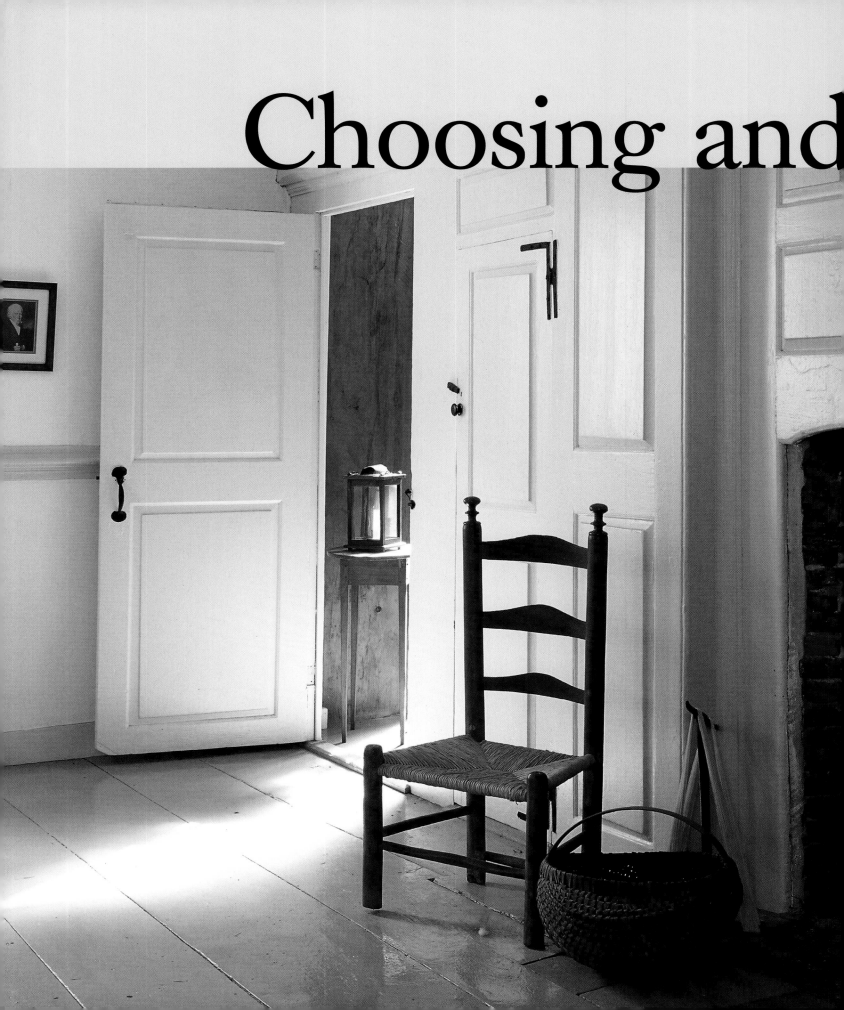

CHAPTER ONE

Specifying Doors

Choosing a door may seem simple, but choosing and ordering the *right* door involves many decisions. First and foremost is the location: Is it an interior or an exterior door? You also need to consider the purpose of the door, its width, and the clearance space around it, which will determine what type of door operating system works best. Next, you'll need to choose the door's material and design by taking into account the style of your house and the décor of the rooms. Finally, you'll identify all the specifications for your door. This chapter explains all the options so that you can select the right door to meet your needs and order exactly what you want.

1 Door Operating Systems, p.4

2 Styles and Materials, p.6

3 Ordering Doors, p. 12

Specifying Door Swing

The safest way to avoid a mistake when ordering a prehung door is to draw a small bird's-eye view of the door swing on the order form. That way, the supplier can call it whatever he or she wants, but you'll be covered. (For exterior doors, indicate the interior and the exterior sides of the opening.) How do you determine the swing? Try the "butt in the butts" method. Stand in the door opening with your butt (as in buttocks) to the butts (as in hinges). Use your arm to mimic the swing of the door. If you use your right arm, the door is a right-handed door; if you use your left arm, it is a left-handed one.

IN DETAIL

Mirrored Bypass Doors

Mirrored bypass doors are sold in kit form to fit standard-size openings. Unlike most interior bypass doors, mirrored doors roll on a floor track, which sustains their weight.

Door Operating Systems

Before you select a style of door or its construction materials, you need to determine the door's location and its intended function. The traditional hinged single door doesn't work in every case. You need to consider the direction in which the door opens and whether you have sufficient clearance. Also, a single large door probably won't work for a very wide opening. Fortunately, there are several door operating systems to suit nearly every application.

The hinged single door

The most common type of door is the hinged single door. For interior applications, hinged single doors are used between rooms and on small- to medium-size closets. If you order prehung hinged doors, you must specify the hand or swing. This is the direction in which the door opens, a critical factor depending on the location of the door. Most exterior hinged single doors open into the interior (called in-swing doors), though out-swing versions are available, too.

Hinged double doors

A hinged single door is often too heavy to use in a very wide opening. A double door solves the problem by dividing the weight in two. When used for closets, hinged double doors permit full access to the closet's interior. Double French doors are often used between a living room and a dining room. They serve as an elegant screen that distributes light between adjacent rooms.

Hinged double interior doors can be secured with catches or locks and bolts. With catches, both doors can be opened and shut indepen-

Door operating systems

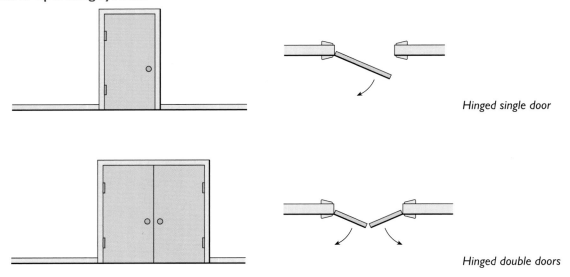

Hinged single door

Hinged double doors

TRADE SECRET

If you don't want to risk a mistake on the hand of a door, you can order a reversible prehung unit. Its hinges are placed equidistant from the top and the bottom of the door, and its lock bore is located in the center of the height of the door. Since a reversible prehung door is symmetrical in height, you can turn it end for end to swing either way. The main drawback of a reversible prehung door is that the lock is located 2 in. higher than the standard 38 in. above the floor.

dently of each other. For a more positive closing arrangement, one door (the *semiactive* one) is secured in position with sliding bolts; the other door (the *active* one) latches and/or locks to the stationary door.

For exterior applications, hinged double doors appear most frequently as French doors that open onto a deck or patio, though solid double doors are occasionally used for front entrances. Exterior double doors are harder to weatherstrip than single doors, because the stile of the semiactive door isn't totally fixed. Consequently, you should avoid hinged double doors unless you really need the wide opening.

Center-hinged double doors have one permanently fixed door and one operating door. The fixed door, which is rigidly attached to the doorframe, acts like a solid jamb for the operable door. This gives the appearance (though not the function) of a double French door, but it has better weather resistance.

Bypass sliding doors

Bypass sliding doors are another solution for wide openings. They are most often used for closets. Bypass doors are easy to install and don't take up space in a room, but they limit access to half of the closet at a time. Most interior sliders hang on a track mounted to the head jamb.

Bypass doors can be installed in a regular jamb-lined opening or, if there are no jambs, from the floor to the ceiling. (Drywall covers the sides of the opening.) The hardware for regular bypass doors includes an overhead track, hangers, and floor guides. It's essential that the hardware be rated for the weight of the doors. The heavier the doors, the sturdier—and more expensive— the hardware.

For exterior use, bypass doors are frequently installed as sliding patio doors, which run on a lower track. Aluminum patio doors are inexpensive, but they lose a lot of heat because of their high thermal conductivity. Clad wood units have largely replaced them in all but the mildest climates.

Pocket doors

Pocket doors, which disappear into a hidden wall pocket when closed, are suitable for only interior applications. Victorian houses often have heavy double pocket doors between a dining room and a parlor. In contemporary homes, pocket doors are common in bathrooms and powder rooms. Retrofitting pocket doors involves major wall surgery, so their use is generally confined to new construction. Repairing pocket doors is especially difficult because the track is hidden inside a wall.

Pocket door kits include rolling hardware as well as the wooden components needed to frame the walls of the pocket. As with bypass doors, it's essential that pocket door tracks and rollers be heavy enough to carry the door. The latches are designed with flush sides so that the handles don't get in the way as the door retracts.

Bifold doors

Another solution for wide openings, bifold doors are used primarily for closets. When open, they

---

Closure Hardware for Double Doors

- Magnetic catches—easy to install but conspicuous.
- Ball catches—neat, hidden appearance; adjustable action
- Sliding bolts, flush or surface mounted; time-consuming to operate; better suited to exterior doors

IN DETAIL

Stationary Double Doors

Stationary doors are bolted to the jamb above and the floor below with either *flush bolts* or *surface bolts*. Flush bolts are mortised (recessed) into the edge of a stationary door, which makes them invisible when the door is closed. Surface bolts are mounted on the face of the door. A strip of molding, called an *astragal*, can be mounted on the stationary door to arrest the active door as it closes. Astragals are a must for weatherproofing exterior doors, but you can omit them on interior doors with catches. If you don't have an astragal on a double door, either door can open first.

Pocket Doorframe Options

Preassembled pocket walls are often flimsy and unstable when made with low-grade lumber, though some manufacturers offer sturdier units made with laminated studs. They are available in specific door sizes.

- Universal pocket frames are shipped unassembled. They have studs wrapped in steel and can be adapted to different door sizes by cutting the track and studs.
- Site-built pocket walls are possible when the surrounding wall is framed with 2×6s instead of 2×4s. Pocket walls are framed "on the flat."

IN DETAIL

An Astragal Seals the Gap

For exterior doors, a wood or metal *astragal* helps seal the gap where double doors meet. The astragal is usually T-shaped and mounted on the outside of one of the doors. Weatherstripping, which is mounted along its inner face, is compressed when the doors are closed. Metal astragals are more durable than wood ones, but they are appropriate only for painted, not stained, doors.

Door operating systems

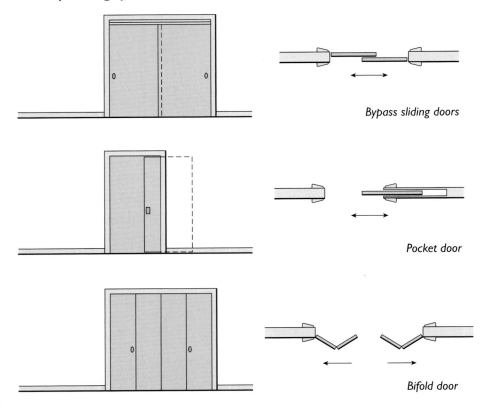

Bypass sliding doors

Pocket door

Bifold door

permit almost complete access to a closet but don't protrude into the room as much as hinged double doors. Depending on the width of the opening, you can use a *two-panel* set (a pair of doors that fold against one side of the opening) or a *four-panel* set (two pairs of doors that fold against opposite sides). You can install larger panel sets with special hardware.

Bifold hardware includes a track and a floor pivot and two top pivots for each pair of doors. Aligners are used to keep four-panel bifolds flush with one another. Bifold doors can be troublesome to operate, mainly because of cheap hardware. To avoid problems, buy the best quality you can find.

Styles and Materials

Interior doors provide privacy, hide things from view, and separate parts of a house. These doors don't need to take pounding from the weather, so they can be made of lighter materials. Exterior doors are thicker to provide better security and durability. They are insulated and weatherstripped to seal out winter's icy chill and summer's fiery

> "The appearance of wood is hard to fake convincingly (though fiberglass doors come close). Wood also permits more latitude in surface treatment than any other material."

Bifold Options

- Spring-loaded pivots have a telescoping action that allows the doors to squeeze into place.
- Fixed-length pivots work on a different principle. Pairs of doors are first folded and then tilted into position. The sockets slide in the track as the doors tilt, and the pivots are held captive when the outboard sockets are locked in place with setscrews.

heat. Weatherstripping also helps exterior doors seal out moisture. In order to select the right door, you need to know all the available styles and materials.

Frame-and-Panel Doors

Wood, the old standby, still has some distinct advantages. Well-built wooden doors age gracefully, acquiring nicks and scratches that become part of a home's legacy. Wooden doors are warm to the touch and close with a mellow "thunk." The appearance of wood is hard to fake convincingly (though fiberglass doors come close). Wood also permits more latitude in surface treatment than any other material.

Since wood moves, it's impractical to make doors out of one solid slab, which will inevitably warp or split. The solution is to make frame-and-panel doors, which are the norm in traditional-style homes. This style of door effectively counteracts the seasonal shrinking and swelling of wood.

The inner edges of the stiles and rails of frame-and-panel doors have molding designs (called *sticking*), usually with a quarter-round profile. Large door manufacturers don't usually offer a choice of sticking profiles, but custom cabinet-makers can match just about anything…for a price. The panels are also raised, or molded, meaning that the panel's center is thicker than its tapered edges. As with sticking profiles, raised-panel designs aren't usually an option unless you're dealing with a custom woodworker. Flat panels, which are common in nineteenth-century

The rich color and deep carving on this mahogany door exemplify the best qualities of solid wood.

farmhouses and early twentieth-century bungalows, are sometimes substituted for raised panels.

Paint-grade, solid wood doors are usually constructed of white pine or fir because of the inherent stability of these woods. Stain-grade doors are often constructed of hardwoods. While some hardwoods, such as mahogany, are as stable as white pine, others, such as oak, have a tendency to warp. Exterior doors are particularly vulnerable to warping because of the extreme differences between interior and exterior temperature and humidity. To make stile-and-rail doors more

TOOLS AND MATERIALS
Wood Moves

Wood expands and contracts across its grain depending on seasonal humidity, but its length remains constant. The width of a 3-ft. slab of solid wood can vary by as much as $3/4$ in., making it unsuitable for a tight-fitting door. A frame-and-panel door, however, maintains a relatively stable overall width because the length of its horizontal rails doesn't vary. Only the cross-grain expansion and contraction of the stiles affects the door's width and amounts to no more than $1/8$ in. Panels fitted inside the frame are free to expand and contract depending on the season. That's why a panel that was painted in the humid summer may show a line of unpainted wood around its edges during the dry winter.

WHAT CAN GO WRONG

The Downside of Wooden Doors

Wood's vulnerability is its biggest disadvantage. Cheap doors come apart at the joints. Softwoods, such as pine, can break off in big chunks. Warping and splitting not only look unattractive, but also waste energy through air leaks. However, the biggest problem of all is rot. The exposed end grain at the bottom of the stiles can wick up water like a straw, causing rapid decay.

IN DETAIL

Sheltering Exterior Doors

A sheltering overhang of some sort is always advisable for wooden exterior doors. This is especially true of stained doors, because natural finishes break down quickly when exposed to sunlight. Some companies offer a factory application of hi-tech natural finishes. When a door is exposed to the weather, this is a good option.

> "Exterior doors are particularly vulnerable to warping because of the extreme differences between interior and exterior temperature and humidity."

Frame-and-panel door (Elevation and horizontal section)

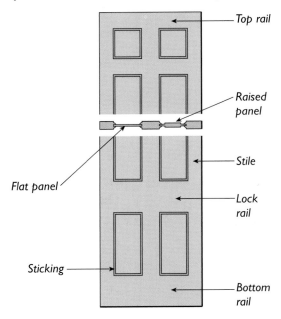

Top rail

Raised panel

Stile

Flat panel

Lock rail

Sticking

Bottom rail

The vertical members of the frame are called stiles and the horizontal members are called rails. The rails are referred to specifically as the top, bottom, and lock (or middle) rails.

stable, manufacturers usually build stiles and rails with a stave core. Another approach is to laminate thin boards together to create thicker boards.

Plywood doors are now available in fancier styles than old flush doors. These new doors have an inner core of steel and foam, a thick veneer of oak plywood, and surface moldings with traditional designs. Hardboard doors, made from compressed wood fibers, can be flush (smooth) or stamped with a traditional raised-panel design.

Steel doors are a good choice if both sides will be painted. Steel is strong, stable, and relatively inexpensive. With the development of raised moldings and embossed wood graining, steel

doors now look more convincingly like wood frame-and-panel doors. Other types of steel doors have a wood-grained vinyl coating that can be stained.

Most steel doors are sold as a unit that includes the frame. When buying a steel door to retrofit in an existing frame, look for a door with wood edging that protrudes slightly beyond the steel skins. These doors permit some trimming to accommodate an out-of-square frame. While steel doors don't rot, they can rust. In exposed

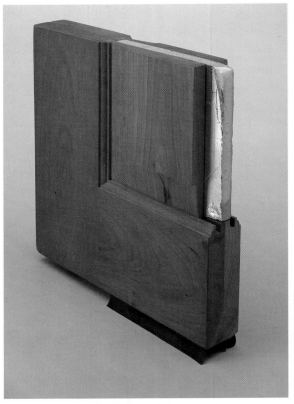

The stiles and rails of this solid cherry door are laminated from thinner boards. The result is a more stable door.

IN DETAIL

Stave-Core Frames

To make wooden doors more stable, the stiles and rails are sometimes built from smaller pieces of wood glued edge to edge, which is called *stave core*. The stave core is veneered on both sides with a thin layer of solid wood for the sake of appearance. The resulting stile or rail looks like solid wood, but it's much more stable.

Stave-core stiles (cross section)

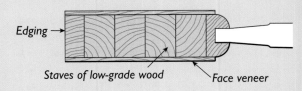

Edging

Staves of low-grade wood *Face veneer*

Stave-core door stiles look like solid wood stiles but are more stable.

locations, steel doors need maintenance, just as wood doors do.

Fiberglass doors offer better weather resistance than wood and steel ones, and they're practically impervious to dents. Because of this, fiberglass door manufacturers offer the longest warranties in the industry—up to 30 years. Fiberglass readily accepts paint and heavy-bodied stains. These should be reapplied every few years, depending on the amount of exposure. Factory finishes can be applied to fiberglass doors for an additional cost.

French doors

A cousin of the frame-and-panel door is the frame-and-glass door, often called *French doors*. Wide French doors typically feature 15 (three wide by five high) individual panes of glass, called

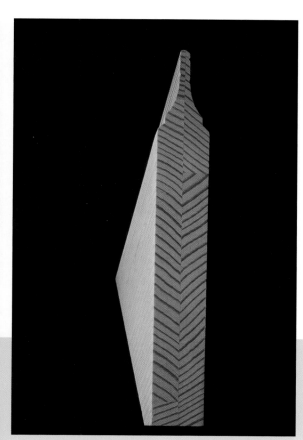

This raised panel is composed of small clear pieces. The growth rings in the pieces are oriented perpendicular to the face of the panel, called "vertical grain." Vertical-grain panels don't expand and contract as much as flat-grain panels do.

Exterior Door Styles

Six-panel colonial doors in wood, steel, and fiberglass are still the most popular door style. Doors with a greater number of panels are associated with romantic styles, such as Mediterranean and Santa Fe, while round-top versions are particularly well suited to Tudor architecture. The romantic styles are also good candidates for board-and-batten doors, which nowadays are made with a foam core for improved energy performance. Black iron hardware, preferably hand forged, is the norm for this style.

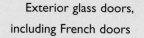

Exterior glass doors, including French doors and patio doors, are more common on the back of a house than on the front. Traditional versions feature multiple panes, whereas contemporary glass doors are single-lite. Half-and-half doors are common for side and rear entries. They are called out by the number of lites on the top half and the number of panels on the bottom half, such as a six-lite over two-panel door. *Dutch doors* are half-and-half doors with upper and lower portions that swing independently of each other.

IN DETAIL
Exterior vs. Interior Doors

Interior doors are often far less expensive than exterior doors but don't ever be tempted to use them for an exterior application. Exterior doors are more expensive because they're made of heavier, tougher materials. Exterior doors take pounding from the weather on one side. Heat, sunlight, rain and snow can take their toll on lighter materials. In nearly every climate there's a need for good insulation to keep the interior cool in summer and warm in winter. And very important is the need for security. You don't want a flimsy door that can easily be broken between you and would-be evil doers.

IN DETAIL

Let There Be Light

Windows are not the only way to bring natural light into a room. Exterior doors can also help bring much-needed light into a dark room or entrance hall. Glass panels both let in light and dress up a door. Certain panel sizes and shapes suggest specific period styles, so choose a glass treatment that harmonizes with the style of the house.

Sidelites are another way to let in light near a door. Technically, sidelites are fixed windows, but they are usually designed to harmonize with the style of the door. Door manufacturers often offer sidelites as accessories to exterior doors. They can be installed on one side of the door (see photo, p. 11) or on both sides.

Remember that safety glass in and around doors is required by code in many regions. And choose a double-keyed lock for security.

These stamped hardboard doors are convincing imitations of solid wood frame-and-panel doors. Four-panel doors (left) and six-panel doors (right) are available.

lites in the millwork industry. Narrow French doors usually have 10 lites (two wide by five high). The narrow wood strips that separate the lites from each other are called *muntins*.

The life of wooden French doors and patio doors can be extended by cladding their exteriors with vinyl or aluminum, which also reduces maintenance. Clad doors are typically available in either white or bronze, though some manufacturers, such as Weathershield, offer greater variety. An effective compromise between cladding and field finishing is a factory-applied paint finish.

Other types of solid wood doors

In rustic settings, *board-and-batten doors* are attractive. They can be made on site with simple tools or produced by a local carpenter or cabinetmaker. Boards that have tongue-and-groove edges obscure seasonal shrinkage better than square-edged boards. If you use rough-sawn boards for their texture, be sure to dry them first or wide gaps will appear as they shrink. It's important with all board-and-batten doors to provide a Z-brace, or a very wide crossbrace, to keep them from sagging.

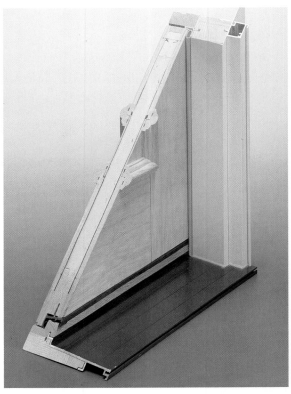

The foam core of this door is sandwiched between steel skins, with a thick oak veneer bonded to the steel. The result is energy efficiency, strength, and beauty.

> "The life of wooden French doors and patio doors can be extended by cladding their exteriors with vinyl or aluminum, which also reduces maintenance."

IN DETAIL

Steel-Door Design

Unfortunately, steel doors can dent (though, like cars, they can be repaired with auto-body filler). Another drawback of steel is its high thermal conductivity. This can cause interior warmth to be wicked to the exterior. In addition to energy loss, the resulting coldness on the door's interior surface may produce condensation that can lead to paint failure. To prevent these problems, steel door manufacturers employ various kinds of *thermal breaks* around a door's edges.

Wood edge
Steel faces are glued and crimped to a wood frame.

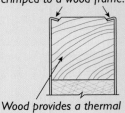

Wood provides a thermal break.

Louver doors are another type of solid wood door, but for obvious reasons, their use is confined to the interior of the house. They are often used for closets or wherever a light, breezy look is desired. Sometimes a panel is used below the lock rail with louvers above, an arrangement known as *louver-over-panel doors*.

Flush doors

Lightweight *hollow-core* flush doors, typically found in Ranch-style and contemporary homes,

Interior French doors look elegant and let adjoining rooms share sunlight. Here a pair of 10-lite French doors separates a library from a hallway.

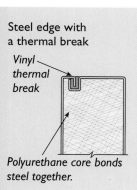

Steel doors are strong, stable, and affordable. This steel door has a vinyl coating with a wood-grained texture.

are inexpensive and easy to install. Heavier solid-core flush doors, which have a core of particleboard or lumber instead of cardboard webbing, are used for soundproofing and a solid appearance.

Plywood skins for flush doors are available in a variety of wood species. Lauan is the least expensive, but it has a porous surface that makes finishing difficult. Birch has a tighter grain, but is somewhat more expensive than lauan. Other hardwood veneers, such as oak, are also used for stain finishes.

Solid-core doors are used for exterior applications. Although plywood doors are stable, they

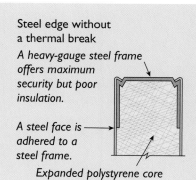

Steel edge with a thermal break

Vinyl thermal break

Polyurethane core bonds steel together.

Steel edge without a thermal break

A heavy-gauge steel frame offers maximum security but poor insulation.

A steel face is adhered to a steel frame.

Expanded polystyrene core

✓ According to Code

Most building codes require steel doors between a garage and a home's interior. Check your local code to see if an all-steel door is required or if a wooden door with a sheet-steel overlay is permissible.

Board-and-batten doors look good in rustic architectural styles. Wide battens and Z-braces prevent sagging.

applying stops, and mounting hinges. If you order a prehung door, you'll need to specify the jamb's width (which depends on wall thickness) and its wood species (which depends on whether the jamb will be painted or clear finished).

The door's operating system determines how it functions (swinging, sliding, etc.). When you order multiple doors, you'll need to describe their configuration, along with which doors are *active* (used all the time) and which doors are *semiactive* (secured in position). Depending on the operating system, you may also need to specify the *hand* of the door, or which way it swings. Another option for interior doors is to order a prehung door *cased* or *uncased*. Finally, you'll need to make decisions about the style and finish of the hardware.

sometimes suffer from delamination and *checking* (small splits on the surface) when exposed to weather. A well-maintained coat of paint is your best line of defense. As with all wooden doors, it's vital that the edges of plywood doors be well sealed.

Ordering Doors

Doors can be ordered without a frame, but the frame is usually ordered at the same time as the door. You can get the frame disassembled (knocked down) or with the door prefitted inside, which saves a lot of time making jambs, applying stops, and mounting hinges. If you order

Sizing interior doors

The standard thickness for interior doors is 1⅜-in., though sometimes you'll find 1¾-in.-thick exterior doors used inside a house. Economical sliding closet doors can be made of ¾-in.-thick medium-density fiberboard (MDF). The fact that sliding doors hang vertically helps them stay straight despite their reduced thickness.

The standard height of both interior and exterior doors is 6 ft., 8 in. tall. Other heights are generally special order. Door widths step up in 2 in. increments. Sizes 1 ft., 4 in. to 1 ft., 10 in. are used for narrow openings, such as linen closets, while sizes 2 ft., 0 in. to 2 ft., 4 in. are used for closets and small rooms, such as powder rooms. The standard widths for most interior

IN DETAIL

What Those Numbers Mean

When specifying an interior door size, it's safest to fully spell out the dimensions, such as 2 ft., 8 in. by 6 ft., 8 in. In practice, however, this is often abbreviated as 2868. The same door may be called out simply as ⅔ to refer only to its width, because 6 ft., 8 in. is almost always the standard height. Whichever system is used, just be sure the measurements are clear between you and the salesperson.

These uncased door units can easily be set plumb in out-of-plumb walls.

A precased door unit speeds up the installation process.

doors are 2 ft., 6 in. and 2 ft., 8 in.; 2 ft., 10 in. and 3 ft., 0 in. are used for heavily traveled doorways. Single doors up to 4 ft., 0 in. wide can be used for special applications, such as a workshop. The only standard width with an odd number is 1 ft., 3 in., which produces a 2-ft., 6-in. pair of doors when doubled.

To avoid confusion, dimensions for doors and windows are always called out, or specified, with the width first and the height second. Interior doors are still universally called out in feet and inches, whereas exterior doors and windows are called out using whatever system prevails in the manufacturer's catalog.

Sizing exterior doors

Most standard-height exterior doors are 1¾ in. thick, though taller doors should be thicker so the stiles don't warp. A thicker stile is also more rigid, thus creating a better seal for weatherstripping. Doors made from 10-quarter stock net out at 2¼ in. thick, while board-and-batten doors with insulated cores may run even thicker. While some old houses have 7-ft. doors, almost all stock doors are now 6 ft., 8 in. The exception is 8-ft. French doors, which are now becoming more readily available.

Most front entry doors are 3 ft. wide, while back and side entrances are sometimes 2 ft., 8 in.

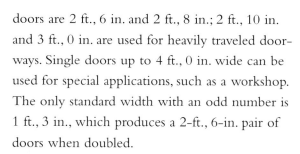

TAKE YOUR PICK

Precased vs. Uncased Units

Prehung door units can be shipped with the casing already applied to one side. This saves a little nailing time. It also makes it easy to set the jamb flush with the wall simply by shoving the unit up tight to the drywall. However, precased units have some disadvantages. First, there's no way to shave the miters without removing them first. Shaving is necessary when the miters open up because a jamb was set plumb in an out-of-plumb wall. Second, precasing makes it impossible to slide wedges in from the precased side. This makes fine-tuning the straightness of the jamb difficult. Finally, preattached casings often get damaged during shipping. If you have a choice, stick with uncased units.

TRADE SECRET

Hinges present a potential security problem for out-swing doors because the pins are outside the house—and so is a potential burglar. Regular removable-pin butts can simply be tapped out to remove the door. The solution is a special hinge with a setscrew threaded into one of its knuckles. The setscrew engages a groove that is milled in the hinge pin so it can't be removed.

or 2 ft., 10 in. Narrower doors may be somewhat less expensive, but I think the initial savings may not be worth the hassle of squeezing through a slim door with a bag of groceries under each arm. When wheelchair accessibility is a consideration, 3-ft., 6-in. doors can be special ordered.

Hardware

Hardware for hinged single doors includes hinges, also called *butts,* and a latchset or lockset. Hinges for 1⅜-in.-thick doors measure 3½ in. by 3½ in. when open, whereas heavier 1¾-in.-thick doors require 4-in. by 4-in. butts. Solid wood and hollow-core doors usually require just two hinges, but heavier solid-core doors should have a third hinge in the middle. Most standard exterior doors are hung with three 4-in. by 4-in. hinges, whereas taller doors have four hinges. Extra-heavy doors may require even larger hinges, preferably with ball bearings. In the arcane language of millwork, three hinges are referred to as a *1½ pair.*

Interior doors that don't need to be locked are closed with *latchsets,* or *passage locks.* Bedroom and bathroom doors are secured with *locksets,* or *privacy locks.* The specific term *bathroom lock* means a lock with a brass finish on the hallway side and a chrome finish on the bathroom side to harmonize with chrome plumbing fixtures. Many other hardware finishes are available, as well.

If you want your supplier to bore the holes for a cylinder lock, you'll need to specify the *backset.* This is the distance from the center of the face bore (the hole in the door's face) to the edge of

Split jambs can be adjusted for variations in wall thickness. A built-in doorstop hides the joint between the two halves of the jamb.

the door. Most cylinder locks for residential use require a 2⅜-in. backset, but certain heavy-duty locks need a 2¾-in. backset (see the drawing on the facing page).

Locks for hinged exterior doors may be of the *cylinder* type or the *mortise* type. Cylinder locks mount in easily drilled round holes, while mortise locks are mounted in square recesses (called *mortises*) that are difficult to make without specialized tools. Since the advent of cylinder locks, mortise locks have been reserved for front doors and other high-end doors. Mortise locks often feature a handle with a thumb lever on the outside.

Hardware for an exterior hinged pair of doors should be installed at the factory, if possible, because it's quite time-consuming in the field. You'll need to specify which leaf (door) is active and which is semiactive. The lock on the active

Choosing a Hardware Finish

Hardware finishes	Typical settings
Bright brass	All types
Satin brass	All types
Antique brass or bronze	Victorian, Craftsmanstyle homes
Bright chrome	Bathrooms, contemporary homes
Satin or brushed chrome	Bathrooms, contemporary homes
Black	Early American

door may be a regular cylinder lock, though a special narrow mortise lock is supplied with better units. If it's up to you to choose the lock, make sure it fits on the stile of the door. French doors have narrower stiles than frame-and-panel doors to maximize the glass openings and may not accommodate an ordinary cylinder lock, so check the dimensions before ordering a lockset.

Interior doorframes

When ordering prehung doors, you'll need to specify the width of the jamb. Jambs are sized to accommodate standard wall thicknesses. The most common interior jamb width is 4 9/16 in., which fits a 2×4 wall with 1/2-in. drywall on both sides, and leaves a little extra room in case the drywall isn't tight or the studs are slightly warped. Many exterior walls and some interior walls are framed with 2×6s, in which case a 6 9/16-in. jamb is required. In remodeling work, oddball wall thicknesses are common. You'll need to specify a custom jamb width or use the nearest standard jamb and then add jamb extensions.

Split jambs consist of two interlocking half jambs. By sliding a half jamb into a groove in the edge of the other half jamb, you can adjust the overall jamb width to accommodate variations in wall thicknesses. A built-in doorstop conceals the joint between the two sides of the jamb. To confuse matters, the term *split jamb* also refers to a different type of jamb used with pocket doors.

A *head jamb* typically fits into *dadoes* (grooves) cut into the leg jambs. Short sections of leg jambs extending above the head are called *horns*. Horns

lock the head jamb securely in place. In some regions, horns are omitted. Instead of a dado joint, the heads are joined to the legs with a *rabbet* joint or simply a *butt* joint. All three types of joints should be reinforced with screws driven through the back of the leg jambs into the head (see the drawing on p. 16).

Exterior doorframes

Exterior door jambs are typically 1 in. to 1 1/2 in. thick with a wide rabbet that houses the edge of the door when it closes (in contrast with interior jambs, which rely on an applied stop to arrest the door). Weatherstripping nests in the corner of the rabbet to seal against the door. You'll need to specify the jamb width when you order your door. Typically, this is the thickness of the wall from the face of the drywall on the inside to the face of the sheathing on the outside (or 6 9/16 in. for a 2×6 wall with 1/2-in. interior drywall and 1/2-in. exterior sheathing). The exception is no-mold jambs, which are used without casings for an adobe look.

Exterior doorsills were once made of thick wooden planks that had to be recessed below the

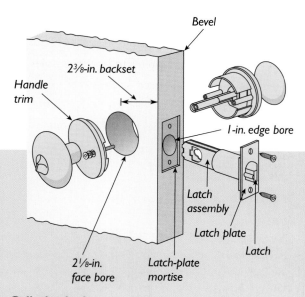

Cylinder lock
A bored lockset is installed by drilling a pair of holes—the face bore and the edge bore—at right angles to each other.

IN DETAIL
Mortise Locks

Before World War II, doors were fitted with *mortise locks,* or box-shaped locks mounted in deep, square holes chiseled into the edge of a door. Cylinder locks have replaced mortise locks for most applications. They are easier to install because they simply mount in a large hole drilled through the face of the door. Mortise locks are still used for high-end exterior doors and occasionally for high-end interior doors.

TOOLS AND MATERIALS

Finger Joints

Jambs are available in either solid or *finger-jointed* lumber. Finger-jointed lumber is composed of short pieces of solid lumber glued end to end. Finger jointing allows low-grade knotty boards to be processed into a clear product that is much less expensive than naturally clear lumber. Although finger-jointed jambs take paint well, they look odd when stained.

WHAT CAN GO WRONG

Conflicting Hardware

In some cases, the handle or knob on a primary door can interfere with a storm-door latch. If the holes for the latch will be drilled at the factory, make sure you indicate the position of your primary door's hardware on the order sketch. If you are mounting the latch on site, be sure to take into account the position of the hardware on the primary door.

Doorframe joinery

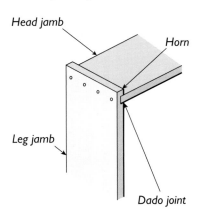

Head jamb · Horn · Leg jamb · Dado joint · Rabbet joint · Butt joint

subfloor in order to be flush with the finish floor. Now most exterior doorsills are made of aluminum and sit directly on the subfloor. Exterior casings are usually applied to doors and windows at the factory, so you'll need to specify your choice of casing style, typically either a narrow brick-mold or a wider plain casing.

Ordering aluminum storm doors

Aluminum doors can be made to order, but if your primary door is a stock size, there's probably a stock storm door available for it. When ordering screen and storm doors, make a sketch of your existing doorway to bring to your dealer. That way there can be no mistakes. Measure the width between the door frame's leg casings, measuring casing at the top, middle, and bottom in case there's some variation. Measure the height from the bottom of the head casing to the sill. The expander at the bottom of the door provides ample adjustment

so accuracy in measuring the height isn't quite as critical as it is for the width. Also, be sure to measure the height of the primary door's hardware above the sill to avoid a conflict with the storm door's hardware.

In addition to your frontal sketch, draw a bird's-eye view that shows the swing of the existing door. The storm door always hinges on the

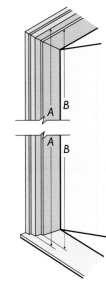

Measuring the height of storm and screen doors
Measure the height of storm and screen doors at the front of the exterior casing (A). Dimension A is slightly greater than dimension B because of the slope of the sill.

> "When ordering screen and storm doors, make a sketch of your existing doorway to bring to your dealer. That way there can be no mistakes."

TAKE YOUR PICK

Aluminum Combination Doors

Door materials	Advantages
Extruded aluminum with wood core	Premium
Hollow extruded aluminum	Low cost
Steel-reinforced aluminum	Maximum security
Vinyl cladding over wood core	Consistent with vinyl siding; doesn't scratch

These wooden screen doors harmonize with the natural look of the porch framing.

same side as the primary door. The hinges on some aluminum doors can be easily reversed to change the swing, but others cannot.

Wooden secondary doors are typically hinged to the edge of the exterior casing. To find the proper door size, measure the width between the casings and the height at the front of the casing where the opening is tallest. If there's glass in the primary door, make a sketch along with the sill-to-glass measurement. You'll want to coordinate the panels or rails in the secondary door with the primary door, if possible.

SAFETY FIRST

To complement the light-duty security of a cylinder lock, exterior doors should be fitted with a separate dead bolt, as well. A dead bolt, which is operated by a key on the outside and a thumbturn on the inside, is tougher to break through because it has a longer *throw* (horizontal travel), which engages the jamb more securely than the bolt of a cylinder lock. A dead bolt is also more resistant to smashing than a knob-type lock because its internal mechanism is housed entirely inside the door. Deadbolts for glass doors should be key-operated from both sides so a burglar can't simply break the glass and use the thumbturn to get in.

Doors

Compared with exterior doors, installing interior doors is a breeze. They don't need flashing or weatherstripping, because they aren't exposed to weather, and they don't require a sloped sill, because they simply stand on the floor. Security isn't much of an issue with interior doors either, so they're generally thinner and lighter, making them easier to handle. Their locksets and trim are simpler to install, too. The process is pretty straightforward if you take it step by step. Start by measuring carefully, so that you prepare the opening accurately. From there, installing a standard, prehung, hinged single door is a simple procedure once you know all the quirks of the job and the ways to work around them.

How R.O. Is Calculated

Adding 2 in. to the width of the door allows for the 5/8-in. thickness of each leg jamb, 1/8 in. of clearance on both sides between the door and the jamb, and 1/4 in. of clearance for shimming on both sides between the jambs and the studs. The height, which is 83 in., is measured from the subfloor up. This dimension includes 3/4 in. for the flooring; 1/2 in. for clearance under the door; 80 in. for the door; 1/8 in. for clearance between the door and the head jamb; 5/8-in. thickness for the jamb; 3/4 in. thickness for the horns; and 1/4 in. for clearance between the horns and the header. In cases where carpet is planned, add 1 in. extra. If there are no horns on the jambs, deduct 3/4 in.

TRADE SECRET

I've found that it's a good practice to write all of the rough opening sizes next to each window and door (both interior and exterior) on the plans. Use a red pen to make the dimensions stand out.

> "Most interior walls don't bear structural loads, but some do. You need to know which kind of wall you have before modifying it and framing the R.O."

Preparing the Opening

Before you frame an opening, you need to take some measurements and do a bit of detective work to determine the size of the space and whether the wall is a bearing or non-bearing one.

Sizing the opening

Doors and windows are installed in oversize openings called *rough openings* (R.O.). While manufacturers' catalogs list the R.O. for exterior doors and windows, they handle the dimensions for interior doors and windows differently. With new construction, a blueprint shows the actual size of each door, or the doors may be keyed to a door schedule. With renovation work, you need to calculate the R.O. Generally, the width of a hinged door's R.O. is the actual width of the door plus 2 in. The height of a typical hinged door opening where hardwood flooring is used is 83 in.

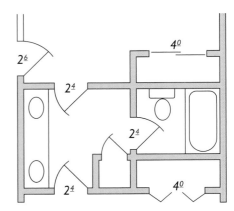

Sample plan detail
A plan may show actual door sizes (top), from which the carpenter calculates the rough openings. In other cases, doors and windows are referenced with numbers or letters that correspond to a schedule (below). The schedule gives the R.O. dimensions, along with other information.

Door Schedule

#	Type	Door Size	Model #	Manufacturer	R.O.	Hardware	Remarks
1	Wood Entry w/sidelights	5'0" × 6'8"	French Entry Door w/2 sidelights	Pella	5'2" × 6'10"	Deadbolt & Lever Handle	Custom Grill 2 over 2 sidelights 1 over 4 see elev. 1-A3
2	Wood Closet	(2) @ 2'0" × 6'8" x 1⅜"	1⅜" solid core birch	Brosco	V.I.F.*	Brass Wire Pulls—4"	
3-4	Wood French Doors	5'2⅜" × 6'10⁷/₁₆"	WFDR5068 × OLHI	Marvin	5'3⅜" × 6'10¹⁵/₁₆"	Deadbolt & Lever Handle	Insul. tempered glass
5-6	Wood French Passage	3'0" × 6'8"	M-5911 Pine	Morgan	V.I.F.	Lever Handle	Tempered glass

*V.I.F. = Verify-in-Field

Doorhanger's Level

A doorhanger's level is 78 in. long, which is just a bit shorter than a standard door. It is made of wood, metal, or plastic. Wood is heavy, but it has the advantage of not bending when dropped. Aluminum bends, which is a particular problem with a doorhanger's level because of its extreme length. On the upside, aluminum is light and inexpensive.

Determining whether the wall is load bearing

Once you know the size of the R.O., you need to determine whether the wall in which the opening is situated is a load-bearing one. Most interior walls don't bear structural loads, but some do. You need to know which kind of wall you have before modifying it and framing the R.O.

Sometimes an interior wall is used to transmit structural loads. The most typical example of an interior load-bearing wall is a partition that runs parallel to the front and back of a house, effectively reducing the depth of the house into two spans. In houses with basements, this wall typically sits over a heavy wood or steel beam supported by columns in the basement.

If you're building a new structure, it's simple to determine whether a wall is load bearing by analyzing the blueprints. When you're remodeling, however, it's not so easy. First, determine which way the roof rafters and floor beams run. They usually run parallel to each other, but not always. In the attic, the rafters (or trusses) are probably exposed. The attic floor joists may be covered with plywood, but you can easily see where the beams are by the nails in the floor. Intermediate floors are more difficult to assess because they are covered above and below by finish materials. In those cases, you can locate ceiling joists the same way you hunt for studs.

Look for posts in the basement and the attic. These indicate the presence of a load-bearing wall above or below. Another telltale sign is a beam that hangs below the ceiling in one of the

Calculating R.O. Dimensions for Interior Doors

Type of Door	R.O. Width	R.O. Height*
Single Hinged	Door width + 20	Door height + 3"
Double Hinged	Combined dr. width + 2¼"	Door height + 3"
2-Panel Bi-Fold	Comb. dr. width + 2¼"	Door height + 4", or use same height as hinged doors to align trim, then cut doors
4-Panel Bi-Fold	Comb. dr. width + 2½"	Door height + 4", or use same height as hinged doors to align trim, then cut doors
By-Pass Sliding	Comb. dr. width + 1" (doors overlap in middle when closed)	Door height + 5", or use same height as hinged doors to align trim, then cut doors
Pocket Doors	Consult hardware manufacturer's instructions	

*To adjust heights shown above, deduct ¾" if jambs don't have horns. For carpet, add ½" to 1", depending on pile.

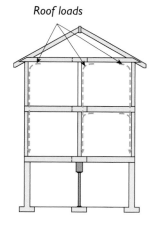

Roof loads

Bearing vs. nonbearing walls
Some interior walls are load bearing and others are not. Load-bearing walls must be identified before a new wall is framed or an existing wall is modified to receive a door or window.

An interior load-bearing wall helps carry floor loads from above. Columns and beams in the basement support load-bearing walls above.

Roof loads

Roof trusses and heavy floor beams span the entire building. The partition on the first floor is non-bearing.

TRADE SECRET

After removing trim with a prybar, remove the finish nails that stick out in back. Driving nails back through the face of the trim will leave holes that are made even uglier by the blowout of paint and wood fibers. It's better to draw the nails out through the back of the trim, which usually leaves the face of the trim unblemished. To draw the nails, use pliers, Vise-Grip® tools, or nippers to lever them out. Nippers work best because they bite into the nail. Don't squeeze too hard, or you'll cut through the nail.

TOOLS AND MATERIALS
Stud Finders

The simplest stud finder is a magnetic one. It works like a compass to point toward metal. This type works best a few inches above the floor where there's sure to be framing nails at every stud. In the middle of a wall, a magnetic stud finder may pick up the presence of drywall nails, but the process is hit or miss. In recent years, a new generation of high-tech stud finders has appeared. They use electronic sensors to find wood as well as metal. The readout is by LED and/or an audible signal. Some models also have warning devices that indicate the presence of hot electrical wires.

TRADE SECRET

The distance from the top of the header to the top of the king stud is the length of the cripples. You can either measure this distance or hold an oversize block in position for marking.

lower stories. If plaster or drywall prevents you from seeing the actual beam, you can drive a finish nail in a few places to see if it's solid inside. If there's a wall above this beam on the next story, it's probably a load-bearing one.

Framing an opening in new construction

With new construction, I precut and assemble all of my frame components for door and window openings, then install them as I'm building the wall. The process I describe here is for a nonbearing wall.

1. Cut the jack studs to the height of the rough opening less 1½ in. to allow for the thickness of the bottom plate. Nail the jacks to full-height king studs to make two double-stud assemblies.

2. Cut the pieces for the header to the width of the rough opening plus 3 in. (the combined thickness of the two jack studs). Assemble the header, and then lay it on the floor on edge.

3. Lay the double-stud assemblies in position at each end of the header and drive four nails through each king stud into the end of the header. Then nail on the top plate and bottom plate.

4. After cutting the cripples and marking their location on the header, toenail (angle nail) them between the header and the top plate.

Nonbearing door opening
A king stud is combined with a jack stud on each side of the opening to form a double-stud assembly. King studs are nailed to the ends of the header. One or more cripple studs are toenailed between the header and the double top plate. The bottom plate is cut and removed from the opening later.

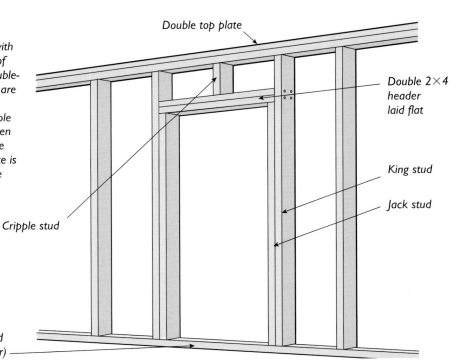

Double top plate

Double 2×4 header laid flat

King stud

Jack stud

Cripple stud

Bottom plate (removed from the opening later)

TRADE SECRET

You can't straighten a crooked stud, but you can achieve a straighter double-stud assembly by orienting the crowns of the king stud and the jack stud in opposing directions. Nail both ends first, and then drive a toenail into the edge of one piece to draw it flush with the other. Use your foot to keep the studs from sliding.

IN DETAIL
An Interior Wall May Support the Roof

Roof trusses are usually designed to span a building's full width, but not always. In some cases, the truss's webbing (diagonal struts) direct part of the roof load to an interior wall. Have an engineer analyze the design of your trusses to see if they're full span. For that matter, take any doubts you have about structural loads to an engineer before you start cutting.

A jack stud is combined with a king stud to make a double-stud assembly for each side of the door opening.

A double-stud assembly is nailed to each end of the double 2×4 header.

The top and bottom plates are nailed to the king studs. The top plate will eventually be doubled, and the bottom plate will be cut out between the jack studs after the wall is raised.

Cripple studs fill the space above an interior doorway. They're toenailed between the header and the double top plate.

Making a rough opening in an existing nonbearing wall

Once you have selected a new door's location and are satisfied that the wall is nonbearing, determine the precise location of the existing studs.

If you can incorporate one of the existing studs into the new framing as a king stud, so much the better. In this case, measure 1½ in. from the side of the stud to the side of the opening. You'll be adding a new jack stud to the existing stud, so the side of the new jack will flush out with the opening. Measure the width of the opening to find the other side and use a level to mark both edges. Measure up from the floor to the top of the opening and mark the top with a level.

The only place you'll be cutting through existing framing is across the top of the opening. The existing studs will be cut off to become cripple studs. To mark these cuts, measure 3 in. (the thickness of the new double 2×4 header) up

Locating Studs

Locating hidden studs is the first step in many remodeling projects. You can use either a stud finder or the low-tech method of rapping on the wall with your knuckles and listening for a change in pitch that indicates solid lumber rather than a hollow space. The variation in tone is most pronounced in the middle of a wall or ceiling, where greater vibration occurs. Make light pencil marks where you think the studs and beams are, and then stretch a tape between the marks to see if they fall on 16-in. or 24-in. centers. Once the spacing, or module, is established, you'll have a pretty good indication of where the rest of the framing members are located.

When you find the approximate location of a framing member, check it by driving a nail. Try to drive it where the trim has been removed to avoid having to patch it later, but stay at least 2 in. above the subfloor, or you'll be nailing into the wall's bottom plate. Probe back and forth across the edge of a stud until you feel the nail poke through, indicating one side of the stud, then measure back ¾ in. to find the stud's exact center.

TOOLS AND MATERIALS

Choosing Studs

Perfectly straight studs are a rarity. Most studs are *crowned*, meaning they have a curve throughout their length. To determine the direction of a crown, eyeball (look down) the stud from one end. If you're sighting a batch of studs at one time, mark the direction of the crown with an arrow on each stud.

Hidden in the Walls

When locating a door, you need to consider hidden pipes, ducts, and wires inside the wall. You can't know for sure until you punch a hole, but you may get some indication of what is hidden in a wall by looking in the basement or the attic. Be especially cautious if there's a kitchen or bathroom in the vicinity. If there's something in the way and you aren't confident of your skill in moving it, consult the appropriate tradesperson.

IN DETAIL

Narrow Trim

If a new door opening will be covered with wide trim, the trim will hide incisions and no patching will be required. However, if the trim will be narrow, you have two choices. You can tape and spackle over the cuts, which will require new paint or wallpaper. Alternatively, you can use a single 2×4 as your header and make the cuts 1½ in. above the opening. Although a single 2×4 header is less than ideal, it is strong enough as long as it carries no structural loads.

"It's a good idea to cut the header slightly oversize and gradually shorten it until you have a snug fit."

from the top of the opening at every stud location. After laying out the opening on one side, use a *bellhanger's drill* (a long, skinny drill bit) to drill through to the other side of the wall in several spots. This provides reference points for laying out the opening on the other side of the wall.

Cutting the opening

Before you cut an opening with a saw, punch holes in the plaster or drywall with a hammer to be certain there's nothing vulnerable inside. Prepare for cutting by setting up dust-control barriers. Remove the baseboard from both sides of the wall and store it somewhere out of the way. It's easier to remove, cut, and reinstall base-board than to try to cut it accurately while it's in place.

1. Cut the plaster or drywall on each side of the wall separately, rather than trying to cut through both sides at once. To cut through drywall, use an old handsaw or a reciprocating saw with a coarse-tooth blade. Holding the blade at a low angle close to the wall makes it easier to cut straight.

2. After removing the wall finish from both sides of the opening, cut the intervening studs at the marks you made 3 in. above the opening. Cut the studs again somewhere close to the floor. Then, gingerly twist and pull to remove the bulk of the stud.

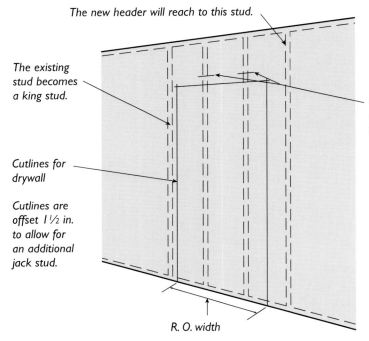

The new header will reach to this stud.

The existing stud becomes a king stud.

Cutlines for drywall

Cutlines are offset 1½ in. to allow for an additional jack stud.

Cut through the drywall and studs at these locations.

R. O. width

Layout for an interior door's rough opening
The location of a new doorway is laid out with regard to the existing framing. Existing studs above the doorway will partially remain as cripple studs.

TRADE SECRET

The impression left by a misplaced hammer blow is called a *ding*. (It's also ironically referred to as a *smile*, because of its crescent shape.) A good way to prevent dings is to use a shield when nailing finish surfaces. The shield is just a cedar shim with a slot in it. After starting a nail, slide the shield around it. Drive the nail most of the way, and then use a nail set to finish the job. If you miss, the shield is damaged, but not your work.

3. Complete the demolition by cutting and removing the plate across the bottom of the opening. Cutting all the way down to the sub-floor can be difficult when there's finish flooring on both sides of the opening. Cut down as far as you can with a handsaw or reciprocating saw. Then, drill a series of overlapping holes to sever the plate. Finally, use a chisel to chop back the ragged edge left by the overlapping holes.

Framing the opening

Measure the header that fits between the two existing studs. If both of these studs are located away from the opening, it may be hard to read your tape measure inside the wall. It's a good idea to cut the header slightly oversize and gradually shorten it until you have a snug fit.

1. Insert the header by angling it into position through the opening. Use a cordless drill to fasten the header inside the wall with screws. Predrill angled holes and start your screws before slipping the header into position.

2. Once the header is in place, fasten it to the ends of the cripple studs (the existing studs you cut off). Use long screws or barn spikes to go through a double 2×4 header. If you used a single 2×4 header, 16d common nails or sinkers will suffice.

3. Make double studs for the sides of the opening and install them between the bottom plate and the header. If you're employing any existing studs as king studs, add jacks to make them into doubles.

Cutting Plaster

Plaster is a lot tougher to cut than drywall. The degree of difficulty depends on the type of plaster system that was used. The oldest type of plaster was applied over closely spaced strips of wood called wood lath. Plaster contains mostly sand and is abrasive enough to strip the teeth right off a reciprocating-saw blade. Instead, chop through the plaster with a wide flooring chisel or a brick chisel. After outlining the cut with a chisel, break up the intervening plaster with a hammer. Once the plaster falls off, cut the wood lath with a saw.

The next type of plaster was used in the early 1900s, when wire lath replaced wood lath. To remove this plaster, score and break it. The plaster will cling to the wire lath, exposing a strip about 2 in. wide. Cut the wire lath using a combination of a chisel, sheet-metal snips, and wire cutters. You can then pry away plaster panels from the framing with a prybar. Wear heavy protective clothing and leather gloves.

The last type, modern plaster, is applied over gypsum lath, a drywall-like product that can be cut with a reciprocating saw. The plaster veneer is quite hard, so you may need to score the surface with a chisel before sawing the gypsum lath.

Once the framing is complete, fasten the wall surfaces to the framing around the opening. Be careful to place the nails so that they'll be covered by the trim.

Installing a Prehung Door

Production doorhangers can install a prehung door in about 15 minutes, including the trim. That kind of efficiency comes from being able to quickly diagnose all the ways in which a door opening deviates from ideal conditions, and then rectifying those problems one by one as the process unfolds.

SAFETY FIRST

The sand in plaster contains silica, which can damage the lungs after long-term exposure. Paper nuisance masks are adequate for short-term exposure. A heavy-duty cloth mask costs a little more but offers better protection from really thick dust. Removing asbestos and working with solvents and finishes requires a rubber respirator with filters specifically rated for the job.

TRADE SECRET

A circular saw fitted with an old carbide blade is best for cutting wood lath, because it doesn't vibrate too badly. A reciprocating saw tends to yank the wood lath away from the framing, which makes the adjoining plaster crack.

TOOLS AND MATERIALS

Nail Sizes

The length of nails is expressed in penny size, which is abbreviated by the letter *d*. The best all-around framing nail is a 10-penny common or a 16-penny sinker, both of which have about the same diameter. I like the 10d common, because at 3 in. long, it doesn't leave a nasty point sticking out the back of a doubled stud. The longer 16d sinker gives you somewhat better holding power when you're nailing into end grain.

Nails for framing

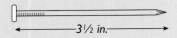

←—— 3½ in. ——→

16d
These nails are good for nailing into the end grain of headers and studs.

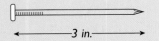

←—— 3 in. ——→

10d
These nails are good for doubling headers and studs.

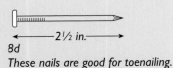

←—— 2½ in. ——→

8d
These nails are good for toenailing.

A doorhanger's level is used to read the hinge side of the opening. If the stud is out of plumb, shims will be required.

Reading and prepping the opening

First, determine how level the floor is. New construction is usually level, but old floors can drop radically from one jamb to the other. Since both jambs were initially the same height, an out-of-level floor produces an out-of-level head jamb—and a tapering margin between the head jamb and the door—unless you take corrective measures.

Sometimes, doors are hung before the finish flooring is installed. In that case, you need to place blocks that are slightly thicker than the finish flooring under both jambs. (These blocks are in addition to any shim you may have used for leveling.) When it's time to install finish flooring, slip the flooring under the jamb for an easy fit.

Use a straightedge in conjunction with a 2-ft. level to read the floor. If the floor is out-of-level, place a shim of the appropriate thickness on the low side (either shim #1 or shim #2). Then use a

doorhanger's level to check the sides of the rough opening for plumb. If you don't have a doorhanger's level, tape a shorter level to a straight board that has parallel edges. If the hinge side of the opening is out of plumb, attach shims where the hinges will be (shims #3 and #4). You'll attach shims to the opposite side of the opening (the strike side) after you set the unit.

Next, check the face of the wall on both sides of the opening to see if it leans out of plumb and, if so, by how much (see photo, top right). The last step in diagnosing a door opening is to see if the jack studs are twisted out of square with the face of the wall (see photo, bottom

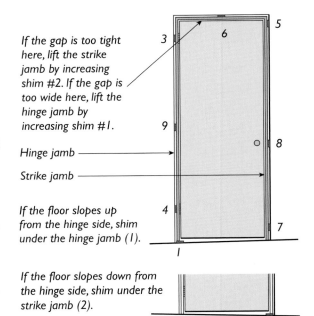

If the gap is too tight here, lift the strike jamb by increasing shim #2. If the gap is too wide here, lift the hinge jamb by increasing shim #1.

Hinge jamb ——→

Strike jamb ——→

If the floor slopes up from the hinge side, shim under the hinge jamb (1).

If the floor slopes down from the hinge side, shim under the strike jamb (2).

Sequence for shimming a door
Rough openings aren't exactly plumb and level, but a doorframe must be. Shims bridge the gap between the two. Shimming in the right order is key to setting a door efficiently.

"First, determine how level the floor is. New construction is usually level, but old floors can drop radically from one jamb to the other."

✓ According to Code

For load-bearing walls, there are often specific codes for the size of headers vs. their length. Check before you settle on your framing layout.

WHAT CAN GO WRONG

Out-of-Level Floors

The simplest approach is to place a shim under the jamb on the low side to bring the head jamb to level. After you hang the door, remove the shim. This leaves a small, inconspicuous gap underneath the jamb. You can also caulk paint-grade jambs. Trim the bottom of the jamb on the high side of the opening before the unit is installed. If the floor drops ¼ in., trim that much off the higher jamb.

right). A twisted jack stud will twist the jamb. This in turn throws the hinges out of plumb. Use tapered wedges to correct this condition.

Setting the unit

Measure the height of the unit to make sure it will fit, trimming off the horns above the head jamb with a handsaw, if necessary. Remove the packing nail or screw that holds the door against the strike-side jamb during shipping. Once the door is set, it will be impossible to remove. If a clip holds the door to the strike-side jamb, you may be able to remove it after setting the unit, which makes handling the unit a little easier.

The face of the wall is checked with a level on both sides of the opening. When a jamb is set plumb in an out-of-plumb wall, the jamb and the wall won't be entirely flush.

Shims are located where the hinges will be. In this case, a single tapered shim was used instead of opposing shims because the stud was twisted.

A square is used to detect a twisted stud. A twisted stud can cause a distorted jamb unless it is corrected with shims.

TOOLS AND MATERIALS
Square-Drive Screws

When screwing in a header, you'll be working "blind," so it may be difficult to drive the screws. Square-drive screws are great in situations like this, because the driver bit tenaciously grips the head of the screw.

WHAT CAN GO WRONG
Out-of-Plumb Walls

If a jamb is set flush with an out-of-plumb wall, the door will be out of plumb too and could possibly swing open or closed on its own. If a jamb is set plumb in such a wall, its edge won't be entirely flush with the drywall. The casing can't lay flat, so the miter joints will open up at the corners. If the wall is more out of plumb on one side than on the other, it makes a twisted, or *cross-legged,* opening. This prevents single doors from closing evenly against the stop on the strike side of the frame.

To keep a door from rattling when it's shut: Set the lock before setting the doorstops. Then set the strike-side stop, nailing it at only the very top and the very bottom. Nail the stop in the middle, but instead of pressing *against* the door, leave 1/16 in. of *clearance* between the door and the stop. When the door closes, it will hit the stop at the top and bottom first, then flex slightly before the latch bolt slips into the striker. The resulting tension holds the door tight. When nailing the hinge-side stop and the head stop, leave about a dime's thickness for clearance.

Solving Out-of-Plumb Problems

Is it better to set the frame flush with an out-of-plumb wall or to set the frame plumb? The best strategy depends on whether the unit has casings. If so, set it flush with the wall, because there's no way to shave the miters without pulling off the casings. If a unit doesn't have casings, set the frame plumb (nonflush), knowing that you'll have to fudge the miters. To guide the setting of a nonflush jamb, preattach a shim to the hinge-side stud and make a mark on it. This mark is plumbed up (or down) from the face of the wall wherever it leans out the most.

The worst case scenario is when one side is more out of the plumb than the other, which is called a cross-legged opening. First, try to bump the entire wall at the bottom with a sledgehammer, using a thick board as a cushion to avoid damaging the drywall. You can also try moving the jambs away from the wall until they're parallel. Moving both jambs a little on opposite sides is less conspicuous than moving one jamb a lot, but it can cause difficulty later when installing the trim. You can offset the jambs from the wall no more than 1/4 in. before it starts to be obvious. With single doors, you can cheat a little by setting the jambs in a somewhat cross-legged condition and then resetting the stop on the strike jamb so it meets the door.

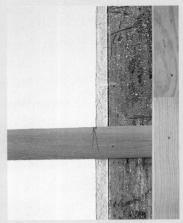

1. Place the unit in the opening. If a floor shim has been set, make sure it's under the jamb. Then, open the door about 90 degrees. The weight of the door will make the top of the jamb tip away from the opening unless it is supported. If the door is light, you can simply hold the jamb in position while you nail through the jamb next to the top hinge. If the door is heavy, it's better to place shims or blocks under the opened door until the jamb is in position.

2. Nail through the jamb next to the top hinge to hold the door in place, then nail next to the bottom hinge with 8d finish nails (see the drawing on p. 26, shims #3 and #4.) Close the door and check the margin between the door and the head jamb. If the gap over the door narrows

SAFETY FIRST

Cutting blindly into a wall with a roaring reciprocating saw can be disastrous. A damaged pipe can unleash a flood. A severed electrical wire can cause a short circuit at best and an electrocution at worst. I once cut into a live gas line. Sparks ignited the gas and I had an instant flame-thrower on my hands. Luckily, a mason standing nearby had the good sense to cut off the gas by kinking the tube. Before you cut into a wall, locate the breaker panel, the main water shutoff, and the main gas shutoff, just in case.

toward the strike side, place a shim under the strike jamb to raise it or drive in the shim that's already there (shim #2). If the gap widens toward the strike side, the hinge jamb needs to be raised. Use a prybar to raise the hinge jamb more, then drive in the tapered shim a little further (shim #1). When the head margin is even at both ends, shim and nail the strike jamb just below its intersection with the head jamb (shim #5). This locks in the end of the head jamb at the correct height. However, the head jamb may be bowed in the center. If it is, shim and nail the head jamb in the middle, straightening it as necessary, until you've achieved a consistent margin (shim #6).

3. Shim the bottom of the strike jamb so that you have a nice even margin between the jamb and the door (shim #7). If you have set the hinge jamb plumb in an out-of-plumb wall, move the bottom of the strike jamb perpendicular to the wall until the door touches the stop evenly from the top to the bottom. This will

The strike-side jamb is shimmed until an even margin appears between the door and the jamb. Then a screw is driven through the jamb next to the striker location. Eventually, the doorstop will hide the head of the screw.

effectively plumb the strike jamb, making it parallel with the hinge jamb.

4. Finish shimming the strike jamb, straightening it as you go. To reinforce the lock, be sure to place shims directly behind the striker plate location (shim #8). Place an intermediate shim behind the hinge jamb, as well (shim #9). When setting a heavy door, run screws and nails next to the hinges and the striker, hiding the screws under the stops. If the unit has preattached casings and you set it flush in a cross-legged opening, pry the stops loose and reset them even with the door.

5. Check the fit all around one last time. You can fine-tune the margins here and there by driving in the shims further or pulling them out. Brace the jamb with your body as you make adjustments or it may be knocked out of plumb. When everything fits right, set all your nail heads and trim back your shims so they are flush with the jambs.

Congratulations. Your door is ready for trim.

The floor is not entirely level here, so a shim is placed under the hinge-side jamb as the door is set.

Off by More Than ½ in.

The ½-in. clearance built into a rough opening affords some tolerance if the framing is out of plumb, but if the opening is more than ½ in. off, the door may not fit. Sometimes a jack stud can be persuaded to make additional room with the help of a sledgehammer. After bumping the stud, trim back the bottom plate and the drywall wherever they protrude into the opening.

TRADE SECRET

When nailing through jambs initially, leave the heads of the finish nails sticking out, in case you have to pull them to make adjustments. Place just one nail next to the stop, on the side away from the door. If you nail on the door side of the stop with the heads sticking out, you won't be able to close the door to test the fit.

Installing Complex

CHAPTER THREE

Interior Doors

Installing complex interior doors involves the same basic principles as hinged single doors, with a few extra challenges. Complex units are often difficult to handle because of their size and additional moving parts. Just moving them around is awkward. When the packing nails are removed and the doors are free to move, you'll have an unruly beast on your hands. But you can tame it by preparing carefully. In some cases, such as with pocket doors, you'll have a very different kind of rough opening to make. For all complex door projects, make sure you understand the entire process before you start, and then take one step at a time. Read up on how to deal with the pitfalls *before* you face them. You'll save yourself a lot of grief in the end.

1 Installing a Pair of Prehung Doors, p. 32

2 Installing a Set of Four-Panel Bifold Doors, p. 35

3 Installing a Bypass Closet Door, p. 39

4 Installing a Pocket Door, p. 41

IN DETAIL
Using Shims in Combination

When shimming between a doorjamb and a stud, the space often varies due to a twisted stud. To create shims with an even overall thickness, combine pairs of wedges with their tapers facing opposite directions. The British call these *folding wedges*. Use different combinations of wedges to accommodate varying degrees of twist.

Installing tapered shims
A twisted stud distorts the shim space between the stud and the jamb. Different combinations of shims can compensate for such irregularities.

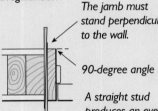

The jamb must stand perpendicular to the wall.

90-degree angle

A straight stud produces an even gap. The shims oppose each other.

A slightly twisted stud produces a tapered gap. A shim is installed from one side only.

A very twisted stud produces a radically tapered gap. Two shims are installed from the same side.

Installing a Pair of Prehung Doors

Just like the installation for a single door, installing a double door begins with preparing a rough opening. After the rough opening has been prepped, shim one of the jack studs plumb. Place the shims directly behind or just above the hinge locations.

After shimming the first jack, measure the exact width of the unit from the outer edges of the jambs. (Take this measurement across the top, where the head jamb fixes the unit's width.) Set a combination of shims at the top hinge location on the other jack. The distance between the shims on both sides of the opening should equal the unit's width.

Preshimming a double door rough opening
Double doors are awkward to handle, so it helps to prepare the opening for a friction fit. Preshim one side of the opening at both the top and the bottom, and preshim the other side at only the top. Additional shims are installed after the unit is set to fine-tune the fit.

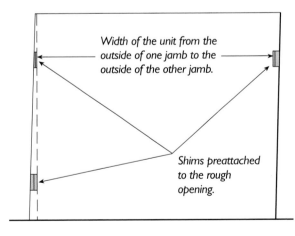

Width of the unit from the outside of one jamb to the outside of the other jamb.

Shims preattached to the rough opening.

A double door is lifted into position. The author's right hand keeps the doors from swinging open. Shims have been preinstalled on both sides at the top of the opening, but on only one side at the bottom. This unit is precased, so the author will tack it through the head casing to hold it temporarily.

This unit isn't precased, so the author angles a nail into the header to hold the unit temporarily.

Shims are adjusted behind one of the lower hinges to make the center margin even.

> "The top of the unit should squeeze into place with a nice whoosh. If not, lay the door back down and adjust the shims."

TOOLS AND MATERIALS
Buy or Make Shims

Cedar shims are a by-product of making cedar shingles. In fact, you can buy a bundle of low-grade, "undercourse" shingles and rip your own shims. Another type of wedge is manufactured especially for shimming. They are more uniform than cedar shims but also more expensive.

IN DETAIL
Shimming Both Jack Studs

When preshimming a single door, it's not necessary to shim the strike side—that's done after the unit is in place. With double doors, however, it's a good idea to completely preshim one jack stud, then preshim the other jack stud at the top hinge only. That way, the door will be friction-fitted in place when the unit is set, which makes handling it more manageable.

Prepping and setting the unit

After the rough opening has been shimmed, you'll need to move the door unit into position and get it ready to install. First, remove all the fasteners used to hold the door during shipment. If a stretcher was used across the face of the unit, leave it there until the unit is set. Align the bottoms of the jambs carefully so they're centered in the opening, and then stand the unit up by lifting the head jamb. The top of the unit should squeeze into place with a nice *whoosh*. If not, lay the door back down and adjust the shims.

To keep the unit loosely in place, drive temporary nails partway into the rough header. Angle these nails just outside the jambs, not through the jambs. Using a prybar, lever the bottoms of the jambs sideways until the gap between the doors is even. If the tops of the doors don't align, add a shim under the lower jamb.

Open the door on the side where the jamb is only shimmed behind the top hinge. Place a temporary shim under the open door to keep the jamb approximately plumb. Squeeze through the opening and nail the other jamb (the one with shims behind the top and bottom hinges).

Drive one nail next to each hinge and leave the heads sticking out. Moving to the side with the upper shims, insert another set of shims behind the bottom hinge until the gap between the doors is even. After shimming the jamb side to side, you may have to move the bottom of the jamb in or out of the wall to make the doors meet flush. Once you've got the bottom of the jamb where you want it, open the opposite door enough to

Locating Shims

Ideally, shims should be located directly behind the hinges to keep the weight of a door from bending the jamb. The trouble is, modern doorjambs typically run about ⅝ in. thick. That leaves standard ¾-in. hinge screws protruding slightly from the back of the jamb. These small nibs are a real pain when you're trying to set a prehung unit tight against the shims. Therefore, I typically shim just above the hinges. If the door is heavy, I shim above and below the hinges to prevent a kink in the jamb.

Whether you shim above or directly behind the hinges, there's a trick that can speed up your layout. Transfer the hinge locations from the unit to your level with a pencil, magic marker, or piece of tape. Then use the marks on the level to locate shims on the jack studs. If you're using a straightedge in conjunction with a shorter level, mark the straightedge.

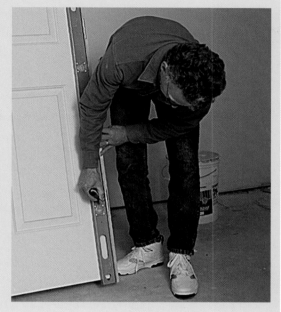

squeeze through. Nail through the jamb next to the bottom hinge. Check the fit. The gap between the doors should be even, and the doors horizontally aligned and flush where they meet.

Shim and nail as necessary to straighten the head jamb and the side jambs. Make sure there's a shim at the middle of the head jamb where closure hardware will be situated. Nail this shim precisely where the doors meet. If you nail to one side or the other, your nails may interfere with the hardware.

TRADE SECRET

Some double-door units have a skid nailed to the bottom. In that case, you can slide the unit to move it. If finish flooring has already been installed, place a strip of carpet under the skid to protect the floor. Sometimes, the unit has a temporary stretcher nailed to the edges of the jambs instead of a skid. Trying to slide this type will damage the jambs, so you'll need some help lifting it into place.

WHAT CAN GO WRONG

An Opening That Is Too Small

The rough openings for double doors are sometimes too tight. After setting the upper shim on the second side of the opening, plumb down from the shim to make sure there's adequate clearance. If not, you'll have to widen the opening. Try bumping the errant stud with a sledge-hammer and trimming the plate if you can move it enough. If that fails, you'll have to gnaw on the stud with a hatchet or a power plane, but be sure to drive common nails well below the surface so they don't nick your cutting tools. Another alternative is to substitute some ⁵⁄₄ stock for the 2×4 jack studs.

Solving Double-Door Alignment Problems

With heavy doors, you may find that the gap between the doors has spread at the bottom and closed at the top. Don't despair. First try driving additional nails through the jamb at the top hinge. If nailing doesn't do the trick, remove the stops, drive screws next to the hinges, and then cover the screws with the stops. You can also replace the hinge screws closest to the stop with long, 2½-in. to 3-in. screws. Replace only the screws closest to the stop, where there's wood behind the jamb. Longer screws placed closer to the barrel of the hinge will hit only drywall.

Moving the hinges to make double doors meet

Moving a hinge out from the jamb shifts the door's opposite diagonal corner inward. When other methods fail, use this trick to adjust warped doors or doors in cross-legged openings.

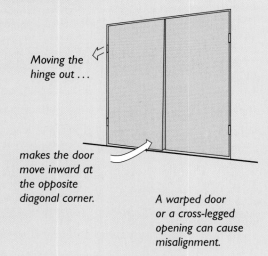

Moving the hinge out . . .

makes the door move inward at the opposite diagonal corner.

A warped door or a cross-legged opening can cause misalignment.

Adjusting a pair of hinged doors

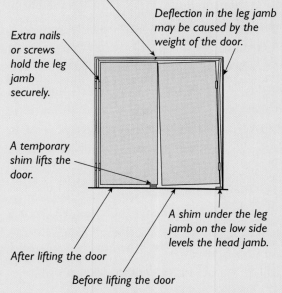

Partially driven nails straddle the head jamb to hold the unit in place.

Deflection in the leg jamb may be caused by the weight of the door.

Extra nails or screws hold the leg jamb securely.

A temporary shim lifts the door.

A shim under the leg jamb on the low side levels the head jamb.

After lifting the door

Before lifting the door

If your opening is cross-legged (the wall is out of plumb more on one side than on the other), the doors won't meet properly and will be out of plane with one another. You can cheat by moving one of the hinges on each door away from the stop. This moves the opposite diagonal corner of the door inward. In this case, you'll need to reset all the stops and patch the hinge gains.

"The gap between the doors should be even, and the doors horizontally aligned and flush where they meet."

TAKE YOUR PICK

Nails for Framing

Framing nails come in two types: common nails and sinkers. Common nails have either a *bright* (uncoated) finish for interior work or a *galvanized* (coated) finish for exterior jobs. Sinkers are for interior framing only. They're coated with a black, sticky film that acts as a lubricant to drive the nail and creates better adhesion with the wood. Common nails are thicker than sinkers, which makes them stronger but also more likely to split a board. Preferences are largely regional. West Coast framers use sinkers exclusively, whereas common nails are still popular on the East Coast.

Shims are placed under both jambs to provide carpet clearance and to even out any slope. If wood flooring were installed instead, the carpenter would use ¾-in. blocks on both sides for clearance and a tapered shim on only the low side for leveling.

Installing a Set of Four-Panel Bifold Doors

If you're using a prepackaged set of bifold doors, compare the manufacturer's specs with your rough opening. If you're using a hardware package in conjunction with standard doors, consult the instructions to figure how to deduct from the opening size to find the door size. Trim the doors, if necessary. Check the floors to make sure they're level and correct any discrepancies with shims on the low side. If carpet or finish flooring will be added later, you'll also need blocks on both sides of the opening that are equal in thickness to the flooring. For carpet, allow ⅜ in. to ¾ in., depending on the pile of the carpet. For hardwood flooring, allow ¾ in.

Weight Distribution of a Bifold Door

In contrast to a hinged door, whose weight hangs on a side jamb, a bifold door's weight is carried by pivot pins in floor brackets, which bear directly on the floor. A metal track mounted to the head jamb guides the doors as they open and close. Like bifold side jambs, bifold head jambs need to be straight but not necessarily all that strong. As a consequence, you can take certain liberties with bifold jambs that would otherwise weaken a hinged door; namely, you can use fewer shims and fewer nails. You can depend mainly on the casings to keep the jambs straight.

Anatomy of a bifold door

A pencil mark on the track helps fine-tune the location of the stationary socket.

A spring-loaded top pivot engages the sliding socket inside the track.

Head jamb

Track

Casing

Leg jamb

L-shaped floor bracket

Shims behind the jamb

A block simulates the thickness of hardwood flooring. If carpet will be used instead, the block becomes permanent.

Valance

The bottom pivot engages the floor bracket.

A shim levels the subfloor, if necessary.

A 1×2 valance is installed flush with the front of the opening to conceal the bifold track.

Leg Jamb Deflection

When setting heavy doors, you may see a bend in the upper portion of both leg jambs. This deflection is caused by the weight of the doors as they pull on the top hinges. To fix this, place temporary shims under the doors to prop them up, which will straighten the jambs.

TRADE SECRET

To center the top of a door or window frame in a rough opening, first push it all the way to the right. Make a mark on the wall along the edge of the casing. Then, push the top of the frame all the way to the left. You can now measure from the mark to the casing to see how much the unit moved. For example, if the unit moved a total of ½-in., move it back halfway, or ¼-in. to the right, to center it in the opening.

TOOLS AND MATERIALS

Checking a Level for Accuracy

To check a level's accuracy, set it on a flat surface and shim it at one end or the other until it reads level. Then spin the level 180 degrees end for end. It should still read level. You can check a level's plumb vial in a similar fashion. Place it against something vertical, shim it perfectly plumb, and then spin it around. It should still read plumb. If not, you may be able to adjust the vial by loosening its mounting screws. Some levels are nonadjustable. When they bend or go out of level, trash 'em.

IN DETAIL

Level Lugs

Some doorhanger's levels have rollers or lugs at both ends. Their purpose is to set a jamb plumb from top to bottom, even if the jamb is bowed toward the level. After setting both ends of the jamb, flip the rollers out of the way so you can use the level as a straightedge.

> *"If you're using a nailer to fasten the jambs, you'll only need three hands; if you're nailing by hand, you'll need four."*

Assembling and installing the jamb

Trim your jambs to the correct length and assemble them as a three-sided frame on the floor. To hide the bifold track, nail a 132 valance (wooden cover piece) to the head jamb. The edge of the valance should be flush with the front of the opening (see photo, p. 35, bottom right). Install casing while the frame is still on the floor.

Of course, you'll be nailing only into the jambs for now; the outer edge of the casing will be nailed to the wall later. Cover the valance with casing as if it were the head jamb. Then stand the frame up and slip it into the opening. After centering it, drive two nails through the casing to hold the frame in place. Place the nails close to the corners of the frame, because you haven't checked the jambs yet for straightness. The top of

A leg casing is applied to the unit while it's still on the floor. The head casing will be installed next, thereby concealing both the head jamb and the valance.

The precased unit is set in the opening. After centering the unit, nails will be driven through the casing near the upper corners.

To plumb the first leg, a nail is driven through the casing near the floor. The carpenter reads his level while nailing.

To plumb the second leg, a measurement is pulled from the first leg. The width of the finished opening must be equal at the top and the bottom.

The casings are checked with a level as they're nailed. If any bowing is detected, a little pressure will fix the problem.

the frame is now fixed from side to side, but the bottoms of the side jambs are still free to move from side to side. Hold your level against one of the side jambs while moving it back and forth. When the level reads plumb, drive a nail through the casing to fix the bottom of the jamb. If you're using a nailer to fasten the jambs, you'll only need three hands; if you're nailing by hand, you'll need four.

Shim the jamb about 2 in. above the floor and nail through the jamb into the framing. Now go to the other side of the opening. To guide you in locating the second side jamb, pull a measurement from the one you just nailed. The width of the finished opening must be equal at the top and bottom. Secure the second jamb by nailing through the casing, just as you did with the first

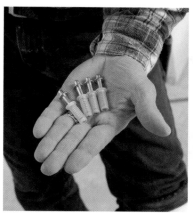

Spring-loaded top pivots will be mounted in the tops of the doors.

Adjustable pins will be mounted in the bottoms of the doors closest to the jambs. The pins engage L-shaped brackets on the floor, and the pins' crenulated surfaces mesh with the serrated openings in the brackets to permit side-to-side adjustment.

jamb. Then nail off the casing around the opening, checking it for straightness as you go with a level or straightedge. If you detect any bowing, a little pressure on the casing as you nail should fix the problem. Install the casing on the other side of the wall, and then drive a nail through the top of each side jamb into the framing.

Installing the track and floor brackets

A bifold track contains sliding sockets that engage pivot pins mounted in the tops of the doors. The outboard sockets are fixed in permanent positions at the ends of the track, while the inboard sockets slide along the track as the doors fold open and closed. Be sure all four of these sockets are inside the track before the track is installed. You can adjust the position of the outboard sockets later with setscrews, but there's no way to get them (or the inboard sockets) *inside* the track after the track is installed. Attach the

The track is screwed to the head jamb directly behind the valance. Just in front of the screwdriver bit is one of the sliding sockets. Spring-loaded pins in the tops of the doors engage the sockets, which are shifted in the track to plumb the doors.

TRADE SECRET

Always check the levelness of the floor before you set a door unit. It's easy to make corrections before you set the unit by shimming or trimming the jambs, but trimming or prying up a jamb after it's installed is an ornery job.

WHAT CAN GO WRONG

Trimming Too Much Off a Hollow-Core Door

Cutting more than 1 in. off the bottom of a hollow-core door removes the bottom rail and exposes the void between the door skins. Fortunately, the door can be repaired. To plug the bottom, you can reuse the piece you cut off or cut a new piece to size on a table saw. To reuse the bottom rail, strip off the plywood skin from both sides with a chisel. Apply glue liberally to the rail and to the inside of the door. Insert the rail into the bottom of the door and clamp it for an hour until the glue dries.

TRADE SECRET

Bifold doors can be difficult to operate from the fully retracted position. Folks usually tug on the back of the leading door to get it started, but this leaves fingerprints. Place a rubber bumper close to the hinges on the back of the outboard doors to keep them slightly flexed and easy to start.

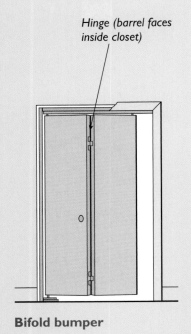

Hinge (barrel faces inside closet)

Bifold bumper

38

track to the head jamb with screws. Short screws are adequate, because the doors aren't suspended from a bifold track—they're just guided by it.

In addition to the two top pivots, each pair of doors has a single bottom pivot that sits in a floor bracket at each side of the opening. The floor brackets have vertical flanges with one round hole and one oblong hole. To attach the brackets to the jambs, drive screws into the center of the oblong holes. Later you can fine-tune the location of the doors by loosening these screws and moving the brackets in or out. When the doors are adjusted to meet flush in the middle, drive screws into both the round and the oblong holes to lock in the adjustments.

If finish flooring has already been laid, set the floor brackets directly on it. If not, elevate the brackets with temporary blocks. Permanent blocks are necessary if carpet will be installed.

Make carpet blocks just slightly bigger than the brackets, and then screw through the bracket and the block into the floor. Use plywood instead of solid wood to prevent splitting.

Installing and adjusting the doors

Hinge the doors together to make two pairs. Drill holes in the doors for the pivots (if this has not been done at the factory) and install the pivots. To place the doors, lift them up as you steer the top pivots into the sockets in the track. You'll have to play with the floating inboard sockets to get them in the right place. Both of the top pivots are spring-loaded, which allows you to lift the door high enough for the floor pivot to drop into the floor bracket. The top pivots will then be captured in the sockets in the track, and the bottom pivot will be captured in

The spring-loaded top pins are steered into the sliding sockets as the door is lifted. Then the door is lowered so the bottom pin enters the floor bracket.

the floor bracket. When both pairs of doors are installed, you're ready to make adjustments.

The bottom pivot has a star-shaped head that engages a series of notches in the floor bracket. To adjust the doors sideways at the bottom of the opening, lift a pair of doors slightly and scoot the floor pivot over a notch or two. To adjust the doors sideways at the top of the opening, loosen the setscrew in one of the outboard sockets and shift it slightly. A little pencil mark on the track next to the socket will provide a helpful reference point as you do this.

Installing a Bypass Closet Door

A bypass door is easier to install than any other type of door. Gravity does most of the alignment work when bypass doors hang from the top, as they usually do. The hardware is mostly mounted

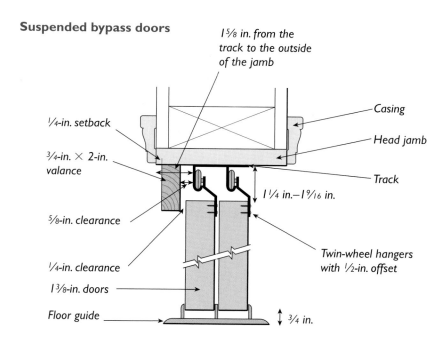

Suspended bypass doors

1 5/8 in. from the track to the outside of the jamb

1/4-in. setback

3/4-in. × 2-in. valance

5/8-in. clearance

Casing

Head jamb

Track

1 1/4 in.–1 9/16 in.

1/4-in. clearance

1 3/8-in. doors

Floor guide

Twin-wheel hangers with 1/2-in. offset

3/4 in.

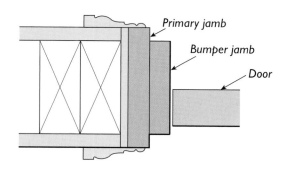

Bumper jamb for bypass doors
Openings for bypass doors are typically undersize, so that the doors overlap. To achieve the same effect with a standard-width opening, a secondary bumper jamb is installed over the primary jamb.

Primary jamb

Bumper jamb

Door

on the surface, so no routing is required, and there's only one main adjustment: up or down.

Preparing the opening

Pocket doors overlap in the middle, which makes their rough opening narrower than a hinged- or bifold-door opening. If your opening is too wide, you can compensate by adding bumper jambs to the primary jambs. On the other hand, the height of a bypass opening needs to be about 2 in. taller than a hinged-door opening to make room for the track. If you already have a standard-height opening, look for a kit with doors that have been specially sized to fit that configuration. If you need to shorten a stock hollow-core door, trim the bottom only. The top rail of the door needs to remain intact to anchor the hanger hardware.

IN DETAIL
About Bypass Doors

Bypass doors can be purchased as a complete unit, which includes the doors, or as separate door and hardware kits. If the doors are included, the strength of the hardware matches the weight of the doors. If you buy the doors separately, make sure you purchase hardware that's adequately rated for the job.

IN DETAIL
Bifold Doorknobs

Bifold doorknobs are located on the outboard doors, just outside the middle of each pair. An *aligner* on each door holds them flush in the middle of the opening. As the doors meet, the aligners cross each other, thereby wedging the doors into position.

Bypass Track Systems

- **Light-duty track with rollers at the top:** The hangers are mounted on the rear face of the door and ride on an open-sided J-track. Double-wheel hangers are preferable to single-wheel hangers.
- **Heavy-duty track with rollers at the top:** Three- or four-wheeled hangers are mounted on the top edge of the door and ride in a U-track or an I-track. This track system is also used for pocket doors.
- **Heavy-duty track with rollers at the bottom:** The rollers ride on a floor track similar to sliding patio doors. The tops of the doors are guided by a U-channel. This system is used for mirrored doors, which are quite heavy, and for hefty antique pocket doors.

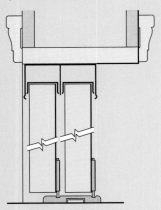

Bypass doors on floor rollers

> *"Like bifold doors, bypass doorframes can be assembled and precased on the floor."*

Prepping and hanging the doors

Like bifold doors, bypass doorframes can be assembled and precased on the floor. You'll need a wider valance, however, because bypass tracks are taller than bifold tracks. Install the valance with its wide dimension in the vertical position rather then the horizontal one. Setting the

To hang a bypass door on a J-track, the door must be tilted as it is lifted. When the hanger wheels clear the lip of the track, the door is lowered to a vertical position.

An adjusting dial on this hanger raises and lowers the door. The adjustment is correct when the sides of the door make even contact with the doorjamb. The door is lifted slightly during adjustment and its weight locks it into place.

valance back a little from the edge of the head jamb looks neater than setting it flush.

The head jamb for a bypass door needs thorough shimming to adequately support the track. To guide you in locating the shims, transfer the location of the prepunched holes in the track to the head jamb. Be sure to install the track far enough from the valance to permit the front

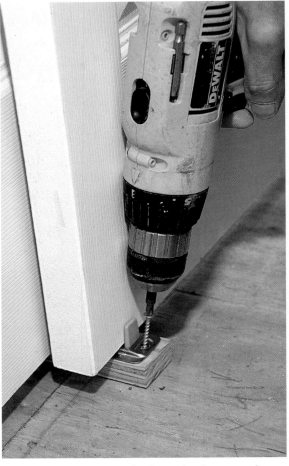

Floor guides are installed where the doors overlap at the middle of the opening. A plywood shim block is placed under the guide if carpet will be installed.

TRADE SECRET

You can consult the instructions to determine the necessary setback for the track, but I often find that it's more enlightening to simply mock up the hardware by slipping the hangers into the track. Then I can visualize the whole assembly, including the offset of the track from the valance.

IN DETAIL

Hiding a Valance

Covering a valance with casing doesn't usually work. A valance is almost as wide as standard casing, so the casing can't reach the header. Of course, if you're using an extra-wide casing, it could cover the valance and still overlap the header. Some bypass tracks have a built-in valance, making a wood valance unnecessary. However, a built-in valance is appropriate only in a paint-grade setting, when the metal will be coated.

door to slide freely. The ends of the track don't have to fit tightly against the side jambs, because the hangers are set back from the edges of the door. The only exception is a track with a built-in valance, which must be cut to fit.

While there are different types of bypass hardware, light-duty, single- and double-wheel hangers are typically used for this type of installation. Mount them on the rear face of the door about 2 in. from each edge. Hook the door onto the track by tilting the top away from you as you lift it into position. When the wheels clear the lip of the J-track, let the door hang down vertically, thus seating the wheels in the track. A large adjusting screw drives a cam that raises and lowers the wheels. The adjustment is correct when the doors contact the leg jambs evenly.

Finishing up

Floor guides are small plastic yokes that guide bypass doors at floor level. Install them where the doors overlap at the middle of the opening. The guide always holds a portion of both doors. To install a floor guide, slide both doors to one side of the opening, then slip the guide under the doors at the exact center of the opening. Now move the guide in or out perpendicular to the wall until the faces of the doors are parallel to the edges of the jambs. You can determine this by cross-sighting the edges of the doors to the edges of the jambs or simply plumbing the doors with a level. When the floor guide's location is correct, screw it into the floor. Elevate the floor guide with a shim-block if carpet will be installed.

TOOLS AND MATERIALS
Pulls for Bypass Doors

The pulls for bypass doors need be recessed so they don't scrape each other. Press fit circular cup pulls into properly sized holes. Another type of recessed pull has an oblong shape that requires some chiseling and drilling to install.

Installing a Pocket Door

A pocket door kit consists of a track, rolling hardware, and the components for the pocket walls. Two types of kits are available. The first type comes with preassembled wall sections sized for a specific width of door. Many builders dislike these kits because of their low-quality wall lumber and light-duty hardware. The preassembled walls are also cumbersome to transport.

The second type of kit employs a universal frame. The studs for the wall are shipped loose, so

Universal pocket door kit

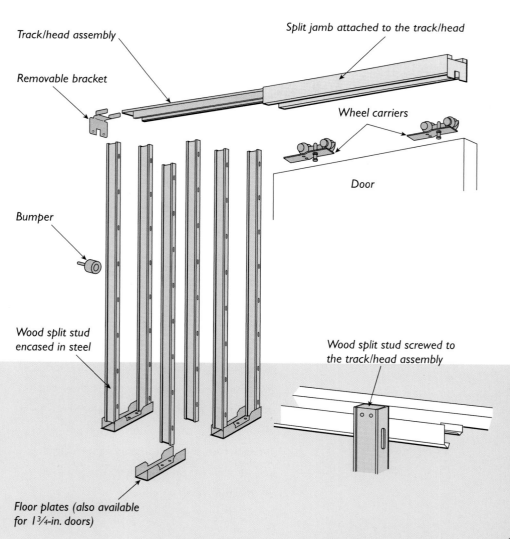

Track/head assembly

Split jamb attached to the track/head

Removable bracket

Wheel carriers

Bumper

Door

Wood split stud encased in steel

Wood split stud screwed to the track/head assembly

Floor plates (also available for 1³/₄-in. doors)

TRADE SECRET

You can avoid buying a kit frame altogether if you're willing to make the wall containing the pocket door a 2×6 wall instead of a 2×4 wall. This will allow you to frame the pocket walls with 2×4s placed "on the flat." Before going this route, though, be sure you can find all the necessary hardware sold without the frame.

IN DETAIL

Mounting the Track/Head Correctly

Unlike the head jamb for a pair of bypass sliding doors, a pocket door head is *not* attached to the structural header above it. Doing so could cause problems if the structural header eventually sagged, and the concealed nature of a pocket door would make adjustment difficult. Instead, the pocket door head is attached to the sides of the rough opening by a removable bracket (see photo opposite, upper left.) This permits clearance between the track/head and the structural header.

> **"Avoid pocket door kits that employ J-tracks, which sometimes allow a hanger to jump off."**

you can space them out to accommodate different door widths. The studs are 1×2s wrapped on three sides with steel to strengthen the thinner-than-normal lumber. Universal frame kits are usually equipped with heavy-duty hangers consisting of two main parts: a three- or four-wheel trolley that rolls in a U-track and a bracket that's mounted to the door. In an arrangement that is somewhat like a hotel coat hanger, a threaded stud with a pair of jam nuts hangs down from the trolley. When the door is installed, the bracket slips onto the trolley's stud. Avoid pocket door kits that employ J-tracks, which sometimes allow a hanger to jump off.

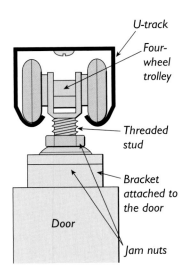

Heavy-duty roller and track

- U-track
- Four-wheel trolley
- Threaded stud
- Bracket attached to the door
- Door
- Jam nuts

Pocket-Door Floor Guides

Several different types of floor guides can be used to keep a pocket door centered. The simplest of these is a plastic U-shaped guide similar to the floor guides used for bypass closet doors. Although easy to install, this type of guide can leave marks on the faces of the door after repeated use. There is another type of plastic guide that just grazes the bottom edge of the door on both sides.

However, the most durable and inconspicuous floor guide is a metal angle that engages a continuous groove routed in the bottom of the door. The groove can be cut with a router and a self-piloting wing cutter. Some kits furnish a metal angle that's as long as the pocket. A long angle ensures that the door is centered throughout the entire pocket. On the downside, though, a full-length angle can cause binding if the door warps or the floor guide isn't exactly parallel with the overhead track. Some carpenters prefer to place a 3-in.-long angle at the mouth of the pocket. In either case, the angle should extend slightly into the opening, so that the door doesn't slip off the angle when it's closed.

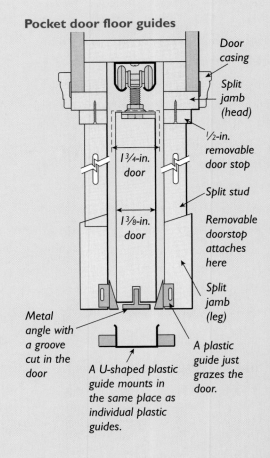

Pocket door floor guides

- Door casing
- Split jamb (head)
- 1¾-in. door
- ½-in. removable door stop
- 1⅜-in. door
- Split stud
- Removable doorstop attaches here
- Split jamb (leg)
- Metal angle with a groove cut in the door
- A U-shaped plastic guide mounts in the same place as individual plastic guides.
- A plastic guide just grazes the door.

The pocket frame track/head is attached with steel brackets to the studs flanking the opening. Some clearance is left between the track/head and the structural header in case the structural header sags.

Installing a universal pocket frame

When you frame the rough opening (your kit should have the dimensions), make sure the double studs on both sides of the opening are plumb in both directions, because a twisted opening is a serious problem. Install the track/head assembly first. The pocket frame header is attached to the studs flanking the opening, usually by means of steel brackets. Before installing a U-shaped track, make sure the hanger trolleys have been placed inside.

Install pocket wall studs next. They're screwed to the frame header at the top and slip onto

Pocket wall studs are screwed to the frame header at the top (top) and slip onto special floor brackets at the bottom (left). The floor brackets provide a flexible connection so the header isn't pulled downward if the floor sags.

IN DETAIL
Putting Hangers in the Track

Hangers must be placed in a U-shaped track before the track is installed, as there's no way to install or remove them later. The exception is a track with keyhole-shaped holes for mounting screws. To remove this type of track, first take out the accessible mounting screws in the opening. Then, shift the track slightly, so that the oversize part of the hole aligns with the screws inside the pocket. The track should then drop off the frame header. When initially installing this type of track, the screws should be seated lightly in the keyhole-shaped holes so that the track can shift laterally.

IN DETAIL

Working with Split Leg Jambs

A split leg jamb is actually two pieces, with one segment on each side of the mouth of the pocket. If stops are used to retain the door, then the split leg jamb can be installed permanently. In that case, the distance between the full-width leg jamb and the split leg jamb equals the width of the door plus ⅛ in. for clearance. This lets you remove the door for repairs. If no stops are used, then removable split leg jambs retain the door. In that case, the distance between the full-width jamb and the nearest pocket frame stud equals the width of the door plus ⅛ in. The ¾-in.-thick split leg jamb then covers the face of the door by ⅝ in. when the door is closed.

special floor brackets at the bottom. The floor brackets space the studs for the correct pocket width and, because the connection between the stud and the bracket is vertically free-floating, the floor brackets keep a sagging floor from pulling down the header/track assembly. Next, snap lines on the subfloor on both sides of the opening to guide the installation of the studs. Finally, slip a temporary spacer between the pocket walls to support them during drywall installation.

Preparing and installing the door

Next, install the flush pulls and/or latchset, since they are very difficult to install after the door is hung. Most pocket door latches are installed by cutting a chunk out of the edge of the door. This weakens a hinged door, but pocket doors aren't subject to the same racking stresses, so a cutout isn't as damaging. Another type of pocket door latch fits the standard face bore and edge bore of hinged doors. If locking isn't a consideration, you can install flush pulls in conjunction with an edge pull.

Screw the hanger brackets to the top edge of the door. Then lift the door and slip the hanger brackets onto the threaded studs suspended from the trolleys. To adjust the door, rotate the lower jam nut up or down with a wrench. The adjustment is correct when the edge of the door makes even contact with the full-width jamb at the outside of the opening. Lock in the adjustment by tightening the upper jam nut against the bracket. To hang a pocket door on a J-track,

The cutout latch (top), which fits into a notch in the door, is the easiest type of pocket door latch to install. An alternative is a mortise edge pull used in conjunction with a flush pull (bottom). The edge pull is grasped when the door is hidden in the pocket; the flush pull is grasped when the side of the door is exposed.

"Floor brackets float vertically, so a sagging floor won't pull down the track."

TRADE SECRET

Pocket wall studs can be knocked out of alignment by too much pressure during drywall installation. A temporary 1×4 stiffener prevents this and makes it easier to drive drywall screws. After the installation, twist the stiffener free and remove it from the pocket.

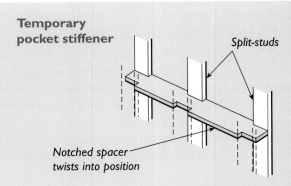

Temporary pocket stiffener

Split-studs

Notched spacer twists into position

tilt the door away from you as you hook it onto the track.

Trimming out a pocket door

There are two common approaches to trimming out a pocket door. One employs stop molding and the other doesn't. In either case, install the *full-width,* or strike, leg jamb first, shimming it if necessary so it stands plumb and is perpendicular to the wall. Next, install the split leg jamb at the other side of the opening.

The head jamb is also split and, like the split leg jamb, can be installed with or without stops. The stops should be nailed lightly or screwed with finishing washers for easy removal.

If you don't use stops, screw the leg and head jambs on one side of the pocket and use finishing washers for easy removal. Nail the split jambs on the other side of the pocket. Nail the casings to the screwed split jambs as scantily as possible, since the casings will be pulled up when you remove the door. If you aren't using stops, then the split jambs and casings can be nailed permanently.

Alternative methods for trimming out pocket doors
Pocket doors need to be removed occasionally for repairs. To allow for this, the trim can be installed in two different ways. Make one of the split jambs removable (bottom) or leave the split jamb fixed but apply a removable stop over it (top).

With stop molding

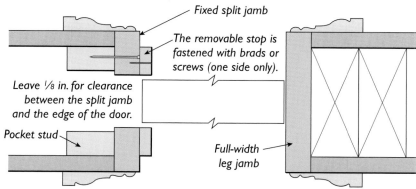

Fixed split jamb

The removable stop is fastened with brads or screws (one side only).

Leave ⅛ in. for clearance between the split jamb and the edge of the door.

Pocket stud

Full-width leg jamb

Without stop molding

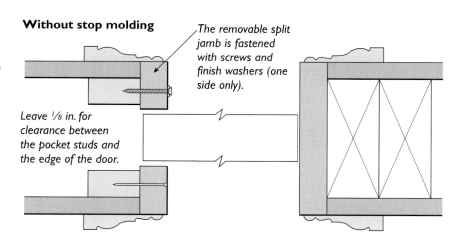

The removable split jamb is fastened with screws and finish washers (one side only).

Leave ⅛ in. for clearance between the pocket studs and the edge of the door.

TRADE SECRET

Stops are seldom applied to a full-width leg jamb because they look unsightly when the door is retracted into the pocket. Stops aren't necessary if the door is adjusted properly, in which case there won't be any gap to conceal.

IN DETAIL

Avoid Setting Screws in the End Grain

Whenever you're mounting hardware that needs to hang and bear a heavy load, try to locate your screws so that they go into the long grain of the wood, which is stronger than the end grain. When setting pocket doors, this means screwing the brackets to the top rail rather than to the end of the stile, where they will eventually loosen.

CHAPTER FOUR

Doors

Installing an exterior door presents some challenges. Unless you have the advantage of installing the exterior door in new construction, you'll need to cut through both the interior and the exterior surfaces. You'll be working in a load-bearing wall and need to make sure you leave it sturdy. You'll also need to make sure everything remains watertight and well insulated. None of this is particularly difficult, if you work in a methodical way. Make sure you take the time to familiarize yourself with all the steps before you begin. Take special care when installing the components that keep water out of the house. Come the first rain storm, you'll be very glad you did.

Framing a Door Opening in a New Exterior Wall

Exterior door openings are framed like interior door openings, except they are mounted in load-bearing walls. For that reason, they require a beefy header to support the structural loads above them.

Structural headers

Headers must be sized properly so they don't *deflect* (bend) appreciably. The wider the opening, the stronger the header must be. A header is usually made stronger by increasing its vertical depth. In cases where a tall header doesn't fit, you can substitute a stronger material. For instance, a steel header is much stronger than a wooden header of the same height.

The most common header in new construction is a double 2×10 placed directly below the top plate, with a 2× packing underneath. In a nominal 8-ft. wall, this setup produces a standard rough opening (R.O.) height suitable for a 6-ft., 8-in. door installed over hardwood finish flooring. Cripple studs won't be necessary above the header. When a solid header doesn't completely fill the wall area between the door and the ceiling, cripples are framed between the header and the top plate to make up the difference.

Assembling the frame

Assemble the wall flat on the floor, making the header first. The header's length equals the width of the R.O. plus the combined thickness of the

Framing a standard-height opening with and without cripple studs

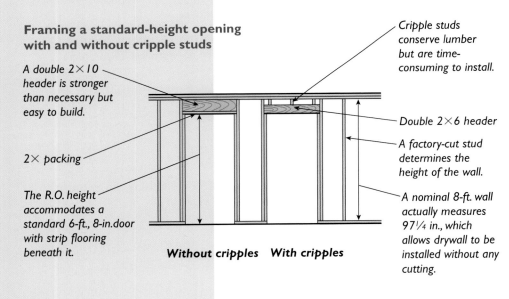

A double 2×10 header is stronger than necessary but easy to build.

2× packing

The R.O. height accommodates a standard 6-ft., 8-in. door with strip flooring beneath it.

Without cripples   With cripples

Cripple studs conserve lumber but are time-consuming to install.

Double 2×6 header

A factory-cut stud determines the height of the wall.

A nominal 8-ft. wall actually measures 97¼ in., which allows drywall to be installed without any cutting.

Cripples have been toenailed to the double top plate. Next the king stud/header assembly will be pulled against the double top plate and the cripples will be toenailed to the header.

IN DETAIL

Header Spans

The following are suggested maximum spans for openings in a conventional wood-frame home. If your local code specifies header sizes, consult it first. Extra loads may be imposed on headers by such factors as special roofing materials, extreme snow conditions, or exceptionally wide floor or roof spans. In those cases, consult an engineer.

Header material on edge	Two stories (Supporting one floor, ceiling, roof)	Single story (Supporting only ceiling and roof)
dbl 2×4	3 ft., 0 in.	3 ft., 6 in.
dbl 2×6	5 ft., 0 in.	6 ft., 0 in.
dbl 2×8	7 ft., 0 in.	8 ft., 0 in.
dbl 2×10	8 ft., 0 in.	10 ft., 0 in.
dbl 2×12	9 ft., 0 in.	12 ft., 0 in.

jack studs (3 in. for a single jack stud one each side, 6 in. for double jack studs). Openings 6 ft. or wider require double jacks to provide adequate bearing for the header.

1. Sandwich the 2×s for the header along with intervening layers of plywood or insulation to produce the needed thickness to match the wall. Then, carefully align the ends and nail the layers together with 16d nails.

2. After the header is assembled, position it against the top plate according to the diagram (see drawing opposite page) and toenail it with 16d nails. Use 16d nails to nail the king stud to both ends of the header, being careful to crown the king studs toward the exterior.

3. Jack studs come next. While you can arrive at their length by subtracting the header height from the length of the king studs, a better way is to hold the jack next to the king stud with its top end butted underneath the header. Then mark the bottom of the jack so it is flush with the bottom of the king.

4. Now the jacks can be nailed to the kings, using a zigzag pattern with 10d sinkers to help clamp the pieces together evenly.

5. Finally, nail the bottom plate to the bottoms of the studs, along with the rest of the studs in the wall. Remove the bottom plate between the jacks after you stand up the wall.

Tipping the double top plate upside-down on the deck makes it easy to toenail the header and attach the king stud.

Nailing patterns for door framing

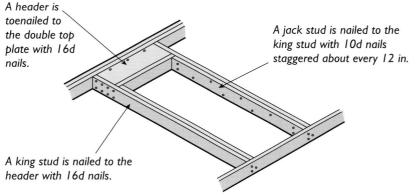

A header is toenailed to the double top plate with 16d nails.

A jack stud is nailed to the king stud with 10d nails staggered about every 12 in.

A king stud is nailed to the header with 16d nails.

You can scribe the jack stud without measuring by holding a stud alongside the king stud and against the underside of the header.

The final step in assembling the wall is nailing the bottom plate to the studs. Layout marks on the edge of the plate refer to the jack studs (the figure O) or common king studs (the figure X).

49

Remove the bottom plate from the door opening after you stand up the wall. This task is easier if you cut halfway through the bottom of the plate with a power saw before assembling the wall. After the wall is up, you can easily finish the cut with a handsaw, chainsaw, or reciprocating saw without marring either the floor or the blade.

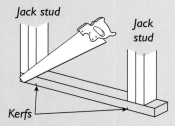

Jack stud

Jack stud

Kerfs

Easy plate removal
Cutting halfway through the plate before raising the wall makes removal easier.

TOOLS AND MATERIALS
Rosin Paper

To protect your finish floor, cover it with rosin paper, a heavy pink kraft paper sold at building suppliers, and tape the joints with clear packing tape. Drop cloths are a poor substitute for paper, since they can't be vacuumed easily and tools and nails tend to hide in the folds.

" Remember to carefully probe the wall for hidden pipes and wires before cutting, and take proper measures to protect the floor and control dust."

Cutting an Opening in an Existing Exterior Wall

When cutting a relatively narrow opening for a hinged single door, you can usually depend on other parts of the building to do the work of the header temporarily. For instance, a band joist at the edge of a floor frame provides quite a bit of temporary support. Wide openings, on the other hand, require shoring for temporary support.

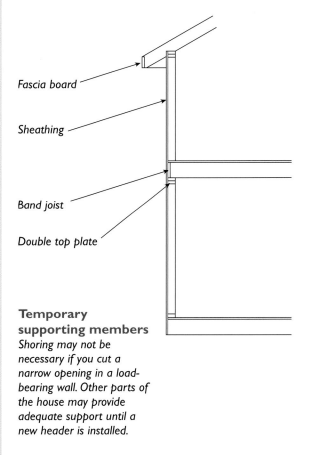

Fascia board

Sheathing

Band joist

Double top plate

Temporary supporting members
Shoring may not be necessary if you cut a narrow opening in a load-bearing wall. Other parts of the house may provide adequate support until a new header is installed.

Locating the opening

The R.O. size for exterior doors is specified by the manufacturer. Once you know the R.O., follow the same procedure for laying out an opening in an interior nonbearing wall (see p. 23). The exception is the top. A beefy structural header can't be sandwiched between the existing wall surfaces. Therefore, make the top cutout

Cutout for a new opening in a load-bearing wall
Openings in load-bearing walls require beefy headers, so the drywall must be removed above the opening.

A new king stud will be added here.

A new header will go here.

Cut intermediate studs here to make cripple studs.

An existing stud becomes a king stud.

New jack studs will go here.

A cutout is made in the drywall.

Remove the plate and studs below the top of the header.

Nails for Framing

Framing nails come in two types: common nails and sinkers. Common nails have either a *bright* (uncoated) finish for interior work or a *galvanized* (coated) finish for exterior jobs. Sinkers are for interior framing only. They're coated with a black, sticky film that acts as a lubricant to drive the nail and creates better adhesion with the wood. Common nails are thicker than sinkers, which makes them stronger but also more likely to split a board. Preferences are largely regional. West Coast framers use sinkers exclusively, whereas common nails are still popular on the East Coast.

about ½ in. above the top of the new header. Align the sides with the new opening, except toward the top, where you need to broaden it just beyond the new jack studs to accommodate the header.

Cutting and framing the interior

Cut out the opening on the inside, using the same cutting techniques as for an interior non-bearing wall (see p. 23). Remember to carefully probe the wall for hidden pipes and wires before cutting, and take proper measures to protect the floor and control dust. After removing the drywall or plaster, cut the studs where the top of the new header will be. Next, pry the studs away from the back of the wall sheathing to remove them from the opening.

Make a king stud/jack stud assembly for each side of the opening and predrill them for screws. Slip them into position between the sheathing and the interior wall finish (drywall or plaster). Fasten them with screws at the top and bottom. Now you can slip the header into position, resting it on the tops of the jacks. Toenail the header thoroughly to the king studs and the cripples above.

If the bottoms of the cripples don't quite sit on the new header, shim the gaps tightly with tapered shims. Do the same if the header sits directly underneath a top plate without cripples and the fit isn't quite perfect. The main concern is that the structural load from above is conveyed to the header.

A circular saw is plunge-cut into the siding above a new window. The saw's depth of cut is adjusted beforehand to cut through the siding but not the sheathing. This makes room for the head trim to overlap the sheathing.

A new header has been seated into position. Shims are used to transfer loads from the cripple studs to the header before nailing.

IN DETAIL
Cutting a Wide Opening

Before cutting an opening in a load-bearing wall, it's a good idea to have an architect, engineer, or experienced contractor inspect the situation. It's often necessary to shore up the floor or ceiling with temporary studs to support the load when cutting a wide opening in a load-bearing wall. When a concentrated load is present, even narrow openings may necessitate shoring.

WHAT CAN GO WRONG
When a Reciprocating Saw Binds

If you're cutting an existing stud and your reciprocating saw suddenly starts to shake violently, it means that the blade is pinched in the cut. There's always a slight bind as a cut is completed, but if you can't free the saw, it's an indication that there's a lot of weight bearing down on the stud. Stop and reassess whether you need to shore up the floor or ceiling above the new opening.

IN DETAIL

Weather Barrier Systems

Flashing, housewrap, exterior trim, and siding each play different roles in a weather barrier system. In order for them to do their jobs, the system's components must be overlapped correctly. Like the skin of a fish, there are big scales and little scales, but they all face in the same direction. In fact, incorrectly installed flashing is worse than no flashing at all, because it actually funnels water into the building instead of shedding it to the exterior. It's not that difficult to figure out the right way to overlap. Use this rule: *That which is above overlaps that which is below.*

TOOLS AND MATERIALS

Plunge-Cutting with a Circular Saw

When plunge-cutting with a circular saw, set the depth of cut to just graze the sheathing. With the front of the saw's shoe on the siding and the back of the shoe raised so the blade clears the siding, retract the blade guard. Start the saw and gently lower the blade into the cut. Reverse the procedure when you reach the end of the cut.

Cutting the exterior opening

Once the new header is installed, drill holes at all four corners of the opening through to the exterior so you'll have reference points outside. Now the trick is to cut back the siding so that the new door's exterior trim fits snugly. Make the lower horizontal cut in both the siding and the sheathing flush with the subfloor. Your reference holes establish the *elevation* (vertical location) of the subfloor on the outside. Connect these holes to lay out the cut, then cut both the sheathing and the siding from the outside with a reciprocating saw. Don't worry about an imperfect cut here, since the flashing will hide it. However, the other three cuts have to be "on the money."

The best tool for cutting into existing siding is a lightweight circular saw, preferably a cordless one. Plunge into the cut, making the top sheathing flush with the underside of the new header. Cut the siding a little higher to accommodate the head casing and flashing. To establish the upper horizontal cut in the siding, start at the subfloor where the doorsill will be located. Measure the overall height of the door unit from the underside of the sill to the top of the head casing, and add an extra ½ in. for some play.

Now make the vertical siding cuts. A circular saw is the best tool to use, because it cuts cleanly and its depth can be adjusted precisely. The problem, however, is that the siding in most cases presents a bumpy surface. A cutting jig solves this problem. After you remove the

siding, connect your reference holes on the sheathing, then cut out the sheathing with a reciprocating saw or a chainsaw.

Prepping an Exterior Door Opening

Most of the prep work occurs at the bottom of the opening. Always keep two goals in mind: Make it level and make it watertight. The sides of the opening are wrapped to make them watertight as well. At this stage, the top of a door or window opening doesn't require any preparation. The weather barrier at the top (usually metal flashing) is installed as part of the siding process, after the door or window is installed. Notice the sequence here: bottom, sides, top. The key to a watertight installation is working from the bottom up.

Installing a floor pan

Unless the door is sheltered by a porch, install a floor pan below the sill to keep out moisture. Pans can be fabricated on site using metal or a flexible membrane. You can also buy manufactured plastic pans that come in standard widths for 2×4 and 2×6 walls. The pan should be turned up at its ends and along its inside edge between the sill and the finish flooring to keep water flowing to the outside of the building envelope.

A floor pan folds down over the exterior wall. When a door exits onto a wooden deck, the pan overlaps the deck flashing. Sometimes a

TRADE SECRET

A circular saw can cut siding cleanly, but you have to provide it with a flat surface. Tack a straight board to the wall temporarily to do so. For greater accuracy, tack a narrow guide strip to the edge of the board as a straightedge. When you run the shoe of the saw against this strip the first time, the board's edge will be made even with the saw's cutting line. Now align the ripped edge of the board with the layout line on your siding for a perfect cut. You're bound to hit at least one nail, so change to an older blade.

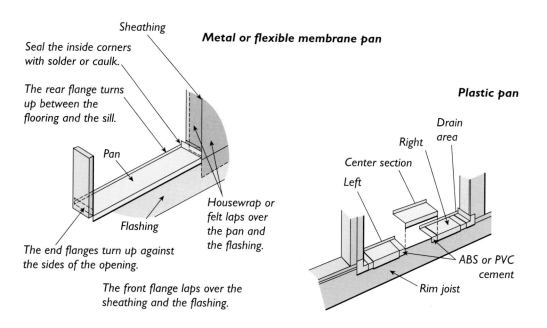

Metal or flexible membrane pan

Seal the inside corners with solder or caulk.

Sheathing

The rear flange turns up between the flooring and the sill.

Pan

Flashing

The end flanges turn up against the sides of the opening.

Housewrap or felt laps over the pan and the flashing.

The front flange laps over the sheathing and the flashing.

Plastic pan

Drain area

Right

Center section

Left

ABS or PVC cement

Rim joist

Floor pans

Floor pans prevent water from seeping into the floor framing below the doorway. Metal pans are custom bent, and their inside corners are sealed with solder or caulk. Flexible membrane pans are folded in place and sealed with caulk. Plastic pans consist of a center section and two end sections that are fused together with solvent-based cement.

masonry stoop or patio is built against a wooden floor. In that case, masonry flashing protects the wooden framing, and the floor pan overlaps the flashing.

To form sheet-metal flashing, you can bend it over a corner with a mallet. A neater job is done with a brake, a device that clamps and bends metal. You can rent a portable brake or make your own. If you're using a sheet-metal brake, turn up the inside edge of the pan before you install the door. Without a brake, it's easier to wait until the sill is installed to turn up the edge, using the sill itself as a straightedge. Flexible membranes, such as waterproof paper, can simply be folded in place. Caulk site-built pans at the inside corners where the upturned flanges meet.

Making a Measuring Rod for Outside Cuts

A measuring rod is a great way to avoid math. Hold a stick with one end against the outside edge of a door's exterior casing. Tick off a mark at the outside of the opposite casing. This is the distance between the vertical cuts in the siding. Now measure the prescribed R.O. width from one end of the stick. Divide the remaining distance in half. This is the offset from one side of the R.O. to the corresponding siding cut. Register the rod against the reference holes, marking the R.O. to locate the cuts in the siding.

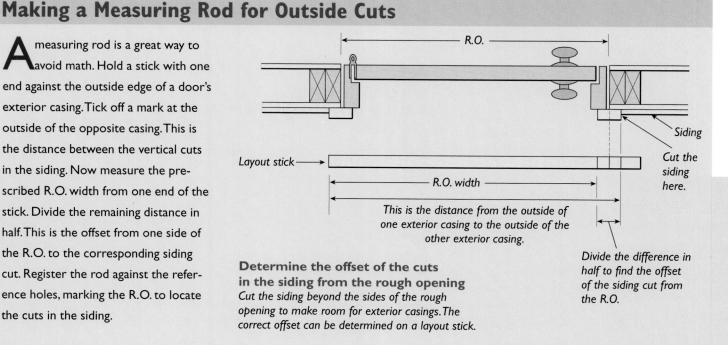

R.O.

Layout stick

R.O. width

This is the distance from the outside of one exterior casing to the outside of the other exterior casing.

Siding

Cut the siding here.

Divide the difference in half to find the offset of the siding cut from the R.O.

Determine the offset of the cuts in the siding from the rough opening
Cut the siding beyond the sides of the rough opening to make room for exterior casings. The correct offset can be determined on a layout stick.

TOOLS AND MATERIALS
Metals for Flashing

While synthetic materials can provide good service, metal is the material of choice for exposed flashing. The primary metals used for flashing doors and windows are aluminum and copper, though galvanized steel, terne (steel coated with tin), prepainted steel, and lead are occasionally used. Aluminum offers good corrosion resistance, is inexpensive, and is available prepainted. Copper is the most durable (and expensive) of flashing metals and is seldom painted. Copper can be soldered, whereas aluminum must be sealed with caulk. Aluminum corrodes quickly in the presence of copper, so never use the two metals together.

Wrapping the sides of the opening

The sides of the rough opening should be wrapped with some type of membrane, in case the caulk between the exterior trim and the siding fails. If you wrap the entire house with 15-lb. asphalt felt or housewrap before you set the doors and windows, then simply fold the wrap into the opening, staple it, and trim off the excess flush with the inside of the framing. Later, when you install the floor pan, be sure to tuck its upturned ends under the wrap.

It's often necessary to install doors and windows before the wrapping is done. In that case, flash the openings with *splines* (strips of waterproof kraft

A brake-formed aluminum pan protects this doorway. The pan overlaps the deck flashing below, and housewrap overlaps the upturned sides of the pan. A dab of caulk seals the inside corners.

Doorway at a wooden deck

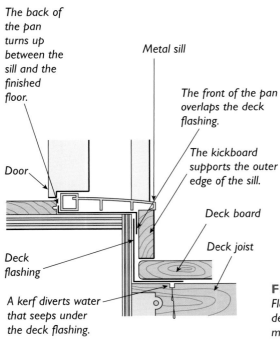

The back of the pan turns up between the sill and the finished floor.

Metal sill

The front of the pan overlaps the deck flashing.

The kickboard supports the outer edge of the sill.

Door

Deck board

Deck flashing

Deck joist

A kerf diverts water that seeps under the deck flashing.

Doorway at a masonry patio

The front of the pan overlaps the masonry flashing.

Masonry paving

Concrete

Masonry flashing

Wooden sill

The bottom of the masonry flashing extends below the top of the foundation.

Top of the foundation

Flashing and kickboard
Flashing below a doorway keeps water at bay. The flashing design depends on whether the adjacent floor surface is wood or masonry. A kickboard supports the overhanging edge of the sill.

> "The sides of the rough opening should be wrapped with some type of membrane, in case the caulk between the exterior trim and the siding fails."

IN DETAIL
About Doorsills

Modern wood and all-metal sills taper in thickness, giving them a sloped top and a level bottom. Unfortunately, tapering weakens the sill right where it needs the most strength—at the overhanging front edge. The kickboard below a tapered sill should support the sill's edge. Some sills have a drip groove. In that case, the kickboard should extend only to the groove. Some sills also have a flashing groove on the underside. You can insert metal flashing, felt, or housewrap into the groove for a positive moisture break. The next line of defense is caulk, which is applied to the bottom of the opening during installation.

A strip of waterproof flashing paper has been folded in place in lieu of a metal or plastic pan. Silicone caulk seals the paper to the underside of the doorsill.

paper or 15-lb. asphalt felt). The side splines overlap the flashing below the door and extend about 6 in. past the top of the opening. After the unit is set, install a top spline over the top of the unit. Later, when the house is wrapped in its entirety, the housewrap or felt will overlap the splines.

The author uses felt splines to prep a doorway when housewrap hasn't yet been installed.

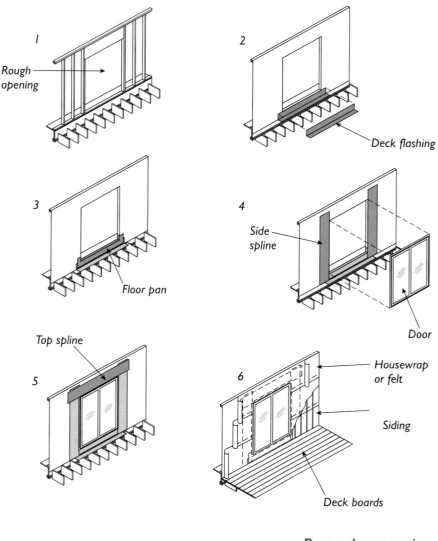

1 Rough opening

2 Deck flashing

3 Floor pan

4 Side spline / Door

5 Top spline

6 Housewrap or felt / Siding / Deck boards

Prep a door opening with splines
Splines are used when doors are installed before the felt or housewrap. Later, the felt or housewrap will overlap the splines.

TRADE SECRET

Some carpenters apply splines to the door unit instead of the opening. Sandwich the splines between the jamb and the exterior casing if the casing wasn't applied at the factory. If the unit has been precased, staple the splines to the back of the casing. Attaching splines to the door instead of the opening makes a lot of sense, because it blocks water before it even enters the wall.

TOOLS AND MATERIALS

Nails for Exterior Trim

The standard nail for exterior casing is a 10d galvanized finish nail. It's long enough to pass through both the casing and the plywood sheathing and still get a good bite into the framing. Various types of siding nails are used, as well. Some of these have spiral shanks or ringed shanks for extra holding power. For maximum longevity, use stainless steel nails instead of galvanized ones. They're expensive, but they won't rust or stain clear-finished cedar or redwood trim.

> *"A crooked casing shows up on the inside as an uneven margin, so you can see which way you need to pry the jamb to straighten it out."*

Installing a Prehung Exterior Door

With a properly sized and framed opening and a level floor, you've already fought more than half the battle of installing an exterior door. Now it's simply a question of placing, plumbing, and securing the unit.

Placing and plumbing the unit

Before placing a door, I like to check the floor for level one more time. If it isn't level, it needs to be accurately shimmed. Dry-fit the unit without any caulk to be sure it fits. With the unit in the opening, check the margins between the door and the jambs. Usually they're even, because manufacturers typically place cardboard spacers on the edges of the door. But if spacers haven't been applied and the margins are uneven, then the frame is racked (pushed out of square). In that case, remove the door from the opening and take out any packing nails that are holding the jamb to the door.

Square the frame by tipping it to one side or the other. With all its weight resting on one bottom corner, pull down on the head jamb at the diagonally opposite corner until the diagonals are approximately equal. At this point, you just want to be sure the unit is going to fit, so plus or minus 1/16 in. is close enough. Final squaring is achieved when the unit is plumbed in the opening.

With the unit back in the opening, check to see if there's at least 1/8 in. of clearance between the jambs and the framing. Try to center it at both the top and the bottom, but it's okay if the bottom is slightly shifted to make the top fit. If the unit is shifted tight to one side at the bottom and the opposite corner still won't fit, the opening is seriously out of plumb and you'll have to make some adjustments.

Once the unit fits, tip it out of the opening, lay it face down and shoot a continuous bead of caulk on the wall around the opening. Also, lay three parallel beads of caulk along the bottom of the floor pan and up the ends. If there's still a packing nail holding the jamb, remove it, and then set the unit back in the opening. Drive one 10d galvanized finish nail through each exterior casing leg, about 4 in. up from

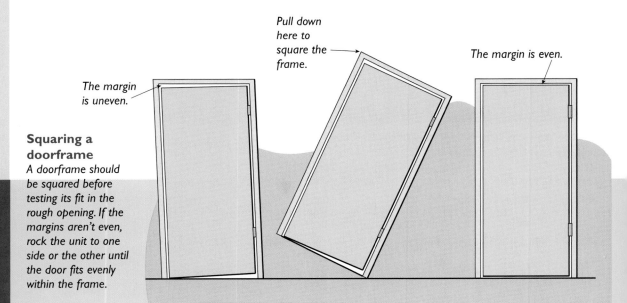

The margin is uneven.

Pull down here to square the frame.

The margin is even.

Squaring a doorframe
A doorframe should be squared before testing its fit in the rough opening. If the margins aren't even, rock the unit to one side or the other until the door fits evenly within the frame.

the floor, but leave the nail heads sticking out a bit.

Next, adjust the top of the unit from side to side (a short pinch bar is ideal for this). If you have a doorhanger's level, use it to check the casing for plumb. If you've only got a short level, you'll need to use it in conjunction with a straightedge to diagnose any warping. When the unit is plumb, drive a nail through each leg casing about 4 in. from the top to lock it. If the sill is sitting level, the frame will be square and the margins will be even.

Next, check the casing legs for straightness. A crooked casing shows up on the inside as an uneven margin, so you can see which way you need to pry the jamb to straighten it out. When the casing legs are straight, nail them every 12 in. or so. Then straighten the head casing and nail it, as well. Finally, set all the nails.

The final check is for in-and-out alignment. If the opening is cross-legged, the door may not close evenly on the strike side. Flexible weatherstripping slightly compensates for this, but you can make an adjustment now that will prevent problems later. If closing the door makes it hit the weatherstripping at the bottom before it hits

Before installing a door, apply a triple bead of caulk to the floor pan. Caulk has been applied here to the side splines, as well, but it could have been applied to the back of the door's exterior casing instead.

Leveling a Sill

An exterior doorsill must be shimmed level and straight if the floor isn't true, and the spacing of the shims must be close enough to prevent the sill from flexing. For instance, shim a heavy oak sill for a hinged door about every 16 in.; shim a thin aluminum sill every 12 in. Sills for sliding doors require the closest spacing (8 in.), because the doors' weight bears directly on them. Apply a bead of silicone caulk as high as or a little higher than the shims to provide additional support and seal out moisture.

The materials for shims should be decay resistant and fairly hard, so they don't eventually compress. Shims placed over a wooden subfloor can be tacked to hold them steady. Use a dab of caulk or construction adhesive to secure shims to a concrete floor.

TRADE SECRET

Brick mold is the most common type of exterior casing. It's only 2 in. wide, so if the rough opening is oversize or out of plumb, the brick mold may be just wide enough to cover it. You need to angle your nails to sink them into the framing, but don't angle them too much, or the nail will exit from the edge of the casing. Use a cordless drill to predrill the holes. Drill from the back, just ¼ in. from the edge, and angle the hole toward the inside. The hole should emerge on the front of the brick mold about ½ in. from the edge.

"To prevent the door from sagging, remove the inside screws from the top hinge and replace them with 3-in.-long screws that penetrate the framing."

the top, move the bottom of the hinge-side jamb out slightly by prying between the exterior casing and the sheathing. If the door strikes the top of the weatherstripping first, move the hinge-side jamb out at the top.

Shimming and securing the jambs

Exterior doors and windows usually have pre-attached casing, which makes shimming tricky, because the shims can only be installed from one side (see left photo, opposite page). I like to use three shims on each side jamb and at least one at the top (more for wider doors). The best places for shims are behind the striker and directly behind all the hinges. To prevent the door from sagging, remove the inside screws from the top

hinge and replace them with 3-in.-long screws that penetrate the framing.

Finishing the Exterior

Your door is in, but you still have some buttoning up to do. First, you'll need to install the exterior trim if it wasn't done at the factory. Then you'll need to flash the top of the unit, so that water coming from above will be shunted safely to the outside. The shim space between the jambs and the framing also needs to be filled with insulation to keep out drafts. Finally, after these "undergarments" are in place, the building is ready for it's outerwear: siding and exposed caulking. If all these components are woven together correctly, water will roll past your door like water off a duck's back.

After centering the unit, nail the leg casings close to the floor.

The author reads a level as his helper inside pries between the unit and the rough opening. When the unit is plumb, the author will nail the leg casings at the top.

The hinge-side jamb is moved out from the wall slightly to correct for a cross-legged opening. The author is watching the gap between the door and the weatherstripping at the diagonally opposite corner of the door.

Installing exterior casing

Contemporary homes with sleek styling look best with no exterior casings. This is achieved by using clad units with nailing fins, which act as hidden casings underneath the siding. When casing is used, it's usually installed at the factory. A precased door lets you quickly set the unit during the rough carpentry phase without installing shims.

Sometimes, the exterior casing is left off, so that special material can be applied at the site to match a particular siding. Unless the manufacturer is willing to preattach special casing, you'll have to apply it yourself. In that case, make sure you order a door unit with long *horns* (extensions of the sill that reach past the sides of the rough opening) to provide a termination for the exterior casing legs

Long screws are driven through the top hinge for extra support. Only the two innermost screws are replaced with long screws, because there is wood behind the jamb at that point. The outermost screws on the jamb leaf have just drywall behind them, so an extra-long screw does no good.

(see the top drawing, p. 60). I usually order the horns slightly longer than necessary, so that I can trim them at the site. (You can use the nominal width of the casing as a guide, since the actual width is ½ in. less.)

The most common type of exterior casing is brick mold. It has a rectangular cross section, with a slightly raised molding on its outer corner. Brick mold looks good on both old and new homes and is neither too skinny nor too wide. Avoid finger-jointed wooden casing, which doesn't hold up well in exterior settings.

Old houses look better with wide casings that are ¾ in. by 4 in. or ¾ in. by 6 in. Use five-quarter stock instead of 1x, so that the siding doesn't stand out beyond the face of the casing. For very thick siding, such as rustic lap siding, you may need to use 2× stock. The wide casing look is now available from some manufacturers in low-maintenance materials, such as aluminum and vinyl. Ask your supplier.

Exterior casing is typically beveled to fit tightly against the sloping surface of the sill. The

This exterior door is precased on the outside, which makes installing shims tricky. Insert a shim with the thick end first. While holding the first shim with one hand, insert additional shims with the thin edge first until they fit snugly.

SAFETY FIRST

Prehung exterior doors are heavy and awkward to move, so installing one is much safer and easier with two people. In addition, a two-person team allows for an inside worker, who pries the unit into its proper position, and an outside worker, who reads a level and fastens the exterior casing. Installing a door solo is possible, too, as long as you work carefully; it just takes a little longer and requires more legwork.

WHAT CAN GO WRONG
Separate Sills

More manufacturers are furnishing the overhanging portion of their sills as a separate piece to fit into the main sill with a tongue-and-groove joint. Having no overhang on the sill enables the unit to nest tightly during shipping, which eases handling and reduces damage. Separate sill extensions can be cut in the field to create whatever length of horn is necessary. However, separate sills have a serious drawback: Water can infiltrate the joint between the extension and the primary sill and lead to decay. To prevent this, set them in a generous bed of caulk.

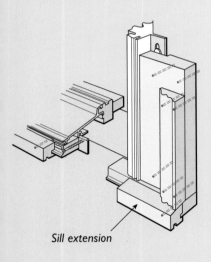

Sill extension

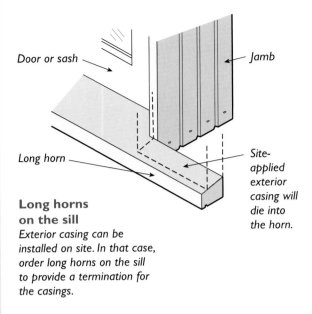

Door or sash

Jamb

Long horn

Site-applied exterior casing will die into the horn.

Long horns on the sill
Exterior casing can be installed on site. In that case, order long horns on the sill to provide a termination for the casings.

exception is a door that takes a full step down to a deck or stoop. In that situation, the casing runs past the sill to the deck, while a durable kickboard fits between the leg casings instead of the siding. A kickboard can take more abuse than siding. Keep the ends of the casings and the bottom of the kickboard at least ½ in. above a deck or patio to prevent decay.

Joining the casing is pretty straightforward. Join brick mold with miters. Flat casings are better joined with butt joints, because large miters tend to open in exterior work. I like to reinforce the joint by driving a screw down from the headpiece into the leg.

Installing head flashing

Head flashing, also known as a drip cap, is a metal strip that tucks under the siding in the back and turns over the casing in the front. Its purpose is

to intercept water from above and convey it to the outside. To keep water from sheeting over the door, the head flashing should overhang slightly so water drips freely to the ground. The ends of the head flashing should reach the outside edges of the casing. Turning over the ends adds a nice finished look.

I prefer to install a wooden drip cap between the casing and the flashing, and then bend the flashing so it pitches forward. A wooden drip cap used to be a standard item at lumberyards, but it's getting hard to find. In a pinch you can fabricate a wooden drip cap on a table saw by ripping a 1×2 at a 10-degree angle (see photo, opposite page).

It's often necessary to slip head flashing under existing housewrap. To do this, slit the housewrap with a utility knife about ¾ in. above the head

This vinyl window trim has traditional styling.
Wide J-channels suggest the look of traditional casing, while a vinyl crown molding duplicates a classic window hood.

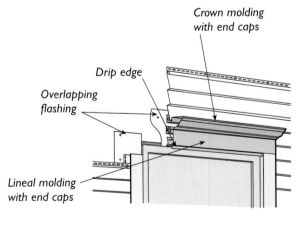

Crown molding with end caps

Drip edge

Overlapping flashing

Lineal molding with end caps

TAKE YOUR PICK
Exterior Casing Options

Brick mold—(Old and new houses)
- wood—clear or finger-jointed
- Vinyl clad over treated wood
- Extruded aluminum
- Solid urethane

Flat—(Old-style houses)
- wood—typically ⁵⁄₄ × 4 or ⁵⁄₄ × 6
- Aluminum extrusion that snaps into the jamb
- Wide vinyl J-channel

None—(New-style houses)
- clad units with hidden nailing fins

casing, being careful not to cut above where the top edge of the flashing will be. Terminate the slit in line with the edges of the leg casings, and slip the back edge of the head flashing under the housewrap. Apply a short piece of housewrap tape over the ends of the slit (see photo, p. 62). If you're using a wooden drip cap under the flashing, raise the slit to allow for its thickness.

Installing siding around doors and windows

Contrary to what you may think, you should leave a gap between an exterior door and the siding. A gap of ⅛ in. is standard, but some of the new fiber-cement sidings require an even bigger gap (follow the manufacturer's installation guidelines). You will fill the gap later with caulk, and a thick caulk bead stretches more than a skinny bead.

To promote drying, there should also be at least a ¼-in. gap between the head flashing and

Head flashing

Head flashing conveys water safely beyond the top of a door or window. Housewrap or felt must overlap the top edge of the head flashing in case rain is driven behind the siding. A wooden drip cap supports the head flashing at a downward pitch.

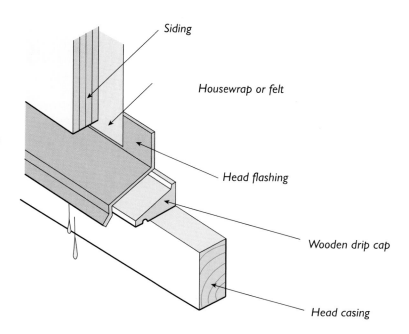

Siding

Housewrap or felt

Head flashing

Wooden drip cap

Head casing

Kickboard

A kickboard supports the sill overhang and resists wear better than siding does. Exterior casing runs past the sill instead of dying into it.

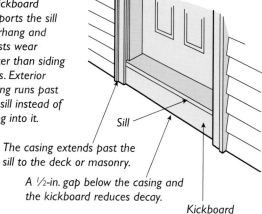

Sill

The casing extends past the sill to the deck or masonry.

A ½-in. gap below the casing and the kickboard reduces decay.

Kickboard

Stop Rot Now

Exterior casing is highly susceptible to decay, especially on the end grain where the legs meet the sill. To prevent decay, always prime the back of casings and treat the ends generously with water repellent, such as Woodlife®. Immersing the pieces overnight is a good idea, too.

To make a drip cap on site, saw a 1×2 in half at a 10-degree angle.

IN DETAIL

Caulking Doors and Windows

Caulking around doors and windows is a two-stage process. During the first stage, sandwich a hidden bead between the exterior casing or nailing fins and the wall. During the second stage, lay an exposed bead where the siding meets the side casing and the sill. To get a neat bead, cut the tube's tip cleanly at a slight angle. Feed the caulk at a steady rate. If caulk starts to build up ahead of the tip, speed up. If the bead starts to pull away from the sides of the gap, slow down. Wipe the tip of the tube frequently. If you do this correctly, you shouldn't have to tool the caulk at all. If you do have to wipe the bead, nothing works better than a wet finger.

TRADE SECRET

Caulk needs to stretch, because the materials it adheres to expand and contract with heat and humidity. A thin surface bead of caulk will break before it stretches, thereby losing its seal, but a thicker bead will stretch as needed. Just don't go overboard.

"If you haven't worked with foam before, practice on a small section first to see how much the foam expands as it hardens. Getting the stuff out of an overfilled gap is not fun."

the siding. If possible, adjust the siding courses so that a *butt line* (the lower edge of a course) aligns with the tops of the windows and doors, which looks better and saves some notching. Sometimes, the courses can also be brought into alignment with the bottoms of windows, but this depends on the height of the windows and the siding's recommended exposed height of the course. The key to harmonizing these dimensions is a good story pole (see sidebar, opposite page).

Vinyl siding exposure is fixed by its interlocking lip, so you won't be able to adjust its spacing. However, it may be possible to start slightly higher or lower in relation to the foundation to make a course even with the tops of the windows. When a new course starts directly above a window, be sure to slip a shim under it. The shim should be flush with the concealed edges of the courses on both sides of the window to produce a uniform bearing surface for the course above.

By the way, the best windows to use with vinyl siding are vinyl windows made specifically for the job. They feature a built-in J-channel that saves time and provides a better seal. These windows also work with bevel siding and clapboards.

Insulating the shim space

The shim space between the unit and its rough opening needs to be filled with either fiberglass "wool" or spray-in foam insulation to prevent drafts. To use fiberglass, cut 1-in.-wide strips from a fiberglass batt using a utility knife and a straightedge or a large pair of sewing shears. Use a screwdriver or the blade of a combination

Head flashing is slipped under a slit in the housewrap. Tape any overcut in the slit with housewrap tape or tuck a small patch of felt under it.

TOOLS AND MATERIALS

Caulk

Latex/acrylic caulk is inexpensive, guns well, and cleans up easily. It's available in a wide range of colors, but you can paint it if you want to change the color down the road. Silicone caulk is more expensive. It adheres about the same as latex/acrylic, except on metal, where it adheres poorly. While silicone caulk is water-soluble fresh out of the tube, it quickly becomes gummy, making it hard to clean up. Most types of silicone caulk are non-paintable. Urethane caulk is another so-called "high-performance" caulk that I haven't found to be much better than latex/acrylic. Avoid butyl caulk, because it's extremely difficult to clean up.

The first continuous course of siding above a window or door should be backed up by a thin strip. The strip sits flush with the siding to the left and right of the window, thereby preventing the siding from bowing inward as it is nailed.

square to stuff the strips into the gaps, filling them fully but not tightly. Gaps that are less than ⅛ in. wide can't be stuffed easily, so caulk them instead.

Instead of fiberglass, you can apply urethane foam from a straw-tipped aerosol can. Non-expanding foam is best, but you can use regular foam if you practice on a small section first to see how much the foam expands as it hardens. Getting the stuff out of an overfilled gap is not fun. After the foam hardens, trim the excess flush with the framing. A bread knife works well for this.

Spray foam is a good insulator around doors and windows, but too much can cause a jamb to bow as the foam expands.

Using a Story Pole for Laying Out Siding

Make a story pole with a straight 1×4. Mark 1 in. up from the bottom to represent the joint between the framing and the foundation. The bottom of the pole then indicates the bottom of the lowest course. With the pole registering at the top of the foundation, mark the pole ¼ in. above the head flashing of the doors and windows. (It's customary to align the tops of doors and windows.) Check all the windows to average out minor discrepancies, and then mark the bottoms of the windows, as well.

If one window height prevails, try dividing it into an equal number of courses, adding or subtracting a course to make the spacing work. Then divide the remaining space below the window. If that doesn't work, evenly divide the total height from the tops of the windows to the bottom of the wall. That means you'll have to notch the siding around the bottoms of the windows but not at the tops. Use a foot/inch calculator to make these computations.

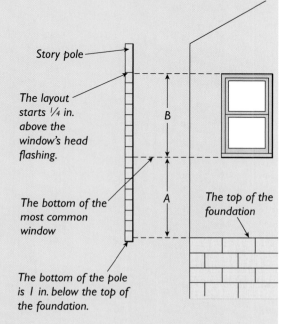

Story pole

The layout starts ¼ in. above the window's head flashing.

The bottom of the most common window

The bottom of the pole is 1 in. below the top of the foundation.

The top of the foundation

Story pole
Ideally, distance A and distance B can both be divided into increments that are close to the siding's recommended spacing. If not, divide the combined distance of A+B into equal spaces, and notch the siding around the bottom of the window.

SAFETY FIRST

Use a dust mask and wear a long-sleeved shirt when stuffing fiberglass around doors and windows. While certain types of fiberglass claim to be less irritating than their predecessors, it's still best to minimize contact with this itchy material.

CHAPTER FIVE
Exterior Doors

oors that open to patios and decks are often wider than front-entry or side-entry doors. Sometimes a larger door is used to give wide access, but more often French doors and patio doors are installed because they bring light into the house. Their open, friendly look brings the outside in and invites us to use exterior spaces for relaxing and entertaining.

Like their interior counterparts, complex exterior doors present a few challenges. As with any door or window project, the best path to success is good planning and preparation. Research your door options in styles and materials before you buy anything. Take the time to make sure your frame is square and plumb, as well. Not only will this make installation easier, it will also ensure that the doors operate properly over the long haul.

1 Installing Prehung French Doors, p. 66

2 Installing Center-Hinged Patio Doors, p. 70

3 Installing Sliding Patio Doors, p. 74

4 Installing Storm and Secondary Doors, p. 78

Installing Prehung French Doors

The key to setting wide exterior door units is leveling the sill. If the floor is out of level and the jambs are plumb, you'll end up with a parallelogram instead of a rectangle, with one door higher than the other. Even if you plane the tops and bottoms of the doors to fit inside the parallelogram, the muntins won't align where the doors meet. Take as much time as you need to get the floor shimmed absolutely level

Make sure the floor is level and straight. Use the longest level you have.

WHAT CAN GO WRONG

Even with careful dry-fitting, problems may not show up until after some nails have been installed. For easy removal it's good to leave all nailheads sticking out until all the nails are driven and everything checks out. Then you can punch the nailheads down with a nail-set.

"Take as much time as you need to get the floor shimmed absolutely level and straight."

Prepping French Doors

If a unit is precased, you can initially fasten it to the wall through its casings, then shim it afterward. If the unit has no exterior casing, lay it flat and preinstall the casing. If that's not practical for some reason, it's good to attach some temporary strips for registering the edge of the jamb flush with the wall. The strips also make handling easier and help hold the frame square. If the doors swing in, mount the strips on the outside. If the doors swing out, mount the strips on the inside. That way, you'll be able to swing the doors to test their action before removing the strips.

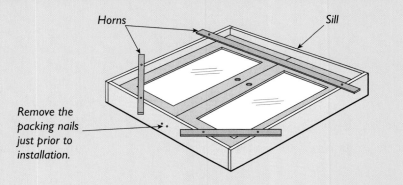

Horns   Sill

Remove the packing nails just prior to installation.

Temporary strips
Door units without exterior casings are easier to handle if temporary strips are screwed into the jambs. The overhanging horns also help make the jambs flush with the exterior wall.

and straight. Use the longest level you have, and spin it 180 degrees from time to time to verify its accuracy.

Placing the unit

After framing the rough opening, dry-fit the unit in the opening to make sure it fits. If the fit looks good, remove the unit and shoot three continuous beads of caulk on the floor pan, extending them 3 in. up the sides of the opening. If the unit has been precased, apply caulk around the opening. If there are packing nails holding the doors where they meet at the head jamb, remove them now, but leave any cardboard spacers between the doors and the frame to keep the margins even.

With a helper, lift and carefully tip the unit into the opening, shoving it in until the casing or the temporary strips fully contact the wall. If you're using temporary strips, nail them to the wall, but leave the heads out for later removal (see sidebar, facing page). Nail the bottom strip first, check the margins to be sure the frame hasn't racked, and then nail the top strips. If racking has occurred, have your helper pry gently between the jamb and the stud until the margins even out, and then nail the top strip. If the unit was precased, fasten the casing on both sides at the bottom first. Then, check the margins all around to make sure they are even, and nail the casing near the upper corners.

Doors must be horizontally aligned where they meet. Check this while dry-fitting the door. If the jambs are plumb but the doors don't line up, then the floor isn't perfectly level.

Setting double doors is a two-person job. Maneuver the bottom of the unit into the opening and then stand the unit up.

WHAT CAN GO WRONG

The Floor is Out of Level

You can forget about plumbing the sides of the unit at this point. If your sill is level and straight, the doors are square, and the margins are even, then the sides will automatically be plumb. If not, it's more important to keep the margins even and the doors horizontally aligned than to keep the unit plumb. The only alternative (and it isn't a good one) is to pull the unit, scrape off all the wet caulk, and reshim the floor to make it level.

TRADE SECRET

If interior doors aren't flush, you can distribute the error by fudging all four corners away from the wall and twisting the casings. Exterior casing won't flex like interior casing, however, so it isn't practical to recess the exterior edges of the jambs. Consequently, one jamb should be flush with the wall and the other jamb should be pried away from the bottom of the wall's outside surface.

Tweaking the jambs to make the doors meet

To make double doors meet flush in the middle, you may have to tweak the jambs perpendicular to the wall, especially if the opening is cross-legged (see p. 74 for more on cross-legging). To tweak a precased unit, pry the exterior casing away from the wall on one side (right or left). To tweak an uncased unit, pry the temporary strip away from the wall. Pry the bottom of the strip, so the discrepancy isn't at eye level. In most cases, the siding will cover any gap between the exterior casing and the wall. Install a few shims behind where the exterior casing has been pried away from the wall, so that the casing doesn't bounce or break when you nail its outer edge.

Moving the casing out also moves the jamb, so the inside edges of the jambs will now be

recessed shy of the interior surface. If it's an out-swing unit, you can add a tapered jamb extension on the inside. If it's an in-swing unit, your only option is to twist the inside casing into position. You may have to shave the interior miters as a result.

Straightening the jambs

If the unit has been precased, the jambs should be straight and the unit can be shimmed later. For an uncased unit, now is the time to shim. Shim behind the upper and lower hinges first, driving just one 10d finish nail through the jambs and the shims at each location, leaving the nail heads proud. Double-check the flushness of the doors where they meet, because nailing through the jambs will lock in this adjustment. When the doors are flush, shim and nail at the middle hinges, at the middle of the head jamb, and at 16-in. increments everywhere else until the margins are perfect all around.

Fastening the sill

Fasten aluminum sills to the floor with either aluminum or stainless steel screws to prevent corrosion. The heads of aluminum screws snap off easily, though, so drill generous pilot holes first. Put a dab of caulk under the heads of the screws to seal them.

Fasten a wood sill with 10d galvanized finish nails where it's exposed and with screws where the threshold will cover it. Oak sills are hard, so you'll definitely need to drill pilot holes. In cases where you fasten the sills to masonry rather than

Double doors set in a cross-legged opening won't meet flush unless one of the jambs is moved out slightly. Here a carpenter pries between the casing and the sheathing until the doors meet flush.

"Fasten aluminum sills to the floor with either aluminum or stainless steel screws to prevent corrosion."

SAFETY FIRST

Prehung French door units are heavy. This is no time to prove how strong you are. Get at least one, preferably more, helpers to maneuver the door into place. Not only are you dealing with extreme weight, but most of these units also have glass, which could be dangerous if it crashes down on you.

WHAT CAN GO WRONG

Don't Try Moving the Hinges

When interior doors don't meet, you can move the hinges in or out as a last resort. That doesn't work for exterior doors, because the doors will no longer contact the weatherstripping evenly.

These French doors have an adjustable threshold that can be raised or lowered with built-in jack screws. The threshold cap (lying on the deck in front of the door) has been temporarily removed while the doorsill is fastened to the floor. When the threshold cap is reinstalled, the fastening screws will be hidden.

flush bolts are connected by hidden rods to operating levers close to the middle of the door, so they're easier to reach.

Usually, the manufacturer mounts the flush bolts in exterior doors. To do the job yourself on an in-swing door, you'll need to rout a deep mortise in the *astragal* (the strip that covers the joint between double doors). Cut the mortise with a router guided by a fence. You won't have a flat surface for the router to run on because of the astragal's shape, but you can make a custom fence that elevates and guides the router. The alternative is to tack a strip of wood to the edge of the door such that the top of the strip is even with the crossbar of the astragal. In that case, you can use a regular router fence.

to a wooden deck, you'll need special fasteners (see sidebar, right).

Installing surface bolts and flush bolts

The semiactive door of a hinged pair is held in place by either surface-mount or flush bolts. Surface bolts are simply mounted to the inside face of the door. Then the door is closed to determine the location of the striker on the head jamb. If the gap above the door is very tight, the striker may have to be recessed into the head jamb with a chisel.

Flush bolts are recessed in the edge of the door at the top and the bottom. Regular flush bolts are only about 6 in. long, so you have to reach down or up to operate them. Extension

Prevent Door Sag with Longer Screws

You may find that heavy doors cause the jambs to deflect at the top hinge, which also makes the doors sag in the middle. To solve this, replace the inner hinge screws with longer screws that bite into the framing. This is a good practice, in general, since it saves adjusting a sagging door later.

Fastening to Masonry

When fastening to a masonry floor, use hardened concrete screws (one popular brand is Tapcon®). This is a fairly new product, so you may have to hunt for it. Rental yards and supply houses catering to commercial construction are a good bet. Concrete screws are predrilled and driven with a special bit, which you can get wherever the screws are sold.

Hardened masonry screws are useful for fastening doorsills to masonry. A special bit is used to drill a pilot hole for the screws.

The old-fashioned alternative to concrete screws is plastic or lead plugs. To use them, first dry-fit the unit and use a 1/8-in.-diameter masonry bit to transfer the locations of the holes from the sill to the masonry. Then remove the unit and use a larger bit to enlarge the 1/8-in. holes. Blow the dust out of the holes with a compressed air nozzle or your drill's motor fan, and then seat the plugs. Caulk the floor pan, reinstall the unit, and run screws through the sill and the pan into the plugs. Unfortunately, plugs will sometimes loosen. As a backup, caulk the floor pan to both the sill and the masonry subfloor.

TRADE SECRET

When setting flush bolts, you need to drill the head jamb and sill to receive the extended bolts. However, it's difficult to mark these points with the door closed. The answer is a strip of sheet metal with a hole whose diameter matches the diameter of the bolt. With the door closed, extend the bolt through the metal and against the sill or head jamb. Then retract the bolt, open the door, and mark the hole.

A flush bolt marker made of sheet metal is used to locate the exact spot where a flush bolt will engage the doorsill.

> "The active door of an exterior pair has a lock just like a single door. The only difference is that the striker is mounted in the edge of the semiactive door rather than in the jamb."

Cremone bolts are fancy, elongated surface bolts. They require less of a reach to operate than plain surface bolts.

Plain surface bolts are inexpensive and easy to apply.

TOOLS AND MATERIALS

Hardware for Double Doors

The latest hardware system for double doors is a five-point lock. This system employs an active lever or handle on both doors. The handle on the semiactive door throws concealed bolts in the top and bottom edges of the door, thereby locking it in position. The handle on the active door works the lock at the center of the door as well as bolts at the top and bottom. The five-point system is more secure and less drafty than a conventional three-point system consisting of a lock and two bolts.

Locks for double doors

The active door of an exterior pair has a lock just like a single door. The only difference is that the striker is mounted in the edge of the semiactive door rather than in the jamb. The semiactive door receives "dummy trim" that matches the knobs or levers on the active door. The dummy trim serves merely as a handle, because flush bolts or surface bolts hold the semiactive door in place. Dummy trim is easy to install; it either screws directly to the door or the trim's escutcheon snaps over a preinstalled mounting plate.

Installing Center-Hinged Patio Doors

Center-hinged patio doors have one fixed panel (or door) and one operating panel. An astragal stiffens the edge of the fixed panel and provides a stop for the operable panel to close against. A fixed panel makes a patio door more energy-efficient because it is always tighter than an operating panel. Fixed-panel doors are less expensive, too, because they require less hardware and weatherstripping. However, if you plan to move large objects such as beds or pianos through the doorway, you're better off with conventional French doors.

Center-hinged patio doors are available in both out-swing and in-swing versions (in-swing is the more common), and in two-panel, three-panel, and four-panel configurations. Three-panel units have a hinged panel in the center with fixed flankers (side panels) on each side. Four-

Flush bolts are mounted in the edge of a door, so that they will be concealed when the door is closed. Shown here is an extension-type flush bolt. The sliding bolt at the top or the bottom of the door is linked to a remote operating lever by a hidden rod. This reduces the reach required to operate the lever.

When routing for a flush bolt, a fence rides against the door to center the bit. A spacer between the fence and the router base allows the router to ride evenly on the astragal.

panel units have a pair of French doors in the middle, with fixed flankers on each side (see photo, below right) In a sense, flankers are just overgrown sidelites. To achieve maximum accessibility in a very wide opening, use foldaway doors. These work on the same principle as bifold closet doors, but they're more heavy-duty.

Prepping the opening and the unit

Prepping the opening for a center-hinged patio door is basically the same as for a French door, except that you don't need as many shims under the fixed panel. There won't be any traffic across the fixed panel side and the panel stiffens the sill, enabling it to bridge a greater distance. One shim at the middle of the fixed panel is adequate.

A four-panel door unit with fixed flankers provides generous access and plenty of light.

IN DETAIL

Astragals

Most astragals are T-shaped, with the leg of the T fastened to the edge of the door. This way, the fasteners aren't exposed when the doors are closed. Astragals for exterior doors are always mounted on the outside, to keep out the weather. Therefore, on an out-swing pair of doors, the astragal is mounted on the active door. On an in-swing pair, the astragal is mounted on the semiactive door.

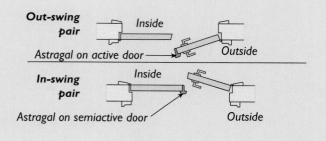

Out-swing pair   *Inside*   *Outside*

Astragal on active door

In-swing pair   *Inside*   *Outside*

Astragal on semiactive door

IN DETAIL

In-Swing vs. Out-Swing Doors

An in-swing door's sheltered location on the interior side of an opening protects it from the weather, and it's easier to open an in-swing door if you're standing on a stoop in the pouring rain. An out-swing door does have some advantages, however. It easily sheds water at the sill, and strong wind presses an out-swing door even tighter against its weatherstripping. In a similar way, a burglar kicking on an in-swing door is resisted only by the door's locks, whereas an out-swing door is reinforced by the entire doorframe. Finally, an out-swing door doesn't take up any interior space with its swing.

WHAT CAN GO WRONG

Specify the Door Swing

When ordering a center-hung patio door, be sure to specify the swing of the door (in or out), as well as which panel is fixed. A simple sketch leaves no doubt.

Foldaway doors provide wide, unobstructed openings.

The operable leaf is removed from a center-hinged patio unit, making the unit lighter and easier to handle.

Always shim under the astragal (where the doors meet), and about every 12 in. under the operating panel. If the unit is precased, it will be easy to secure the unit initially by nailing through the casing. If the unit has no casing, precase it now, or nail on temporary strips as described on p. 66.

Center-hinged patio doors are usually shipped fully assembled and are very heavy. You may want to reduce the weight of the unit by removing the operable door. To do this, remove any fasteners that are holding it on the strike side to the jamb, then disconnect the hinges. If it's an in-swing unit, you can simply remove the hinge pins. If it's an out-swing unit, remove the hinge pins by first loosening the setscrews in the hinge knuckles; however, it's usually quicker to simply remove the hinge screws from the astragal.

Setting the unit

1. Dry-fit the unit to make sure it fits and that all the margins are even. The fixed panel will hold the frame square. If the operable panel side of the unit shows uneven margins, there's probably a bump or a dip in the floor, so you'll have to remove the unit, shim the floor, and try again.

2. When the fit looks good, caulk the floor pan and set the unit. Assuming the floor is level, you won't need to rack the unit plumb as you did for single doors and French doors. Just drive one nail through each casing leg near the top, or nail the upper temporary strips.

3. Remount the operable panel (if you've removed it) and check the fit against the weatherstripping on the strike side. If the wall is plumb on both sides of the opening, or at least out of plumb the same amount in the same

"Center-hinged patio doors are usually shipped fully assembled and are very heavy. You may want to reduce the weight of the unit by removing the operable door."

TRADE SECRET

Here's a trick for holding a door in place temporarily while you adjust it from side-to-side. First, cut a 2×4 block about 6 in. long and fasten it to the wall an inch or two above the opening. Then cut a second block about 12 in. long and nail it to the first block with just one nail. The second block is free to pivot like the hand of a clock. The first block acts as a shim so the second block will clear the door's exterior trim.

Before setting the door, swing the pivoting block to the 3 o'clock position. Then set the door and swing the pivoting block down to the 6 o'clock position. Now you can let go of the door to make adjustments.

Sidelites and Transoms

Sidelites are narrow panels mounted next to a door. They're usually designed to echo the look of the door itself, though solid wood entry doors often have glazed sidelites. When the door itself is glazed, align the muntins in the sidelites with those in the door. Two sidelites per door is typical, but you can use just one if space is tight.

Sidelites don't affect the installation of a prehung unit other than to make it somewhat heavier and bulkier. Although most sidelites are fixed, you can make them operable and attach a screen for ventilation, which alleviates the nuisance of a screen door at the entry.

Mullions (or "mulls," for short) are the heavy vertical columns between the door and the sidelites. They look like solid posts but are actually composed of two jambs fastened back to back. The mullions are housed in dadoes (cross-grained recesses) cut into the head jamb above and the sill. Mull casings cover the joint between the two halves of the mullion. The exterior mull casing is usually applied at the factory, and the interior mull casing is applied on site.

Transoms are glazed panels installed above a door or window. They're often used at entryways to bring light into a foyer. Operable interior transoms were a popular way to provide ventilation in the days before air conditioning.

This unit (left) has operable sidelites with screens but no screen door in front of the primary door. This arrangement makes coming and going fast and easy.

Two jambs (below) fastened back-to-back form a mullion. Interior and exterior casings will be applied to the mullion to hide the connection. A dado cut in the sill houses the bottom of the mullion.

Entry door with sidelites

Sidelites bring additional light into a foyer. They also let the homeowner inspect visitors before opening the door.

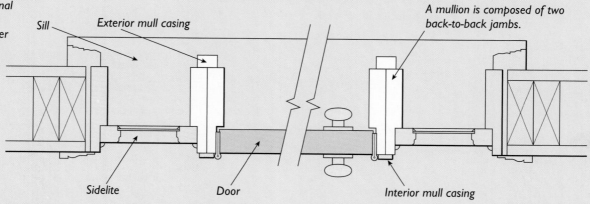

Sill

Exterior mull casing

A mullion is composed of two back-to-back jambs.

Sidelite

Door

Interior mull casing

WHAT CAN GO WRONG

Cross-Legged Openings

If an opening is cross-legged (one wall is more out of plumb than the other), there will be a tapering gap between the door and the weatherstripping. In that case, pry the casing or the lower temporary strip away from the exterior wall on one side until the door seals evenly against the weatherstripping. Shim between the jambs and the rough opening, and then nail through the shims.

Shimming a crooked floor

A crooked or out-of-level floor distorts a doorframe. The bottom of the entire opening must be shimmed to the floor's highest point if the door is to fit correctly.

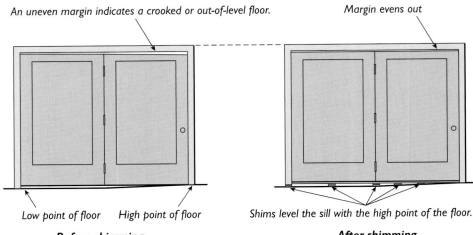

An uneven margin indicates a crooked or out-of-level floor.

Margin evens out

Low point of floor   High point of floor

Before shimming

Shims level the sill with the high point of the floor.

After shimming

Check the diagonals to make sure the frame is square before nailing it off.

direction on both sides of the opening, the door will seal tightly.

4. Finally, fasten the sill to the subfloor. If the unit was precased, nail off the casing now. If the unit is uncased, remove the temporary strips and install the casing.

Installing Sliding Patio Doors

A straight and level sill is absolutely essential for sliding doors. Without it, the panels won't close tightly, the lock won't catch, and the weatherstripping won't seal. Carefully follow the procedure described in Chapter 4 for leveling and waterproofing the floor. The shims should coincide with the screw holes in the sill.

Sliding door frames are usually shipped knocked down (KD), so you'll need to

"A straight and level sill is absolutely essential for sliding doors. Without it, the panels won't close tightly, the lock won't catch, and the weatherstripping won't seal."

 According to Code

Safety glass must be used for the glazing in all doors, sidelites, and transoms.

WHAT CAN GO WRONG

An Uneven Floor

Before ordering sliding doors (or any wide, multidoor unit, for that matter), always check the floor with a straightedge. If there's a hump in the middle, measure the R.O. height from the top of the hump. Similarly, check the header for a dip, and measure from its lowest point. More than one sliding door has been returned because it didn't fit.

Temporary strips are tacked or screwed into the sheathing to hold the unit in position until the jambs can be shimmed and nailed.

assemble the door before installing it. Screw the parts together, adding a dab of silicone caulk in each joint. Wooden sills should have two coats of primer on the ends and underside before installation; wooden jambs should be back-primed, as well.

Dry-fit the assembled frame in the opening and shim it into position at the top. Adjust the shims until the diagonal measurements of the frame are equal, meaning that the unit is square. (Units that are shipped preassembled with the fixed panel in place are already square.) If the unit can't be squared, you'll need to enlarge the opening or buy a smaller unit. If there's adequate clearance all around the opening, drill pilot holes through the screw holes in the sill and mark the sill's side-to-side location so you can later reset it in exactly the same place.

Setting the frame

After dry-fitting the unit, remove it from the opening and lay down a triple bead of caulk on the floor pan and 3 in. up the sides of the opening. If the unit has nailing fins or preattached exterior casings, caulk around the opening, as well. Hold this bead tight to the edge of the opening so it doesn't ooze out too much when the unit is pressed into place.

Tip the unit back into position and fasten the sill to the floor, using the procedure described above (see Setting the Unit, p. 72). Make sure that the sill is located where it was previously. Shim the jambs snug at the top again, so that they're plumb and the unit's diagonals are equal. After the sill has been fastened down, it's a good idea to double-check it for straightness.

Now check the frame to make sure it isn't cross-legged (see sidebar, p. 77). If it is, move one jamb toward the outside at the top, and

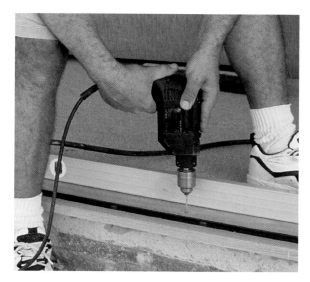

After dry-fitting and centering the unit, drill pilot holes through the sill into the floor. You can then relocate the unit in just the right spot after you've applied caulk to the floor

SAFETY FIRST

A sliding patio door may be the only thing between your toddler and the deep end of your swimming pool. If that's the case, you may want to consider a hydraulic closer that shuts the door automatically.

A self-latching lock called Latchmatic can be mounted high on a patio door to keep kids from wandering outside.

For even greater childproofing, mount an auxiliary lock out of reach. Both of these products, respectively called the Slidematic and the Latchmatic, are available from Slideline, Inc. (4079 Oceanside Blvd., Suite A, Oceanside, CA 92056; 760-325-7655).

TRADE SECRET

For a sliding door to roll smoothly, the sill must be perfectly straight. Initial shimming is done with a straightedge before the unit is installed. However, it's a good idea to check the sill after the door is installed, in case the shims have moved or been compressed. You can use a regular chalkline or dry line for this, but they're too thick and fuzzy for precision work. A better alternative is 20-lb. braided Dacron® fishing line. Attach the string to small finish nails driven into the leg jambs. If additional shims are needed, slip them between the sill and the floor pan with a dab of caulk to hold them in place. A stringline also works well for straightening the head jamb.

move the other jamb toward the inside at the top. Nail through the jambs at the top, and then shim the legs straight, nailing through the jambs as you go. Shim and nail the head jamb, too, being careful to verify that it is as straight as the sill. If the unit has nailing fins or preattached casings, nail them off when everything is straight and true.

Installing and adjusting the panels

Panels are installed by first lifting their tops into the channels in the head jamb, and then lowering them onto the track. If the fixed panel wasn't

installed at the factory, it will be the first panel installed on the job. Slide it against the correct side of the opening and secure it in place with the screw or clip provided. An insert snapped into the threshold also locks the fixed panel in position.

Now install the operable panel. The wheels under the operable panel adjust up and down. The adjusting screws are sometimes accessed through the edge of the door, but more often they're housed in little pockets in the panel's bottom rail. Raise or lower the wheels until the panel glides smoothly and lines up parallel with the jamb. The adjusting screws will be easier to

After caulking around the opening, tip the unit into place.

Install shims between the jambs and the opening to straighten the jambs. Then, drive nails or screws through the jambs and shims to hold them in place.

"The adjusting screws will be easier to turn if you first lift the panel slightly to relieve some of the weight resting on the wheels."

SAFETY FIRST

The safest way to cut a short piece on a power saw is to cut it off a longer one. There are times, however, when you have only a short piece. In that case, place the short piece on the bed of the saw and line it up with the blade. Place another piece of the same thickness at the other end of the bed. Use a third piece as a bridge to apply pressure to both pieces simultaneously, then make the cut. This keeps your hand a safe distance from the blade.

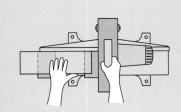

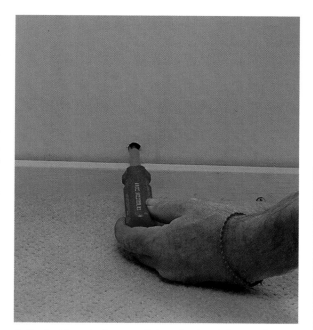

Adjust a door to be parallel to the jamb by turning a screw in the lower rail.

turn if you first lift the panel slightly to relieve some of the weight resting on the wheels.

Installing screens, locks, and hardware

Like primary panels, screens are installed top first. The simplest type of sliding door screen has fixed wheels on the bottom and curved springs on the top (which should be periodically lubricated with silicone spray to keep them from binding). Use a putty knife to gently pry the screen up onto its track.

Better quality screens have adjustable wheels on the bottom. Use a screwdriver to raise or lower the wheels until the screen contacts the jamb evenly. If there are guide wheels on the top

Diagnosing a Cross-Legged Frame

When the walls flanking an opening aren't parallel, the opening is *cross-legged,* or twisted. The problem is especially insidious with sliding doors because the doors may close, but friction between the panels and the upper channel will make operation difficult. At the floor, a cross-legged frame causes uneven wear on the wheels and the track.

There are two good ways to diagnose cross-legging in a sliding door or sliding window frame. First, cross-sight the

Strings stretched from one corner to the other will just touch in the middle if the jambs are parallel. If not, the opening is cross-legged and the doors may not ride smoothly.

opening diagonally from opposing sides. Move your line of vision toward the wall until the opening is foreshortened into a narrow strip of light. If the light tapers in width, the opening is cross-legged.

Cross-stringing is a more scientific approach. Set nails at the corners of the frame and run strings diagonally across the opening. Make sure the strings touch the frame at all the corners. If the jambs are parallel, the strings will just kiss in the center. If not, there will be a space between the strings or one string will press on the other, depending on how they overlap. To detect pressure, bend one of the strings where they cross and see if the other string follows.

Cross-sighting a jamb

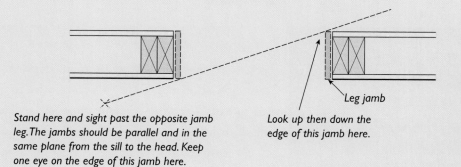

Stand here and sight past the opposite jamb leg. The jambs should be parallel and in the same plane from the sill to the head. Keep one eye on the edge of this jamb here.

Leg jamb

Look up then down the edge of this jamb here.

TOOLS AND MATERIALS

A Better Sliding Screen Door

Marvin sliding doors employ a top-hung suspended screen that resists binding better than rolling screens do. Spring-loaded, nonbearing wheels guide the bottom of the screen. A cam adjustment on top aligns the screen with the jamb.

Out-of-Square Screens

Occasionally, you'll encounter an out-of-square screen with nonadjustable wheels. To get it to fit correctly against the jamb, you may need to rack it slightly. First, measure the screen's two diagonals to determine which one needs to be shortened to improve the fit. Then stand the screen on one corner and pull down gently on the opposite corner until the diagonals are equal and the screen is square.

"There's no way to plane an aluminum door, so it wouldn't be practical to mount it directly to an existing doorway where there may be irregularities."

as well, adjust them to make light contact with the overhead track.

Usually, the handles and locks are installed in factory-bored holes, but the striker has to be set on the job so it aligns properly with the lock. After installing the lock, study the way in which it engages the striker. Extend the tongue of the lock, slide the door against the jamb, and mark the height of the tongue. Then set the striker accordingly.

The tongue on some locks is recessed inside the mechanism even when the striker is engaged. In that case, place the striker inside the lock and lock it. You'll see a little nib on the back of the striker. Press the striker against the jamb so the nib leaves an impression. Remove the striker from the lock and mount it to the jamb, using

Screens with spring-loaded wheels can be adjusted with a screw at each lower corner. The screens should contact the jamb evenly and there should be just enough pressure on the wheels to keep the screen from binding.

TRADE SECRET

Before installing a storm/screen combination door it's a good idea to remove the storm panels and the screen panels. This makes the door lighter, and there's less risk of damage during installation.

the impression left by the nib as a guide. Then, lock the door and see how it fits. If there's, say, a ¼ in. gap between the door and the jamb, mortise the striker ¼ in. deep into the jamb. Don't set the striker too deeply, or it will be difficult to lock the door. The weatherstripping should be just slightly compressed.

Installing Storm and Secondary Doors

Installing an aluminum storm door is a simple project that takes a couple of hours. There isn't much woodworking involved, and everything is prefinished. Most of the work is done with just three tools—a measuring tape, a hacksaw, and a cordless drill.

To locate the striker, extend the tongue of the lock. Then, slide the door next to the jamb and mark the height of the tongue.

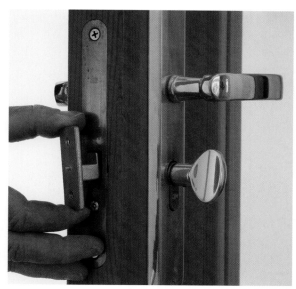

Some strikers are housed inside the lock. To locate them, first engage the striker inside the lock. Then, shut the door. A nib on the back of the striker leaves an impression on the jamb for reference.

There's no way to plane an aluminum door, so it wouldn't be practical to mount it directly to an existing doorway where there may be irregularities. Instead, the door is mounted on an adjustable aluminum frame, and then the aluminum frame is mounted on the existing exterior casing. The aluminum frame has a *Z-bar* (a Z-shaped aluminum extrusion) on each side and a drip cap at the top. At the bottom, a U-shaped *expander* slides up and down to adjust the height of the door. Vinyl sweeps underneath the expander make a tight seal with the existing sill.

Installing a storm door and frame

The first task is to measure and cut the Z-bars to length. The doorsill is sloped, so you'll need to

Mounting an aluminum storm door
An aluminum storm door is hinged to its own extruded frame. The frame is then mounted on the primary door's exterior casings.

Stagger the height of the primary door lock and the height of the storm/screen door lock to avoid conflict.

Primary door

Storm door

Exterior casing

Hinge-side Z-bar

Latch-side Z-bar

Plus or minus 3/16 in.

Hinges are screwed to the storm door on the same side as the primary door.

When ordering a storm door, measure from the inside of one casing to the inside of the other casing.

TRADE SECRET

Sliding screens are sometimes furnished with bumpers to muffle noise and cushion impact. Always install one bumper at the top and one at the bottom. A single bumper can make the screen rise up and jump its track upon impact. If the hardware kit supplies only one bumper, you can make a second one by gluing together a few layers of felt or sheet rubber, using silicone caulk as an adhesive.

TOOLS AND MATERIALS

What You'll Need: Installing Exterior Doors

- Power drill/driver
- Twist bits
- Spade bit (for some types of locks)
- Screwdriver bits (slotted and Phillips)
- Hacksaw
- Caulking gun with caulk (optional)
- Tape measure
- Square and level
- Hammer
- Pencil
- Pliers
- Sawhorses or door buck
- Small wood chisel

cut the bottoms of the Z-bars at the same angle as the sill. To do this, measure the front and back of the exterior casings on each side, and transfer these measurements to the front and back of the respective Z-bars. Be sure to deduct ⅛ in. from your measurements to leave space at the top for the drip cap, which will be slipped under the head casing.

Some units come with Z-bars prehinged to the door, while other units are completely disassembled for shipping. Either way, place the Z-bars on sawhorses and cut them with a hacksaw. Save

Screen doors can be more than utilitarian, as this custom-made door shows.

A wood-composite core strengthens this aluminum storm door and helps prevent dents. The door is hinged to a Z-bar (right side of photo), which features compressible weatherstripping.

the cutoff to use later as a gauge. If the Z-bars have been shipped loose, find the Z-bar with hinges on it and rotate it to expose the hinges. Lay it on the door so that the top end of the Z-bar sticks out ¹⁄₁₆ in. beyond the top of the door. This will provide clearance between the door and the drip cap. Then, drill pilot holes through the edge of the door and drive the screws.

Next, slip the expander onto the bottom of the door and screw it in temporarily to a fully raised position (it can be adjusted later to meet the sill). Slide the sweeps into the channels on the underside of the expander and crimp the ends of the channels to hold the sweeps in place. Mount the hinge-side Z-bar (with the door attached) tightly against the exterior casing, using

---

"Some units come with Z-bars prehinged to the door, while other units are completely disassembled for shipping."

WHAT CAN GO WRONG

When replacing an old aluminum storm door with a new one it can be difficult to remove the old aluminum mounting screws. These screws are soft, so they are easily chewed up by a screwdriver. In that case just shear the screw-heads off with a wood chisel.

TRADE SECRET

The expander at the bottom of an aluminum storm door has a replaceable rubber sweep. To make the sweep slide easily into the expander, coat the retaining channels with silicone spray.

Anatomy of an aluminum storm/screen door

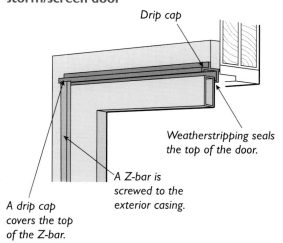

Drip cap

Weatherstripping seals the top of the door.

A Z-bar is screwed to the exterior casing.

A drip cap covers the top of the Z-bar.

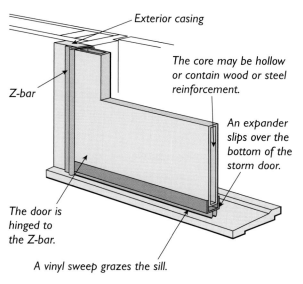

Exterior casing

Z-bar

The core may be hollow or contain wood or steel reinforcement.

An expander slips over the bottom of the storm door.

The door is hinged to the Z-bar.

A vinyl sweep grazes the sill.

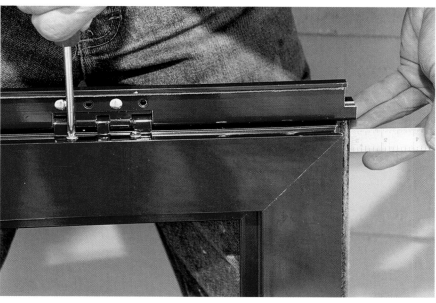

A Z-bar with an integral hinge is screwed to the edge of the door. The Z-bar overhangs the top of the door by 1/16 in. to provide clearance between the drip cap and the door after they're installed.

The hinge-side Z-bar is fastened to the exterior casing with the door attached. The strike-side Z-bar and the drip cap (standing up) are installed afterward.

The U-shaped expander at the bottom of the door is lowered until its flexible sweep just contacts the sill. The screws are tightened to lock in the adjustment.

IN DETAIL

Sagging Problems with Wood Screen Doors

Wood screen doors are built very light, so they have a tendency to sag—or "rack"—after a few years of service. Eventually the bottom of the door will scrape the sill. One way to prevent sagging in the first place is by nailing a thin plywood panel to the outside face of the door. This reduces ventilation somewhat, but it greatly strengthens the door. If you have a dog, the panel will also stand up to his claws much better than screening will. Instead of a plywood panel you can use hardware cloth (heavy wire mesh) to maintain maximum ventilation. Apply the hardware cloth with its weave running diagonally to brace the door and thereby prevent sagging.

Another way to fix a sagging screen door is to apply a turnbuckle brace. The brace should run from the upper corner of the door on the hinge side to the lower corner of the door on the strike side. Gradually tighten the turnbuckle until the door resumes its rectangular shape and clears the frame.

just one screw next to each hinge. Then insert one of the saved Z-bar cutoffs into the gap between the door and the exterior casing on the latch-side of the opening.

Ideally, there should be a ³⁄₁₆-in. gap between the door and the cutoff. If the gap is greater than ¼ in., you'll need to reduce the width of the opening by packing out the edge of the latch-side casing with a wooden spacer strip. If you have to reduce the opening more than ¼ in., remove the hinge-side Z-bar to add a spacer on the hinge side, as well. If you add spacers, use longer screws through the Z-bar into the edge of the casing. Finally, install the drip cap at the top of the opening. Lay a bead of caulk behind the drip cap and the Z-bars to improve the seal.

A leftover scrap of Z-bar is inserted between the door and the exterior casing to see how much clearance there will be after the strike-side Z-bar is installed.

Installing hardware

Once the door has been mounted, adjust the expander downward so the sweeps just graze the sill. Then, install the latch and striker so the door closes easily but doesn't rattle. Install the hydraulic closer, adjusting it so the door closes at the desired speed. Some closers have two pin settings, one for the screen and one for the glass storm panel. The latter setting makes the door accelerate as it closes, thereby overcoming the air pressure that builds up behind the glass. Finally, install the wind-safety chain.

Installing a wooden secondary door

Some trimming will probably be necessary to fit your new wood screen door to an existing casing. If you install a screen door and don't plan to alternate it with a storm door, you can use special screen-door hinges. These screw into the surface of the door and the casing, which makes installation easier. They are also spring-loaded, so a separate closer isn't required. Unfortunately, they look very utilitarian, which may be okay for the back door but not for the front.

A *nonmortise hinge* is more attractive, lightweight, and easy to install. This compact hinge screws into the edges of the door and casing without chiseling a gain. The margin around the door won't be too wide, either, because the leaves of a nonmortise hinge nest together when the door is closed.

> "If you install a screen door and don't plan to alternate it with a storm door, you can use special screen-door hinges."

IN DETAIL

Closure Hardware for Wooden Secondary Doors

Wooden combination doors and dedicated wooden storm doors may be equipped with hydraulic closers. They should also have a wind chain. Before installing any type of closer, however, ask yourself if the extra hassle of coming and going through a spring-loaded door is worth the benefit of keeping out a few more bugs or saving a few extra BTUs.

SAFETY FIRST

Installing a wind chain is essential. It has a spring on the end that absorbs most of the impact if a storm door suddenly flies open in a strong wind. Without this device, a door could be torn off its hinges and become a dangerous projectile. Another possibility is the door could slam, breaking the glass.

Secondary Door Hinges

Wooden storm doors are heavy and need regular 3×3 butt hinges. Ordinary brass-plated hinges soon rust outdoors, however, so if the screen door will be left natural, use solid-brass or galvanized butts. If the door will be painted, use brass-plated butts and paint them, as well.

Removable-pin brass butts (upper left) are standard for house doors. This sample has square corners. Galvanized butts (upper right) are used for exterior work. This sample has round corners. Spring-loaded screen door hinges (lower left) are self-closing. Nonmortise hinges (lower right) don't require routing, because one leaf nests inside the other when the door is closed.

A hydraulic closer and its bracket are mounted separately. Slip the closer arm into the bracket and lock them together with a pin.

The closer arm has two holes for the bracket pin. You can vary the force of the closer by moving the pin from one hole to the other. When the screen is in place, use the innermost hole so the door closes gently. When the storm panel is in place, use the outermost hole so the closer has enough force to overcome air-pressure buildup.

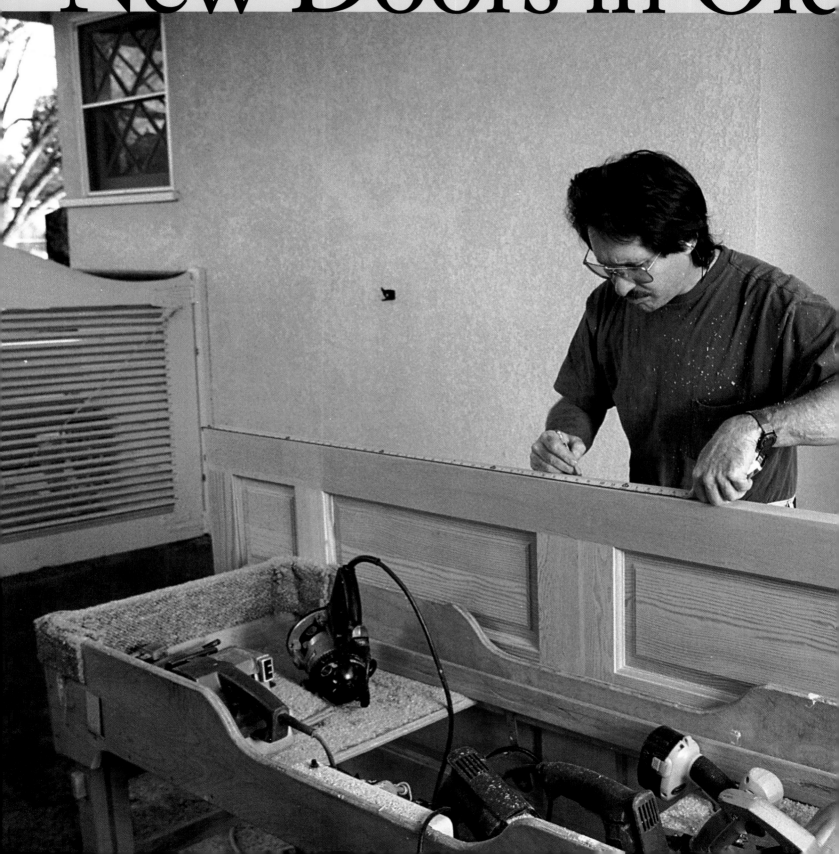

CHAPTER SIX

Frames

1 Fitting a New Door to an Existing Opening, p. 86

2 Hinging a New Door to an Existing Frame, p. 89

3 Installing Locksets and Deadbolts, p. 94

Hanging a door so it fits just right is a tricky undertaking. The gap between the door and the frame shouldn't be more than the thickness of a nickel. Setting hinges also requires precision. The *gains* (hinge recesses) on the jamb must align perfectly with those on the door. In addition, the hinges must be perfectly located for the right amount of clearance between the door and the head jamb. The accuracy required for this job seems daunting, but it doesn't need to be a mystery. With a little guidance, the right tools, and an extra helping of patience, you'll be able to fit and hang a door like a pro.

TOOLS AND MATERIALS
A Homemade Door Hook

A door hook is basically a strap with a hook on each end. One hook slips over the door and the other hook bites into the jamb, with the strap stretched tightly in between. The strap is cut from a bicycle inner tube and the hooks are fashioned from aluminum flat stock.

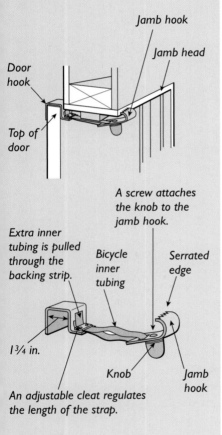

Jamb hook

Jamb head

Door hook

Top of door

A screw attaches the knob to the jamb hook.

Extra inner tubing is pulled through the backing strip.

Bicycle inner tubing

Serrated edge

1³/₄ in.

Knob

Jamb hook

An adjustable cleat regulates the length of the strap.

Fitting a New Door to an Existing Opening

There are several ways to fit a door to an existing opening. The most direct way is to simply prop the door in front of the opening and *scribe* (trace) the outline of the opening onto the door. This method is popular on the West Coast, even in new construction. It only works if no casing has been applied to the opening. The casing won't allow the door to lay tightly against the jamb for scribing, which makes this method impractical for remodeling jobs. If the door has been cased, you have three choices: a) remove the casing; b) make a template for the new door; or c) carefully transfer the opening's measurements.

Scribing a door

Use a door hook to hold a door tightly against the opening so you can scribe it. If you have a helper, he or she can hold the door for you instead. Mark the hinge side of the door at the top with an X. (Use tape on a stain-grade door so you don't have to remove the mark later.) The X indicates the correct edge of the door for the hinges and locks as well as the side of the door that faces the stop. The unmarked side of the door faces the hinge barrel. This is important when routing the hinge gains. Shim the door at the bottom, so that the top of the door overlaps the head jamb by no more than ¼ in. You may have to trim the bottom of the door initially to bring the top of the door down to this height. If

The door is carefully centered before scribing, so that the stiles will remain equal in width. The bottom of the door is leveled with shims and a homemade door hook holds the top of the door firmly against the jambs. A large **X** taped to the stop side of the door provides a reference so edge bevels and hinge gains can be cut correctly.

the top of the opening is square, drop the door to ⅛ in. below the head jamb. In that case, the top of the door won't need to be trimmed.

After establishing the height of the door, shift the door from side to side so the stiles are even. Make sure that the stile on the lock side remains wide enough for the lock you're using. This is often a problem with French doors, which have narrow stiles. Some cylinder locks require a stile to be 3⅞ in. wide, which doesn't leave much room for trimming even standard-width stiles. When the door is where you want it, scribe it, making sure your pencil mark is offset slightly from the jamb so there will be clearance around the door after it's hung.

TRADE SECRET

I use a *scriber* (also called *dividers*) to produce the proper offset to trim a door. My scriber has a wing nut that locks in a given offset between the scriber point and the pencil point. Another way to produce an offset scribe line is to hold a short pencil flat against the jamb as you trace. This produces a fixed ⅛-in. offset, as opposed to the adjustable offset produced by a scriber.

Fitting a door in a cased frame

If you're confident that the opening is square, you can transfer the opening's measurements to the door. Then, reduce the measurements as above to achieve the desired margins. Doorframes aren't always square; make sure you check the diagonals, the width, and the height. If you find that the opening is out of square, the safest course is to make a template.

Start with a sheet of plywood that's 1 to 2 in. smaller than the opening. Have a helper hold it in position while you tape overhanging cardboard strips around the edges to correspond exactly with the doorframe. Transfer the template's shape to the outer face of the door, and then use a straightedge to draw trim lines that are offset to produce the proper clearance.

Trimming the top and bottom

Always trim the top and the bottom of a door before planing the edges. The side planing removes any splintering on the edge of the door. Trim the door with a circular saw, cutting just a whisker beyond the knife cut to avoid splintering. A fine-tooth crosscut blade produces the smoothest cut. A light pass with a block plane will clean up any saw marks.

For greater accuracy, run your saw against a straightedge. Measure the distance from the edge of the saw's shoe to the blade, and clamp your straightedge that distance (or a hair less) from the knife cut. Reducing the offset by a hair ensures that you cut just beyond the line. To avoid measuring, make a cutting guide.

Figuring the Offsets

The necessary offset between the opening and the scribe line varies from the top to the bottom to the sides. The top of the door is simply scribed 1/8 in. away from the head jamb. The bottom of the door is scribed according to the finish floor. If the finish floor has already been laid and there's no carpet, scribe about 1/4 in. above the finish floor (more may be necessary if the floor is out of level). If carpet will be installed, allow enough room for it (this depends on the pile). If the finish floor hasn't been laid yet or if there will be a raised threshold, allow for that, as well.

The offset for the scribe line on the sides depends on the thickness of the door. Door edges are usually beveled slightly to allow the door to open and close more easily. Beveling a door's edges makes the door's inner face slightly narrower than its outer face, so if you want an 1/8-in. margin on the outer face of the door, you'll need to scribe the inner face with a slightly wider offset. The difference grows as the door increases in thickness, so you'll have to set the scribe wider for a thick door than for a thin door. A 13/4-in.-thick door is scribed with a 1/4-in. offset on the inner face, while a 13/8-in.-thick door is scribed with a 3/16-in. offset.

To eliminate tearout on a stile-and-rail door, score across the grain of the stiles with a knife. Scoring the rails isn't necessary, because the grain runs parallel to the cut. When trimming plywood doors, score the entire face before cutting.

WHAT CAN GO WRONG
Overtrimming Wooden Doors

You don't want to take more than 1/2 in. off the top of a frame-and-panel door, or the top rail will be noticeably narrower than the stiles. In the case of a flush door, the concealed internal top rail is only 1 in. wide, so cutting off more than 1/2 in. will affect its structural integrity.

TRADE SECRET

Heavy doors are awkward to maneuver into an opening by yourself. You can get help from a short length of pipe or an electrical conduit. Lay the pipe on the floor as a roller to nudge the door to the left or right. Then you can tip the door slightly to align the hinge knuckles, using the pipe as a fulcrum.

TRADE SECRET

Use a saw blade as an alternative to scoring with a knife. Clamp the straightedge in position, set the saw's depth of cut to just graze the surface, and then make an initial scoring pass. The surface won't splinter because of the shallow angle of the blade. Then loosen the clamps, bump the straightedge or cutting guide toward the end of the door a hair, and make a second pass with the saw at full cutting depth.

Planing Bevels the Wrong Way

Make sure your edge bevels face the right way. I make slash marks on the end grain of the stiles with a pencil or crayon to indicate the direction of each bevel. The bevels on the hinge side and the strike side are always opposed, not parallel.

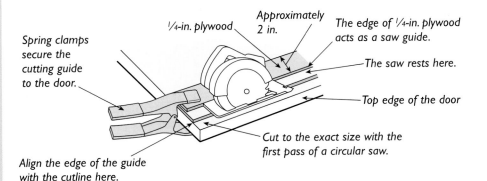

Spring clamps secure the cutting guide to the door.

1/4-in. plywood

Approximately 2 in.

The edge of 1/4-in. plywood acts as a saw guide.

The saw rests here.

Top edge of the door

Cut to the exact size with the first pass of a circular saw.

Align the edge of the guide with the cutline here.

Cutting guide
A cutting guide ensures a straight cut. If you make two passes with a saw—an initial grazing cut followed by a cut all the way through the door—scoring with a knife can be eliminated.

Planing the edges

To hold the door while you plane, use a low sawhorse and extend its crossbeam by tacking a 2×4 on top. Then clamp the door to the overhanging end of the 2×4. A power plane is the ideal tool for planing the edges of a door. The longer the plane, the more accurate it will be. Some power planes have an adjustable fence, but others have a fixed 90-degree fence. Experienced doorhangers gauge the edge bevel by eye as they plane, but a wide fence attached to the power plane will help ensure accurate results.

You can also use a handplane on door edges. A jointer plane with its long sole works best, but a jack plane will do, as well. Tip the plane to one side until you've established the correct bevel, then check the bevel frequently with a try square. For a straight cut, keep pressure on the front of the plane as you start the pass and on the *tote* (handle) as you reach the other end. This applies to both handplanes and power planes.

When the jambs are out of plumb, taper the stiles. Starting at the end of the door that needs the most planing, make a 10-in.-long pass. Then

A power plane makes short work of planing a door. The door bench in the foreground holds all the tools a professional doorhanger needs.

A sharp handplane is the traditional tool for planing doors. Notice the stick clamped to the far end of the sawhorse. The stick butts into a wall to prevent the work from sliding forward.

"If you don't use a template for routing, you can still use a router to remove the bulk of the gain. Then clean up the edges of the gain with a chisel."

SAFETY FIRST

Be careful when you lift a door that's lying flat. It's easy to strain a muscle with your back extended. Instead, lift the edge that's closest to you first, rolling the door onto its opposite edge. This makes the sawhorses carry half the weight while your back stays straight.

TRADE SECRET

When I bevel doors with my power plane, I attach a piece of bevel siding to the plane's regular square fence, which tilts the tool at the correct angle.

Checking for the right bevel
Use a carpenter's square to check the bevel while planing the edge of a door.

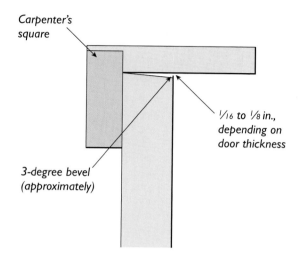

Carpenter's square

1/16 to 1/8 in., depending on door thickness

3-degree bevel (approximately)

Hinging a New Door to an Existing Frame

When I'm called upon to fit a new door in an existing frame, it's usually just one door, so it doesn't pay to haul out a multihinge template. Instead, I use a simple shop-built template and a router to help accurately cut the hinge gains. If you don't use a template for routing, you can still use a router to remove the bulk of the gain. Then clean up the edges of the gain with a chisel.

First, rout the hinge gains on the door using the template. Rout the gains one at a time, clamping the template to the door and moving it from hinge to hinge. After routing the gains on the door, separate the hinge leaves by removing the pins. Affix the hinge leaves to the door, then shim the door into position. Transfer the hinge locations from the door to the jamb, and then rout the gains on the jamb. Finally, mount the leaves on the jamb, and then hang the door by mating the hinge leaves and reinstalling the pins.

The procedure is slightly different if you're replacing an old door with a new one. In that case, the jamb has already been routed and you'll probably be reusing the existing hinges. Shim the door in the opening, transfer the hinge locations to the new door, and then rout the gains for the door.

Routing the gains in the door

On a frame-and-panel door, I usually set the top of the upper hinge 7 in. from the top of the door and the bottom of the lower hinge even with the bottom of the lower panel. When a third hinge is

make a second pass that starts about 20 in. from the end and continues to the end of the door. Make successive passes, with each one a little farther from the end than the previous pass, until you reach the opposite end of the door. Stop tapering when you're parallel to, but just outside of, the pencil line. The successive passes will leave the edge slightly bumpy. Take one final pass over the entire edge to smooth it out and to cut right to the pencil line.

As a finishing touch, slightly round the edges of the door to help them resist nicks, dings, and splintering. A rounded corner also holds paint better than a sharp corner. Use sandpaper to knock down the edges slightly, or round them with a few passes of a block plane or a router with a 1/8-in.-radius roundover bit.

TOOLS AND MATERIALS

Door Bucks

If you have a number of doors to plane, make a door buck with a gap that's just slightly wider than the thickness of the doors. The weight of the door makes the bottom of the buck deflect, which forces the uprights to pinch the door firmly in place.

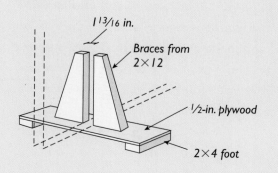

1 13/16 in.

Braces from 2×12

1/2-in. plywood

2×4 foot

Door buck
A door buck holds the door securely for planing. The door's weight makes the door buck sag slightly, which makes the uprights pinch the door.

Removable Pin vs. Nonremovable Pin Hinges

Hinges come with *removable* or *nonremovable* pins. Non-removable pin hinges are mounted to the door first, and then the door is held in position by shims or a helper while the hinges are fastened to the jamb. This is quite awkward, especially for one person. Fortunately, nonremovable pin hinges are a rarity.

TOOLS AND MATERIALS

The Importance of Pilot Holes

Always drill pilot holes before screwing hinge leaves. Start the drill slowly to center the bit before plunging it down. Coarse-grained woods have a tendency to pull the bit sideways, so compensate with a little side pressure. Sometimes one of the holes will be off center after drilling. Run the screw into that hole last, so that the leaf won't be pulled astray.

"When a third hinge is used, I center it between the top and bottom hinges. When four hinges are used, I distribute them evenly, as well."

A Homemade Hinge Template

A homemade hinge template is simply a scrap of plywood with a rectangular cutout on one edge. A router bit with a ball bearing collar travels around the edges of the cutout to rout the hinge gain, and a fence tacked to the underside of the template regulates the hinge gain's breadth from front to back. The breadth of the cutout from front to back isn't critical, because the fence actually controls the breadth of the hinge gain. This dimension varies depending on the thickness of the door casing, so screw or lightly tack the fence to the template to make adjustments easy.

1. Draw the cutout with a sharp pencil. Using ½-in. cabinet-grade plywood, cut a blank about 8 in. by 12 in.

2. Make the end cuts with a sliding compound-miter saw or a radial-arm saw. Overcut slightly so you can remove all the waste. If you use a table saw, initially make the blank longer to give you better control, then trim the template to a smaller size afterward.

3. Use a jigsaw or bandsaw to make the back cut and file or sand it smooth. Overcut the corners slightly to remove all the waste.

Use a ½-in.-diameter straight bit with an overhead ball bearing pilot to rout the gains. You can also use a regular straight bit with a guide bushing. In that case, enlarge the cutout by the difference between the bushing's outside radius and the bit's outside radius.

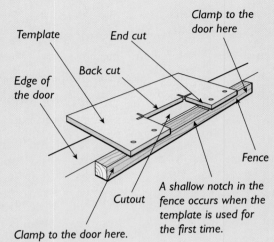

Template · **End cut** · **Clamp to the door here** · **Back cut** · **Edge of the door** · **Fence** · **Cutout** · **A shallow notch in the fence occurs when the template is used for the first time.** · **Clamp to the door here.**

Homemade hinge template
A simple template can guide a router bit to cut a perfect hinge gain. The ends of the cutout are made on a radial-arm saw or slide saw. The back cut is made on a band saw or with a jigsaw. The fence extends past the template to produce horns at both ends. The horns can be clamped to a door or jamb, or the template can simply be held in place with brads.

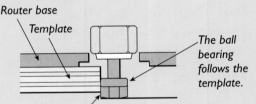

Flush template
Router base · Template · The ball bearing follows the template.
The hinge gain follows the template exactly.

Offset template
The guide bushing follows the template. · A threaded collar retains the bushing in the router base.
The hinge gain is offset from the template.

Flush template vs. offset template
Flush templates are used with a special router bit that is piloted by an overhead ball bearing. This type of bit follows the template exactly. Offset templates are used with ordinary straight bits. A guide bushing that surrounds the bit follows the template, but the template must be oversize to compensate for the difference between the bushing's radius and the bit's radius.

used, I center it between the top and bottom hinges. When four hinges are used, I distribute them evenly, as well.

Mark one side of each hinge to register the template. To find the location for the middle hinge, divide the distance between the top of the top hinge and the bottom of the bottom hinge in half, and then measure out to one side half the length of the hinge. In other words, for a 4×4 hinge, measure 2 in. away from the center to locate one side of the gain. Place an *X* to indicate which side of the mark to cut. Make the *X* close to the open side of the gain, so that you don't rout from the wrong side.

After locating the hinges, you're ready to rout. First, make sure that the template's fence is set for the correct width of the hinge gain. The more the template overlaps the edge of the door, the wider the gain will be. The correct width depends on the size of the hinge, the thickness of the door, and the thickness of the casing. Clamp the fence to the door as you align the template's cutout with the mark.

To set the depth of cut, retract the bit completely. Then set the router over the template and lower the bit until it contacts the edge of the door. Swing the router sideways so the bit clears the wood, and then lower it a little more according to the thickness of the hinge leaves. Rout a small area—just enough to lay a corner of the hinge leaf into the resulting recess to test the depth. When the leaf sits flush with the edge of the door, the depth is right. After routing the gains on the door, chisel out their corners with a bench chisel or a spring-loaded corner chisel.

Mounting the hinges

When the gains in the door are finished you're ready for the hinges. To make hinges easier to mount, separate the leaves. First open the hinge about 90 degrees and stand it upside-down on the edge of a bench or sawhorse, with the barrel sticking out in midair. Then use a finish nail to drive the pin out.

Hinge layout

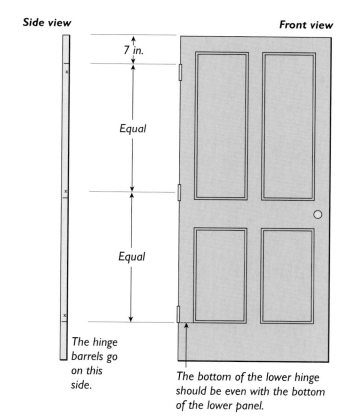

Side view

Front view

7 in.

Equal

An X indicates which side of the mark to rout and which side of the gain is open. The open side faces the hinge barrel.

Equal

The hinge barrels go on this side.

The bottom of the lower hinge should be even with the bottom of the lower panel.

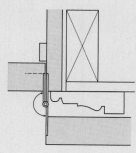

IN DETAIL

Width of Hinge Gains

Folding a door back against a thick casing may make it bind. To provide better clearance, the hinge can be positioned further away from the stop. This reduces the width of the hinge gains. On the other hand, if you move the hinge too far out, it won't have a good purchase on the door's edge. At that point, it's better to jump up to a larger hinge. A good rule is to leave 3/16 in. of wood between the edge of the hinge and the rear face of the door. This provides adequate clearance for standard doors with standard hinges and standard casing.

WHAT CAN GO WRONG

Routing a Hinge Gain from the Wrong Side

Hinges extend beyond one face of the door (the barrel side) and stop short of the other face of the door (the stop side). It's easy to rout a hinge gain from the wrong side. To avoid this, mark the face opposite the gain with a big X so you'll remember not to cut there.

TRADE SECRET

A little wax on the sole of a handplane or power plane makes it glide easier. I apply Butcher's® wax, let it dry for a minute, and then buff it to a nice sheen. When planing resinous woods, such as pine, clean the sole occasionally with lacquer thinner to remove pitch, then rewax it.

> "Sometimes the door trim gets in the way or there is casing but no stop. In that case, remove the fence from the template and tack the template to the jamb."

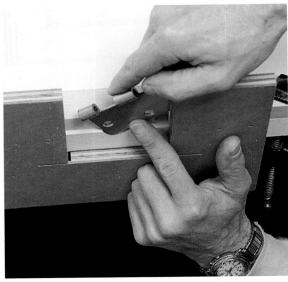

A homemade template is clamped to a door for routing a hinge gain. After routing a small portion of the gain, test the depth against a hinge leaf.

A spring-loaded corner chisel is struck with a hammer to clean out the corners of a hinge gain.

Freehand Routing

Sometimes you might not have the right template on hand, but you can rout gains freehand. Use a utility knife to score a little nick on both sides of each gain. To mark the long edge of the gain, set an adjustable square to the correct width. Holding a sharp pencil against the end of the adjustable square, scribe a line parallel to the face of the door that extends slightly past the nicks at each end of the gain.

Hold a hinge leaf in place and use it as a straight-edge to deeply score the ends of the gain. Then make another cut near each end of the gain to remove V-shaped slivers of wood. This makes crisp shoulders against which to set your chisel. Before you do any chiseling, however, carefully remove most of the gain with a router. The V-cuts at the ends of the gain are easy to see, so you won't overshoot the ends as you rout. After routing, it's easy to chisel out the remaining wood around the perimeter of the gain.

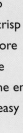

The long edge of a hinge gain (left) is laid out using an adjustable square.

A shoulder (below) is formed at the end of a hinge gain with a chisel. A V-shaped sliver is removed after incising the shoulder with a sharp knife.

One of the leaves has three knuckles and the other has two. If the three-knuckle leaf is mounted on the jamb, the two-knuckle leaf will be on the door, and vice versa. To determine which is which, hold the hinge in its approximate position before you split it, and make a note of the correct orientation. If you lose track, reorient yourself by looking for the manufacturer's trademark; the stamped mark indicates the right-side-up position.

Routing the gains in the jamb

After hinging the door, set it in the opening, shimming it tightly against the hinge-side jamb with the correct margins above and below the door. Then, use a utility knife to transfer the locations of the hinges from the door to the jamb, marking both the top and the bottom of each hinge.

If the opening doesn't have casings or stops, or if they can be removed easily, fasten the template to the jamb with the fence registering against the jamb's edge. Use brads to hold the template in place. Then, without changing the router's depth of cut, rout the jambs just like you did for the edge of the door.

Sometimes the door trim gets in the way or there is casing but no stop. In that case, remove the fence from the template and tack the template to the jamb. To position the template horizontally at each hinge location, draw a plumb line on the jamb from just above the floor to just below the head jamb. This plumb line is set back from the edge of the jamb by the desired width of the gains. Then, set the template cutout's long edge even with the plumb line. After routing the cut, make any adjustments with a chisel.

Mounting the door

When all the hinge leaves are installed, lift the door into place and mate the leaves of the top hinge first. When the top hinge is engaged, start a pin into it and then nudge the door to line up the knuckles. When they're aligned, tap in the pin about halfway. If you've routed accurately, the

A nail is used to drive the pin out of a hinge so the hinge leaves can be separated.

After carefully shimming the door into position, use a knife to transfer the locations of the hinges from the door to the jamb.

Replacing an Old Doorsill

Occasionally, you'll run across an old door during a renovation or remodeling job that needs a traditional wooden sill. To install one, cut out the subfloor, then taper the ends of the framing with a chisel and a hatchet. Make shallow saw cuts at the appropriate angle every 3 in. to guide you as you hew, then use a power plane to refine the surface. Check the angle frequently with a T-bevel (a folding angle gauge). The depth of the recess depends on the design of the sill and the thickness of the flooring. In some cases, you'll need to bevel the floor joists slightly; in others, you'll have to take a hefty notch out of the joists.

other hinges will fall sweetly into place as you ease the door into position. If they resist, tap them up or down with a hammer handle to align them. If they're more than 1/16 in. off, you'll have to dismount the door, enlarge the offending gain, and remount the hinge leaf. When all the leaves mesh properly, drive the pins home.

Installing Locksets and Deadbolts

The procedure for installing locksets and deadbolts is basically the same. A large-diameter *face bore* contains the turning mechanism and a small-diameter *edge bore* contains the latch bolt. The main difference is that locksets are spring-loaded, whereas deadbolts are driven in both directions by a key or thumbturn. Locksets keep the door shut and, in some cases, provide light security, while deadbolts are for security only.

Locating lockset bores

Find the horizontal centerline of the bores. This is typically located 35 in. to 38 in. above the floor. If it is a frame-and-panel door, try to center the lock in the door's middle rail. When you've found the horizontal centerline, use a square to mark and draw a line at that height. Wrap the line around the edge and both faces of the door.

Usually the manufacturer provides a paper template to locate the vertical centers of the face bore and the edge bore. A line on the template indicates where to fold it to fit over the edge of the door, with the wide side of the template

showing the *backset* of the face bore (the distance from the door's edge) and the narrow side of the template showing the centerline of the edge bore. Fold the template over the corner of the door, aligning it with the horizontal centerline of the lock. Mark the center of the face bore with an awl. The short side of the template shows the edge bore's center for different door thicknesses, so measure your door's thickness before marking it.

Locating bores for locksets and deadbolts

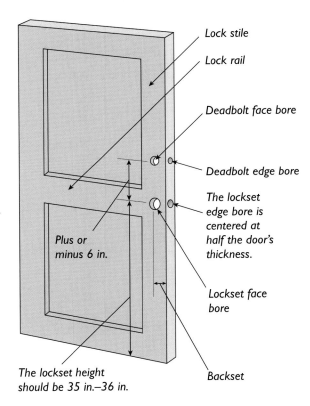

Lock stile

Lock rail

Deadbolt face bore

Deadbolt edge bore

The lockset edge bore is centered at half the door's thickness.

Lockset face bore

Plus or minus 6 in.

Backset

The lockset height should be 35 in.–36 in.

SAFETY FIRST

Using a router in a horizontal position on an upright door jamb is tricky, whether it is guided by a template or guided by hand. To keep the router's base seated firmly on the template, apply some extra pressure on the uphill side. Always wear eye, ear, and lung protection, too.

TRADE SECRET

When fastening leaves to the jamb, initially drive just one screw into each leaf. This makes it easy to shift a leaf if it doesn't fit its mate. Drive the rest of the screws after the door is hung.

A Stop on the Jamb

You can't use a template when there is a stop on the jamb. Instead, build a makeshift template around the gain, using the stop itself as part of the template. First, lay out the gains with a sharp pencil, being careful to leave enough space between the gain and the stop so the door doesn't rub. For instance, if I've left a ¼-in.-wide strip of wood between the hinge and the rear face of the door, I'll leave ⁵⁄₁₆ in. between the hinge gain on the jamb and the door stop. This produces a ¹⁄₁₆-in. gap for clearance between the stop and the door.

After laying out the gains, rip some scrap stock about 2 in. wide by as thick as the door stop. Cut off two 4-in. pieces of this stock and fasten them to the jamb above and below the gain with their ends right on the pencil line. That way, the ends of the strips will guide the router bit as it cuts the top and bottom of the gain. The strips are the same thickness as the stop, so the router will have an even surface on which to bear. Make sure to increase the depth of cut by the thickness of the stop, because the router will be running on the strips and the stop instead of on the template. Rout in from the edge a little at a time, but stop about ¼ in. away from the vertical layout line. Finish the gain with a sharp chisel.

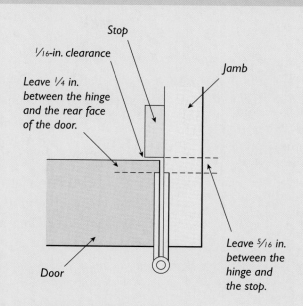

Stop
¹⁄₁₆-in. clearance

Leave ¼ in. between the hinge and the rear face of the door.

Jamb

Door

Leave ⁵⁄₁₆ in. between the hinge and the stop.

Leaving clearance between the door and the stop
To prevent a door from rubbing against the stop, place the hinge a little further from the stop than from the rear face of the door.

The stop isn't removable from this door jamb, which makes routing a problem. To provide an even surface for the router, tack strips to the jamb. The ends of the strips also guide the router like a template. The long edge of the gain will be trimmed by hand with a chisel after most of the waste has been routed away.

A paper template is folded over the corner of a door to mark the centers of the face bore and the edge bore.

Backsets

A cylinder lock's backset is the distance from the edge of the door to the center of the face bore. Most residential locks have a 2⅜-in. backset, whereas heavy-duty commercial locks have a slightly wider 2¾-in. backset. A combination lock can be positioned with either backset. Before committing to a 2¾-in.-backset lock, make sure your door's stile is wide enough. Otherwise, the lock's escutcheon may stick out beyond the stile's edge.

TOOLS AND MATERIALS

Bits for Deadbolt Face Bores

Deadbolt face bores are typically 1½ in. in diameter. You can buy a spade bit in that size, but anything larger requires an auger or a hole saw.

TRADE SECRET

Lockset striker plates have a little tang that bends inward. If the door rattles when it's closed, bend the tang toward the doorstop. If the door won't latch, bend the tang away from the stop.

"You may have to jiggle the key to engage the two halves of the lock."

Remove the template and check the layout with a tape. The face bore should be 2⅜ in. or 2¾ in. from the edge of the door, depending on the lock, while the edge bore should be centered exactly in the thickness of the door.

Boring lockset holes

Drill the face bore with a 2⅛-in.-diameter bit. The quickest type of bit is a self-feeding auger that removes shavings as it cuts and pulls itself into the hole as it drills. These bits are expensive, however, so for occasional use you may prefer to use a hole saw. Start drilling from the face of the door that you marked, stopping when the point of the augur or hole saw just peeks through the opposite face. Drilling all the way through from one side will make the face of the door splinter as the bit exits, so finish drilling the hole from the opposite side.

Drill the edge bore with a 1-in.-diameter spade-bit (never use an augur bit for drilling the edge bore). Brace the edge of the door with your foot to steady it. Use moderate pressure as you drill and eyeball the drill from the side and from above to make sure you're holding it both level and in line with the door.

Installing the lock and striker

Slip the latch bolt into the edge bore and use a sharp pencil to trace the outline of the latch plate. Then score the top and bottom of the latch-plate mortise with a utility knife, holding a square against the door to guide the knife. Chisel into the top and bottom cuts to remove a little

sliver. Then make cross-grained scoring cuts about every ¼ in. with a chisel.

Excavate the mortise in successive layers, shaving off about 1/16 in. per layer. Always work from the center outward, with the chisel's bevel facing the door. After you've removed most of the waste, use a knife to pare the side cuts cleanly. When the latch plate sits flush with the edge of the door, drill pilot holes, then fasten the latch plate with screws. The latch plate is designed to wiggle slightly, so that it will seat itself in the door's beveled edge.

After mounting the latch bolt, install the knobs. If one of the knobs is keyed, put the key in the keyhole. You may have to jiggle the key to engage the two halves of the lock. When the lock is seated properly, fasten it with the machine screws provided. Some locks have screws that pass right through the escutcheon, whereas other

A hole saw is used to drill the face bore. When the center bit of the hole saw pokes through the back of the door, the carpenter finishes drilling from the back to prevent tearout.

locks hide their mounting screws beneath a removable escutcheon. A removable escutcheon snaps into place over a hidden mounting plate, with the lock screws bearing on the plate.

Close the door and mark where the center of the latch bolt strikes the edge of the jamb. Extend this mark across the face of the jamb, and draw a vertical centerline halfway between the doorstop and the edge of the jamb. Center the striker plate on the lines and trace its outline on the jamb. Where the centerlines cross, drill a 1-in.-diameter hole to receive the latch bolt. The hole shouldn't be more than ⅝ in. deep or you'll break through the back of the jamb. After drilling the latch bolt's hole, mortise the strike plate into the jamb. Then, drill pilot holes and fasten the strike plate with screws.

Installing a deadbolt

Deadbolts are installed in much the same way as locksets. The backset and hole diameters are different, but the procedures are similar. Instead of a knob on the outside, deadbolts have a key cylinder. A *cylinder bar,* or little metal tongue, slips into the cylinder before it is installed. As the key is turned, the cylinder bar throws the bolt. A thumbturn throws the bolt from the inside, unless it's a double-cylinder deadbolt.

Make sure the striker hole is deep enough to allow the bolt to be thrown all the way. Otherwise, the bolt may spring back as a result of vibration. The mounting screws for deadbolt striker plates are extra long, so that they'll extend into the framing to provided added strength.

TOOLS AND MATERIALS
Strike Boxes

A strike box is a sleeve mounted underneath the strike plate. Its purpose is to make the hole neat and keep out dust. If a strike box is provided with your lockset, it's okay to drill through the jamb when you're mounting the strike plate.

A spade bit is used to drill the edge bore. The bit must be eyeballed carefully from above or it could break through the face of the door.

The latch bolt is slipped into the edge bore and the latch plate is traced onto the edge of the door. The latch plate will then be recessed with a chisel.

The striker plate is traced onto the jamb after transferring the latch bolt's centerline from the door to the jamb.

CHAPTER SEVEN
Problems

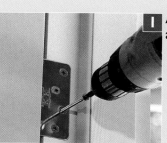

1 Adjusting Doors for a Better Fit, p. 100

2 Weatherstripping Door Jambs, p. 103

3 Sealing Door Bottoms, p. 105

4 Repairing Doors, p.108

There's nothing more annoying than a door that always sticks in summer's humidity or sags because its hinges are coming loose. Maybe the problem you face is an icy blast coming from under the door in the winter. Even if you haven't noticed it, you could be heating your yard in the winter and cooling it in the summer because your door isn't properly weatherproofed. If you have children who slam or bang doors while they play, chances are you have nicks or gashes in your doors, especially if you have hollow-core doors. This chapter explains how to diagnose and fix these problems. I'll tell you how to troubleshoot and adjust doors that don't fit right. We'll also look at ways to save on energy by upgrading weatherstripping. Finally, I'll explain how to repair doors damaged by ordinary use.

The most common hinge failure is loosening. This occurs when the pilot holes for the hinge screws weren't properly sized in the first place. Too large a hole reduces the bite of the screw threads into the surrounding wood; too small a hole causes the wood to split. In either case, the integrity of the wood surrounding the screw is damaged. Use a longer screw to penetrate deeper into the edge of the door or reach beyond the damaged wood and penetrate the stud behind the jamb.

TRADE SECRET

Sometimes a screw head gets chewed up beyond all hope. You can remove the head of the screw by drilling it out with a drill bit that's slightly smaller than the head of the screw. After removing the hinge, use vise grip pliers to remove the screw shank.

"When a door sticks, it may seem sensible to plane the edge of the door that rubs. Wrong. The real problem is at the hinge side."

Adjusting Doors for a Better Fit

Perhaps there's a world where every door is a perfectly flat rectangle, every door jamb is straight and plumb, and every entryway has a uniform ³⁄₃₂-in. gap between the door and the frame. If there is such a world, it isn't this one. In reality, we have a host of forces conspiring to loosen hinges, warp stiles, distort openings, and otherwise disturb the proper functioning of a door.

The head margin is too wide on the strike side of the door.

Rubbing here…

…is caused by loosening here.

Tighten old screws or drive new screws here for a tighter margin.

The hinge-side margin is too wide at the top and too tight at the bottom.

Shim here for a wider margin.

Rubbing caused by loose or bent hinges
Loose or bent hinges can make a door sag. Tightening the top hinge and shimming the bottom hinge is one solution. Another solution is to bend the hinge knuckles with a wrench.

To tighten a margin on the hinge side, replace the screws furthest from the hinge barrel with long screws driven into a stud.

A longer screw here won't hold because it would penetrate only the drywall.

To widen a margin on the hinge side, insert cardboard shims between the jamb and the hinge.

Cut the excess off the shims here with a knife.

Tightening and shimming hinges
The best cure for a loose hinge is to drive a long screw through the hinge into a stud. This narrows the margin between the door and the hinge jamb. To widen the margin between the door and the hinge jamb, insert cardboard shims behind the hinge.

Tightening hinges

When a door sticks, it may seem sensible to plane the edge of the door that is rubbing against the jamb. Wrong. Nine times out of ten, the real problem is located on the opposite side of the door—at the hinge. As the hinge gives way, the gap between the hinge side of the door and the frame opens up. Meanwhile, the gap between the strike side of the door and the frame closes, until the door starts to rub.

To diagnose the problem, open the door slightly and pull upward on the knob while looking at the uppermost hinge. See if there's play between the hinge and the jamb, between the hinge and the door, or both. Note also whether

Door edges are usually planed with a bevel of about 3 degrees, so that the inner corner of the door's strike-side edge clears the jamb. The hinge-side edge is beveled as well, but for a different reason. A jamb that's out of square with the wall may bind against the hinge-side edge of a door as it closes. This makes closing the door difficult and eventually loosens the hinge screws. A screw head that isn't seated properly in its hinge leaf produces the same symptoms. A preemptive bevel on the hinge side of the door compensates for these irregularities.

An oversize pilot hole may loosen hinge screws over time. Reinsert the screws with a dab of epoxy on the threads.

there's movement in the middle and/or lower hinges. A loose lower hinge makes the door move *toward* the jamb, further exacerbating the cockeyed condition.

If the hinges are loose, open the door as far as it will go and shim under the door to temporarily relieve the strain on the hinges. Then remove the loose screws and replace them one by one with screws that are about 1½ in. longer than the old ones. Make sure you drill pilot holes of the correct size. There's no point in replacing the screws closest to the hinge barrel on the jamb leaf. Longer screws penetrate into the drywall or plaster, which don't hold screws. The screws closest to the doorstop should be long enough to reach the stud behind the jamb.

TOOLS AND MATERIALS
What You'll Need for Adjusting Hinges

- Screwdriver (or power drill mounted with correct driver)
- Shims
- Extra-long screws (1½ in. longer than the original screws)
- Five-minute epoxy
- Adjustable wrench

If the door leaf on a hollow-core door has loosened, longer screws may not work. The wood stiles at the edges of this type of door are only 1-in. thick, and a longer screw will just poke into a void. Instead, try reinserting the screws with a dab of five-minute epoxy on the threads. Keep the door propped upright until the glue dries. If that doesn't work, consider relocating the hinges or replacing the door. The same problem may occur with solid-core doors. The core of these doors is usually particleboard, which doesn't hold screws well. Try using very long screws (3 in. to 4 in.), and drill your pilot holes smaller than you would for solid wood.

Shimming and bending hinges

Typically, a door's weight makes the gap at the top hinge open up. To fix this, first raise the hinge pin until it engages only the top knuckle. Then use an adjustable wrench to gently bend the knuckles on the door leaf toward the lock

Removing Old Hinge Screws

Removing old slotted screws can be a real chore. First you need to clean the paint and rust out of the slot so you can get a grip on the screw. Starting at one end of the slot, hold a screwdriver at a 45-degree angle to the head of the screw. Tapping gently with a hammer, use the corner of the screwdriver blade to plow out any gunk. You want to restore the slot to its original condition, meaning a square, flat-bottomed groove. To do this, you need the right size screwdriver with a crisp, square tip.

After plowing, drive the screwdriver squarely into the slot. Maintain as much pressure as you can while turning. It helps to brace your body against something fixed, such as the doorframe. To gain extra leverage, clamp vise-grips to the screwdriver handle. A brace and bit also works well. If you're using a power drill, set it on low for maximum torque (turning power) and better control.

Fixing a Severely Racked Door

You may have to add a tapered filler strip to the top or bottom of a severely racked door. Saw the strip off the edge of a thick plank and attach it to the door with brads and glue. Then sand the strip flush with the door.

Tuning Up Slotted Screwdrivers

To restore the blade of a slotted screwdriver, scrape it on a grinder or a belt sander mounted upside-down in a vise. Hold the blade perpendicular to the grinding surface with one hand, and support the blade close to the tip with your other hand. Use gentle pressure and cool the tip frequently so it won't lose its temper. You can also file a screwdriver blade. Restore the taper and adjust the thickness of the tip by grinding a little bit off of both faces.

> "Widening the gap at the bottom hinge has the effect of narrowing the gap between the door and the head jamb on the strike side of the door."

To adjust margins, bend the hinge knuckles with an adjustable wrench. First lift the pin until it engages only the top knuckle. Leave the knuckles on the jamb leaf alone, but gently bend the knuckles on the door leaf. Moving the knuckles toward the lock narrows the margin on the hinge side. Moving the knuckles away from the lock widens the margin on the hinge side.

side of the door and reinstall the pin. This will draw the door back toward the hinge jamb. Ideally, the gap should be equal on both sides of the door. If you overshoot the mark, simply reverse the procedure.

One way to *increase* the gap at a particular hinge is to insert cardboard shims between the hinge leaf and the jamb (see top drawing, p. 100), which moves the door away from the hinge jamb

at that point. This is most often necessary at the bottom hinge, which is under compression (the top hinge is under tension, which opens the gap there). Widening the gap at the bottom hinge has the effect of narrowing the gap between the door and the head jamb on the strike side of the door (see bottom drawing, p. 100).

To shim a hinge, open the door and loosen the screws on the jamb leaf a few turns. Cut shims about ½ in. wide and almost as long as the hinge is tall. Lift the door on the strike side with one hand, which opens a gap between the hinge and the jamb. (For heavy doors, use a prybar for lifting.) Slip a shim or two into the gap with your other hand, then ease off the pressure slightly until the shim is just barely pinched under the leaf. Poke the shim in until it presses against the hinge screws. Tighten the screws and test the fit. When you have installed the correct number of shims, trim off any excess with a utility knife.

Trimming existing doors

Sometimes, no amount of hinge adjustment makes a door close properly. That's usually because the frame, which was originally a rectangle, has become a parallelogram. The door, meanwhile, has stayed rectangular. Distortion of a

Racking of Door Frame and Door

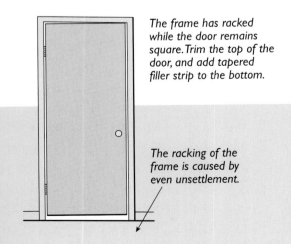

The frame has racked while the door remains square. Trim the top of the door, and add tapered filler strip to the bottom.

The racking of the frame is caused by even unsettlement.

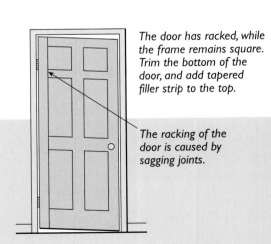

The door has racked, while the frame remains square. Trim the bottom of the door, and add tapered filler strip to the top.

The racking of the door is caused by sagging joints.

rectangular structure, called *racking*, can be caused by foundation settlement or by uneven shrinkage in a house's framing. Sometimes the opposite can occur—a door sags as its joints loosen, while the frame remains square.

Racking makes a door bind on its lock side, either at the top, against the head or at the bottom, against the sill. You'll need to trim off a tapering amount of wood, starting from zero at the hinge side of the door and increasing to ⅛ in. or more on the lock side of the door. Rather than using a straightedge to lay this out, set a pair of scribers to ⅛ in. and trace along the head or the sill. If there's any waviness in the frame, the scribers will transfer that waviness to the door so the gap remains constant.

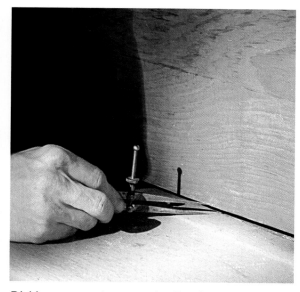

Dividers are used to scratch a line for trimming an ill-fitting door. The line will be perfectly parallel to the sill even if the sill isn't quite straight. Dividers are similar to scribers but without a pencil.

Swelling caused by severe humidity can make a door stick in its frame. Check first to make sure that the gap on the hinge side is correct. If the hinge-side gap is an even ⅛ in. and the door is sticking on the lock side, remove the door for planing. If the entire edge needs planing, remove the lock. After planing, chisel a new gain for the lock face. You may have to enlarge the face bore for the lock, as well. Paint immediately dulls a plane, so remove the finish first.

Weatherstripping Door Jambs

Few home improvement jobs pay as big a dividend as weatherproofing. The few dollars spent on new weatherstripping will be repaid in energy savings, and your home will be more comfortable, as well. Weatherstripping comes in four basic types.

Kerf-in weatherstripping

Weatherstripping that has a continuous fin pressed into a groove around the perimeter of the frame is called *kerf-in weatherstripping*. A big advantage of

Adjusting a Striker

One problem often caused by racking is misalignment of the latch bolt and striker plate. If a door closes but refuses to latch, this is probably the reason. Bring the door up to the edge of the jamb and mark where the latch bolt contacts the jamb. Open the door to see if you need to move the striker up or down. Remove the striker, enlarge the gain with a chisel, and reinstall the striker to align with the latch bolt.

Move the striker at least ¼ in. so you can drill a fresh pilot hole for the striker screws. This may be slightly more than necessary, but the opening in the striker is usually oversize, so it won't be a problem. If you try to move the striker less than ¼ in., the screws will wander back into the old holes. Sometimes a striker hole is sized very tightly, so that moving it even ¼ in. puts it on the opposite side of the latch bolt. In that case, the striker hole must be enlarged. Remove the striker, clamp it in a vise, and file it. To fill the exposed portion of the old gain, use epoxy filler.

IN DETAIL

Compensating for Warpage

There are two ways to fix a warped door. You can pry the stops loose and renail them alongside the twisted door, or you can move one of the hinges away from the stop on the hinge jamb. If the gap between the door and the stop is at the top on the strike side, reposition the bottom hinge. If the gap is at the bottom, shift the top hinge. To move the hinge, first place shims under the open door. Remove the screws, nudge the hinge over, and drive one screw. Test the door; if it closes evenly against the stop on the strike side, drive the remaining screws. Patch the oversize gain with epoxy filler or glue in a small Dutchman.

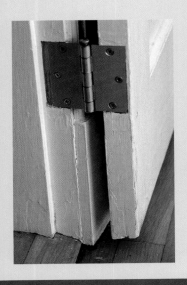

> "A big advantage of kerf-in is that it can be easily replaced when worn. Just take hold of one end and pull."

kerf-in is that it can be easily replaced when worn. Just take hold of one end and pull. Kerf-in is used primarily for new doors because the groove is easily cut during manufacture.

To apply kerf-in to an existing doorframe, you'll need a special router to cut the groove. Then, work the new strip into the groove with your fingers, or use a pizza-cutter-type splining tool. It's also good to remove kerf-in temporarily

Foam kerf-in weatherstripping is pressed into a groove, or kerf, in the doorstop. This type of weatherstripping is concealed when the door is closed, and it can easily be removed to paint the jamb.

Kerf-In Weatherstripping

Kerf-in weatherstripping is available in two materials. Silicone bulb is smaller, so it's completely hidden when the door is closed. Foam kerf-in is larger than the silicone variety, so it remains partially visible when the door is closed, but it seals better than silicone and it's cushy enough to conform to any unevenness in the door or jamb.

when painting an exterior jamb, because paint makes weatherstripping rough and brittle. Don't get paint in the empty groove, however, or it will be difficult to reinstall the kerf-in.

Leaf-type weatherstripping

A metal product nailed to the frame with tiny brads every 3 in. is called *leaf-type weatherstripping*. The springiness of the metal presses the weatherstripping against the door to seal out drafts. Aside from being tedious to install, leaf-type weatherstripping eventually flattens from repeated clos-

A splining tool is used to quickly apply silicone-bulb-type kerf-in weatherstripping.

Leaf-Type Weatherstripping

Leaf-type weatherstripping is available in different metals (bronze, brass, and stainless steel) and in different profiles (flat and V-shaped). Both bronze and stainless steel resist corrosion. Bronze mellows with age to a brown hue, whereas stainless remains silver. V-shaped types are generally acknowledged to perform better than flat types.

ings. You can restore its performance—at least for a while—by running a nail set underneath to pry it away from the jamb (see photo below). On the upside, leaf-type is invisible when the door is closed, and you don't need special tools for the installation.

Rigid-jamb weatherstripping

The easiest type of weatherstripping to add to an existing door, *rigid-jamb weatherstripping* is composed of an extruded seal bound in a wood or metal strip. Most types have elongated mounting

Fit is critical with rigid-jamb weatherstripping. If it's too tight on the hinge side, the door will pinch the seal as it closes, eventually tearing the seal out of the strip.

holes so that you can adjust the strip by loosening the screws. Types that use round holes with nails, including those with wood strips, are not adjustable and should be avoided.

The safest way to cut metal rigid-jamb weatherstripping is with a hacksaw. Jigsaws also work well, and you can even miter cut aluminum on a chopsaw with the proper precautions. The seals for rigid-jamb are made of silicone or vinyl. Silicone is more expensive, but it performs better than vinyl because it's softer and springier.

Interlocking weatherstripping

Seen mostly on older homes, *interlocking weatherstripping* is highly effective and dependable, but it's complex and very difficult to install. It employs special configurations of metal strips at the hinge jamb and around the lock that are different from those used at the top and lock jamb of the door (see photos, p. 106). Interlocking weatherstripping is trouble-free as long as it's not painted and the metal isn't bent. To remove paint buildup, use a scraper and sandpaper. To straighten bent stripping, pry it gently with a putty knife or pound it with a mallet until the door closes smoothly.

Sealing Door Bottoms

Unless a door is protected by some sort of roof or overhang, moisture can seep in through the bottom, flow to the floor below, and cause serious hidden decay. There's also heavy foot traffic through a doorway, so the weather barrier at the bottom must be highly durable.

IN DETAIL
Retrofitting Kerf-In Weatherstripping

Kerf-in weatherstripping can be installed in an existing doorframe, but you may want to hire a carpenter with a special tool to do it. The tool, which costs about $215, is a small router equipped with a V-shaped shoe. The shoe rides along in the jamb rabbet to cut a perfect *kerf*, or groove, for the weatherstripping. The result looks a lot better than rigid-jamb weatherstripping, and it lasts longer because the seal is sheltered from traffic.

Kerf-in weatherstripping can be retrofitted on an existing doorframe by cutting a groove with a special router. The router's tilted motor allows the bit to reach all the way into the corner. A vacuum hose connects to a shop-vac for dust removal.

TRADE SECRET

The seals used in rigid-jamb weatherstripping tend to shrink away from the ends of their aluminum binding, letting air enter. To prevent this, use a pair of pliers or side cutters to crimp the binding tightly around the seal.

Side cutters are used to crimp the end of metal weatherstripping. Otherwise, the strip's flexible seal may shrink away from the ends.

Interlocking weather-stripping is durable but requires professional installation. At the top and hinge side of the door, a strip on the door interlocks with a strip on the stop (left). On the hinge side, a groove in the edge of the door engages a strip mounted on the jamb (right).

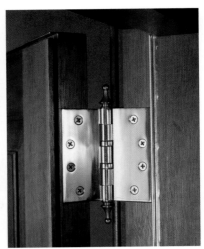

Installing sill covers

Before installing a new metal threshold in an old doorway, you may want to cover an existing wooden sill with an L-shaped aluminum sill cover. This eliminates sill maintenance and conceals any previous deterioration.

To install a sill cover, first determine its length. The length depends on how far the cover extends toward the exterior, because the width of the opening steps outward according to the configuration of the frame. To be on the safe side, make a cardboard template, and then trace the template onto the sill cover. After cutting the cover to its longest dimension, hold it in the

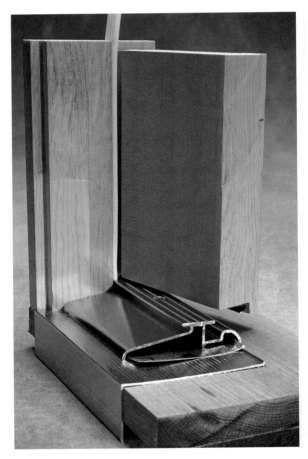

An aluminum sill cover (foreground) is fitted over the old wooden sill before installing a new threshold (center). A drain pan is sandwiched between the sill cover and the threshold. The pan's upturned lip turns away water that seeps through the threshold.

"*A simple V-shaped saddle isn't appropriate for a door that is pelted by rain or snow, since water tends to infiltrate under the sweep and drain into the interior.*"

IN DETAIL
Using a Template

The ends of saddles and thresholds often require a series of notches to fit around the jambs and trim. Use cardboard, sheet metal, or heavy paper to make the template in three segments—two ends and a middle. Use scribers to transfer the notches on the jamb to each end piece. Cut the ends until they fit, place them in position, and tape the middle section to the ends to complete the template. Then trace the template onto your workpiece for cutting. Use a scratch awl or a felt-tip pen for metal.

Part of a template is scribed for fitting a threshold (right). Another part has already been fitted (left). A middle section will join the two ends and the template will then be traced onto the threshold.

A sill cover is notched to fit around the doorstop.

A **U-shaped aluminum threshold** mates with a U-shaped sweep. The sweep features an integral drip bar that diverts most of the runoff to the exterior. Water that seeps past the sweep will drain to the interior, however, so this type of threshold is best suited to sheltered locations.

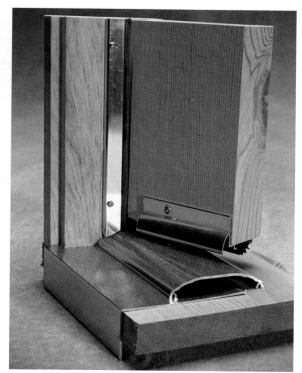

opening on an incline (so it fits between the jambs) and mark the notches that will fit around the doorstops and/or the exterior trim. Use a jigsaw with a metal-cutting blade to cut notches in the sill cover.

Installing thresholds

Exterior thresholds are made from bronze, aluminum, or a combination of aluminum and wood or aluminum and vinyl. Interior thresholds, often referred to as *saddles,* are made of wood. The simplest type of metal threshold has a U-profile and is reversible (see photo, above right). The top of the threshold meets a vinyl sweep on the underside of the door. A U-profile saddle provides an

effective thermal seal for doors that are already protected from the weather. A simple V-shaped saddle isn't appropriate for a door that is pelted by rain or snow, since water tends to infiltrate under the sweep and drain into the interior.

A more effective barrier is a *water-return threshold* (see center photo, facing page). It has a gutter extruded into its profile to collect infiltrated water and return it to the outside through weep holes. While a water-return threshold can be mounted directly to a wooden sill, it's better to apply a sill cover first to prevent seepage. An additional layer of protection known as a *drain pan* can be sandwiched between the threshold and the sill cover. The rear upturned lip of the

TRADE SECRET

Sill covers have other applications. Remodeling sometimes adds to the thickness of a finish floor, such as when changing a kitchen floor from thin vinyl to thick ceramic tile. When this occurs, the doors must be trimmed and the thresholds raised. Rather than replacing the entire sill, use a sill cover to create a neat step from one level to the next.

SAFETY FIRST

Although you can cut rigid-jamb weatherstripping and sill covers with a hacksaw, the quickest and most accurate way is to miter them on a chopsaw. Check to make sure that the metal is aluminum, which you can generally identify by its light weight and softness when pricked with a sharp object. To be absolutely sure, test it with a magnet—aluminum is nonmagnetic. Use a fine-toothed blade (the type for cutting plywood and nonferrous metals) and feed the saw very slowly to prevent kickback.

An Oak-Top Threshold

Instead of combining a threshold with a sill cover, buy a one-piece unit called an *oak-top threshold*. This is a wooden threshold mated to an aluminum sill cover. It's aesthetically desirable for complementing a wooden floor or a wooden door.

This one-piece unit combines an attractive oak threshold with an aluminum sill cover. Fitting a combined unit such as this is more difficult than fitting a threshold and a sill cover separately because there are more notches that must be dealt with at one time.

"The simplest type of sweep is a flap that mounts to the face of a door. This type of sweep is effective for out-swing doors and for in-swing doors."

drain pan keeps water from creeping back toward the interior.

Thresholds seal against door bottoms in different ways. Some have a flat top that mates with a vinyl sweep. Another type has a lip that fits a U-shaped metal hook strip mounted to the underside of the door. The sweep seal is more forgiving of misalignment than the hook strip, but the hook strip is more durable.

Most thresholds have a fixed height, so you need to raise or lower the sweep to adjust the fit. However, some thresholds have a wooden or vinyl insert that can be raised or lowered with adjusting screws to achieve a perfect seal. When trimming a door to fit this type of threshold, adjust the threshold to the middle of its range when accounting for its thickness.

Installing sweeps

Sweeps are mounted to the face or underside of a door and provide a resilient surface that mates with the hard surface of the threshold. A vinyl seal is bound in a metal extrusion that is screwed to the door. Slotted mounting holes shift the extrusion up and down. The simplest type of sweep is a flap that mounts to the face of a door. The flap should press against a rounded corner of

Water-return thresholds catch water that seeps toward the interior, and the seepage is then drained back to the exterior through weep holes. This water-return threshold mates with an L-shaped sweep. L-shaped sweeps are less conspicuous than U-shaped sweeps because they're concealed in a rabbet in the door bottom.

Not Too Tight

When adjusting the height of an under-mount sweep, the seal should make light contact with the threshold. Too much friction makes the door difficult to operate and wears out the seal prematurely.

the threshold. This type of sweep is effective for out-swing doors and for in-swing doors that are sheltered from the weather.

In-swing doors employ a *combination drip/ under-mount sweep.* A curved fin, or *drip,* shelters the top of the threshold from wind-driven rain, while diverting water from the face of the door to the exterior. A bulb-shaped seal underneath the door presses against the top of the threshold. U-shaped and L-shaped extrusions are available. U-shaped sweeps wrap around the door bottom on three sides, with the bottom of the door cut square (see right photo, p. 107). This is the simpler of the two versions to install. L-shaped sweeps are concealed from the interior by a rabbet underneath the door. You can cut the rabbet with a circular saw, but a router does a neater job (see photo, below).

Repairing Doors

It's not surprising that doors take a beating, since virtually all household traffic is channeled through them. Considering the high cost of replacements, it pays to have a few door-repair tricks at your disposal. These techniques can also help you resurrect old doors found at tag sales and salvage yards.

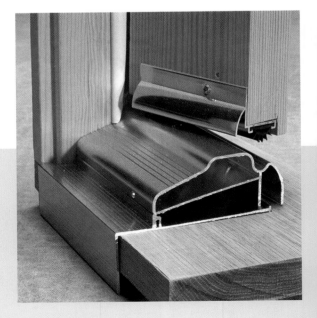

Sealing the Bottom of a Door

There are many systems for sealing door bottoms, most of which involve two basic components. The first component attaches to the bottom of the door. It may be a flexible rubber sweep or a rigid metal hook strip. The second component is the threshold, which is fixed along the bottom of the opening. Some thresholds are applied on top of a wooden sill, while others are an integral part of a metal sill. The sill is the bottom of the doorframe. When the sweep or hook strip meets the raised threshold, it creates a seal. In addition to sealing out drafts and moisture, thresholds elevate a door bottom for floor and carpet clearance.

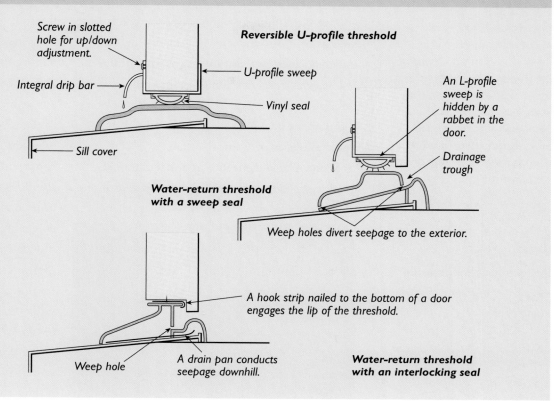

Screw in slotted hole for up/down adjustment.

Integral drip bar

Sill cover

Reversible U-profile threshold

U-profile sweep

Vinyl seal

An L-profile sweep is hidden by a rabbet in the door.

Drainage trough

Water-return threshold with a sweep seal

Weep holes divert seepage to the exterior.

A hook strip nailed to the bottom of a door engages the lip of the threshold.

Weep hole

A drain pan conducts seepage downhill.

Water-return threshold with an interlocking seal

Making repairs with epoxy

Epoxy fillers are strong and waterproof and shrink very little, making them terrific for filling deep cavities. You can even rebuild missing edges and corners if the patch is properly anchored to the door. When using epoxy to repair wood, it's important to create a good mechanical bond between the damaged area and the filler, rather than relying solely on the filler's adhesive qualities. Epoxy sticks tenaciously to wood at first, but as the wood expands and contracts seasonally, the bond weakens.

Flap-type sweeps
Flap-type sweeps are easy to install and work fairly well for out-swing doors. Flap-type sweeps aren't recommended for in-swing doors unless the door is sheltered from the weather.

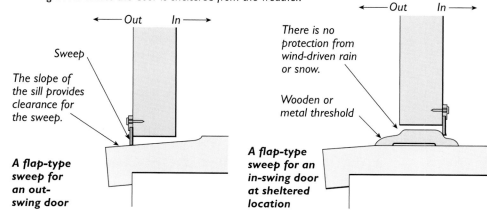

Out ← | → In

Sweep

The slope of the sill provides clearance for the sweep.

A flap-type sweep for an out-swing door

← Out | In →

There is no protection from wind-driven rain or snow.

Wooden or metal threshold

A flap-type sweep for an in-swing door at sheltered location

TOOLS AND MATERIALS

Exterior Doors without Thresholds

A sophisticated cousin of the sweep is the *automatic door bottom*. A plunger on the hinge edge of the door lowers a neoprene seal when the door closes. When the door opens, the seal retracts into the door. To install an automatic door bottom, you need to cut a deep channel in the bottom edge of the door. Although difficult to install, an automatic door bottom operates with no friction whatsoever and is useful on doors without a threshold, such as when a tile floor extends uninterrupted from a kitchen to a patio.

An automatic door bottom is housed in a groove along the bottom edge of the door. When the plunger (sticking out from the edge of the door) is depressed, the neoprene seal drops down. The screw seated in the door jamb provides a durable striking surface for the plunger.

To prepare a crater for filling, remove all loose material. Blast the crater with compressed air if you have a compressor. To anchor the patch, drill a series of ⅛-in.-diameter holes radiating from the crater into the surrounding wood. Drill the holes about ½ in. deep, but be careful not to drill through the door. Filler squishes into these holes and hardens into little tentacles that hold the patch in place.

Epoxy filler is activated by mixing a small quantity of hardener with a large quantity of resin; follow the directions carefully for the correct proportions. Mound the filler above the surface, and then sand it flush when it dries. For a head start on sanding, use a Surform tool to remove the bulk of the excess material. A Surform tool works best when the epoxy is still in a semihardened state. This lasts for only a few minutes before the filler hardens completely, so be ready. Don't try to sand partially hardened epoxy—it will just clog your sandpaper. After about 20 minutes, sand the area with 50-grit paper and finish with 80-grit to 120-grit paper, depending on the desired smoothness. Finish the surface with the appropriate primer and paint.

You can do other repairs with epoxy, as well. For instance, when you move a lock from one side of a door to the other, use epoxy to fill the old lock bore or mortise. To reduce the amount of epoxy required, embed chunks of wood within the patch.

You can also use epoxy to repair a door that has been damaged by decay. Rather than excavating all traces of decay, firm up the softened wood with liquid consolidator. This form of epoxy has a syrupy consistency that allows it to soak into decay-softened wood. Thick-bodied epoxy filler is used to rebuild missing areas after the consol-

To anchor epoxy filler, a series of small holes is drilled into the sides of the crater.

A Surform tool is used to remove most of the excess epoxy from a patch. Sanding completes the job.

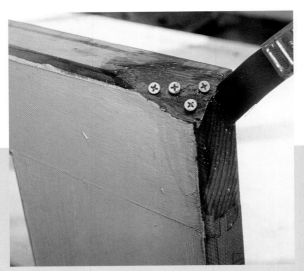

Screws are driven partway with their heads sticking out to anchor an epoxy corner patch. Liquid epoxy consolidator is brushed on to harden the surrounding partially decayed wood.

idator is applied. To improve the chemical adhesion between the filler and the wood, apply the filler as soon as the consolidator becomes tacky.

When building up an edge or a corner, you need to anchor the repair to the door especially well. Drive screws or lag-bolts into the door with their heads sticking out. The farther the screws extend into the patch the better, but don't let them extend beyond the projected face of the door. Apply epoxy to the area, then grind the patch back to its final dimension after the filler hardens.

Installing wooden patches

A wooden patch, sometimes referred to as a *Dutchman*, is a good way to make a surface repair in a door with a natural finish. The repair won't be 100% invisible, but it's the next best thing to a new door. A well-executed Dutchman can even add character.

To excavate the damaged area, use a router with a straight bit. Insert a guide collar into the router's baseplate, and then use a plywood template to guide the collar. Make successive passes with the router, lowering the bit about ⅛ in. for each pass until you reach the necessary depth. After routing, remove the corners of the recess with a sharp chisel.

To make the patch, select a piece of wood with matching grain and color. Rip the patch to the correct width on a table saw, and then cut it to length. The thickness of the patch should be slightly more than the depth of the recess. Taper the edges of the patch ever so slightly with a sanding block, just a hair smaller than the recess below the surface, so that the patch will be tightly seated.

Apply glue to the bottom of the recess and the bottom of the patch, but don't glue the edges. Then clamp the patch for at least eight hours. To trim the patch down to the surface of the door, start by planing across the grain. Planing with the grain may tear the wood. When you get to within ¹⁄₁₆ in. of the surface of the door, switch to a sanding block or a power sander to finish up. Completely sand any squeeze-out before staining or finishing with a clear coat.

Sometimes you need to patch hinge gains when you reverse the swing of a door (or when the carpenter goofs in the first place). The patch needs to be only about ⅛ in. thick, but such a thin wafer of wood will warp as soon as you apply glue to one side. It's better to leave the patch ½ in. to ¾ in. thick. After the glue dries, saw or plane off the extra thickness.

A tight-fitting Dutchman is the best patch for a naturally finished door.

A router fitted with a guide collar is used to excavate damaged wood before installing a Dutchman. The collar rides against the edge of a plywood template to control the cut.

Choosing

CHAPTER EIGHT

Windows

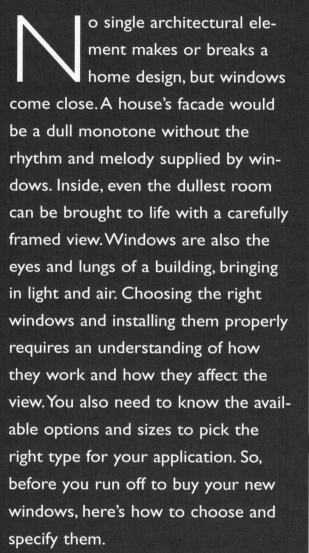

No single architectural element makes or breaks a home design, but windows come close. A house's facade would be a dull monotone without the rhythm and melody supplied by windows. Inside, even the dullest room can be brought to life with a carefully framed view. Windows are also the eyes and lungs of a building, bringing in light and air. Choosing the right windows and installing them properly requires an understanding of how they work and how they affect the view. You also need to know the available options and sizes to pick the right type for your application. So, before you run off to buy your new windows, here's how to choose and specify them.

Order Windows Early

Nothing will bring your job to a grinding halt like missing windows. To avoid construction delays, order them as early as possible. This is especially critical in boom times, when orders can literally be backed up for months.

Where to Use Sliders

Sliding windows are associated with contemporary architectural styles. That's because sliders weren't feasible until the development of weather-resistant materials for the wheels and track. On traditional homes, sliders are sometimes used on the back of the house where stylistic purity isn't as important.

Window terminology

*A **window** is comprised of movable **sashes** inside an immovable **frame**. The frame is composed of a **sill**, **leg jambs**, and a **head jamb**. **Sill horns** are narrow extensions at both ends of the sill. The tracks on double-hung frames have three narrow strips: the **blind stop** on the outside, the **parting bead** in the middle, and the **window stop** on the inside.*

*The sashes have vertical **stiles** and horizontal **rails**. The rails are further differentiated as the **top rail**, **bottom rail**, and **check rails**. Check rails, also called **meeting rails**, are adjoining rails that meet when the window is closed. Individual panes of glass are called **lites**, and the narrow bars that separate the lites are called **muntins**.*

*The **exterior casing** covers the gap between the frame and the outer surrounding wall. The **interior casing** (not shown) does the same thing on the inside. The inner edge of the sill is finished with a **stool**.*

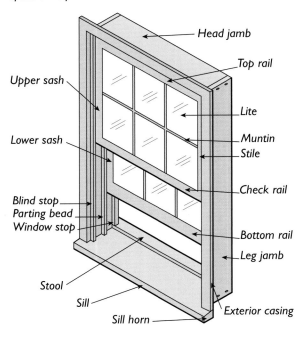

Head jamb
Top rail
Upper sash
Lite
Lower sash
Muntin
Stile
Check rail
Blind stop
Parting bead
Window stop
Bottom rail
Leg jamb
Stool
Sill
Exterior casing
Sill horn

Window Operating Systems

A **wide variety of window** types and sizes have become available in recent years. There's a window type to suit any style of home and any operating application.

Double-hung and single-hung windows

Double-hung windows have upper and lower sashes that slide up and down. A *single-hung* window has only an operable bottom sash. In both types, the ventilation is limited to 50% of the window area. On the plus side, they resist rain easily because the top sash overlaps the bottom sash and they are both sheltered inside the wall.

Contemporary (or "modern") double-hung windows slide in tracks called *jamb liners,* which double as weatherstripping around the sashes. Jamb liners contain spring balances that assist the upward sliding of the sashes. Spring balances have replaced the weights and pulleys once used to

Fixed upper sash
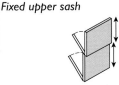

Double-hung windows
Both the upper and the lower sash slide up and down.

Single-hung windows
The upper sash is fixed while the lower sash slides up and down.

Tilt double-hung windows
The sashes slide up and down, and tilt in for cleaning.

"Most casements swing out on a special hinge that lets you reach between the sash and the frame for cleaning."

Lumberyards often retain a millwork specialist on their sales staff. It seems like he's always a middle-aged guy with a bad complexion and a frog in his throat, but he's worth his weight in gold. Cut through the greenhorns at the counter and go straight to him for answers to your millwork questions.

Casements for Tight and Hard-to-Reach Spots

The ease of cranking a window rather than lifting it makes casements preferable to double-hung windows in hard-to-reach places, such as over a sink. If you'll be installing window blinds over casement windows, order low-profile cranks that won't interfere with the blinds.

balance sashes. Double-hung windows require a *sash lock* where the check rails meet; they may also be equipped with sash lifts (handles) to raise the lower sash. *Tilt double-hung* windows pivot into the interior to make cleaning easier. Some tilt windows employ a latch mechanism, whereas others have flexible tracks that allow the sash to wiggle out.

Awning
This window is hinged on the top and tilts outward.

Hopper
This window is hinged on the bottom and tilts inward.

Awning and hopper windows

An *awning* window is hinged at the top and swings outward. It is often used below fixed windows to pull in cool air. A *hopper* window is the opposite of an awning window, and is hinged at the bottom rather than at the top. Like casement windows, awnings and hoppers provide 100% ventilation. Awnings offer partial protection from wind-driven rain when they're open. Hoppers collect rain, so they're best used in sheltered locations. Awnings are opened with a crank like casements and by a pole or motorized operator for out-of-reach places.

Casement
The sash opens like a door and can swing in or out.

Casement windows

Casement windows are second only to double-hung windows in popularity. Most casements swing out on a special hinge that lets you reach between the sash and the frame for cleaning. Out-swing casements are exposed to rain if left open, so cladding is advisable to prevent decay. In-swing casements are sometimes found in old houses. A *crank,* also called a *casement operator,* lets you open out-swing casements without removing the screen. *Casement locks* draw the sash tightly against the frame and compress the window's weatherstripping. *French casements* are pairs of sashes in a single frame. They usually meet without a center bar, like French doors.

A wooden sliding window illuminates this cozy breakfast nook. Sliders are easy to operate and don't interfere with foot traffic outside.

TRADE SECRET

If you can't find an awning window that is the right size, look at casement windows. In some cases, you can turn a regular casement into an awning window simply by turning it sideways.

 According to Code

Building codes require that every bedroom have an emergency exit in case of fire. For a window to qualify, it must afford an opening of no less than 5.7 sq. ft. The opening must be at least 20 in. wide and 24 in. high. The sill cannot be more than 44 in. above the floor. These provisions allow occupants to escape through the window and allow a fireman with a backpack to enter. The window must also permit an emergency escape to a public way and be no less than 3 ft. from a property line.

Polygons

In some cases, the geometry of a polygon is simple enough that you can use a drawing rather than a template to order it. Make sure you provide each of the critical dimensions on your sketch, and if the shape isn't symmetrical—a trapezoid, for example—specify the viewpoint of your sketch (inside or outside). Order more complex polygons with the help of a template made of plywood, cardboard, or heavy paper.

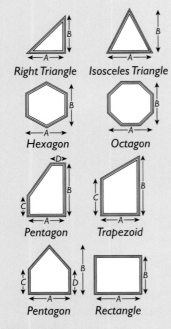

Right Triangle   *Isosceles Triangle*

Hexagon   *Octagon*

Pentagon   *Trapezoid*

Pentagon   *Rectangle*

Polygons
The lettered dimensions shown (A, B, etc.) are necessary when ordering.

> **"Fixed glass units are less expensive than operable windows because you save on hardware, weatherstripping, and assembly time."**

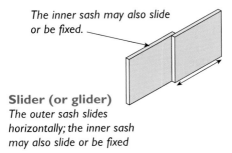

The inner sash may also slide or be fixed.

Slider (or glider)
The outer sash slides horizontally; the inner sash may also slide or be fixed

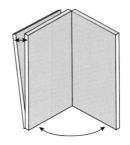

Tilt/turn
The sash swings open like a casement and tilts in like a hopper.

Sliding windows

Sliding windows, also called *gliding* windows, roll horizontally like sliding patio doors. Sliders are easy to operate, and they're especially useful where a casement sash would be in the way, such as on a deck. They employ a sash lock of the type used for double-hung windows. Sliders aren't as tight as casements because their weatherstripping doesn't compress when the window is shut. They are best used in warm, arid climates where a tight weatherseal isn't as crucial.

Tilt/turn windows

Tilt/turn windows were invented in Europe and have gained some popularity in the U.S. They employ a sophisticated hinge that allows them to swing like a casement *and* tilt in at the top like a hopper window. The sash's movement is limited to a few inches in the tilt mode, which lets you leave the window open when your house is locked. Tilt/turn windows are typically used in large sizes that qualify as emergency exits.

Fixed glass windows

Fixed glass units are less expensive than operable windows because you save on hardware, weatherstripping, and assembly time. Fixed units also help you save energy dollars over the long haul because they're tighter than their operable cousins are. A *fixed casement* is an inoperable unit built to match nearby operable casements. *Window walls* are walls containing lots of fixed glass, often extending all the way to the roofline. The frames for *site-built* fixed glass units can be

Fixed glass captures the big picture. These wide horizontal windows harmonize with the wide open horizon beyond. The fixed-glass units on the ends are coordinated with operable units in the center.

fabricated on site rather than in a factory. Fixed glass windows can also be built on site with no sash whatsoever.

A simple yet highly effective use for fixed sashes is the ordinary picture window. Picture windows can be arrayed along with operable units of the same height to mix a lot of light with a little ventilation. The gable end of a room with a cathedral ceiling lends itself to stacked windows, with fixed units stacked over operable units of the same style and width.

Nonrectilinear units called *polygons* are frequently used below a pitched (or sloping) roofline. Polygons are classified according to their

The lower casements in this gable wall are operable, but the units above them are fixed. Note the center post between the two tallest windows that supports the structural ridge beam above it.

These stacked units seem to be alive as they tumble down a stairway.

The diamond-shaped lite in this tiny eyebrow dormer winks at passersby on the outside and illuminates a bathing alcove on the inside.

Fixed windows are sometimes used alone. Here, a small window with an offbeat muntin configuration is the focal point of a beautifully crafted nook.

117

IN DETAIL
Bay Window Flankers

Usually, bay window flankers
are set at a 45-degree angle to
the wall, but 30-degree and
90-degree angles are also
common. A 30-degree bay is
shallower than a 45-degree bay,
so it becomes more like a picture window than an alcove.
A 90-degree bay provides *more*
space than a 45-degree one,
so it's well suited for a seating
nook or small greenhouse.

> "Mullion windows are
> multiple-window units
> assembled from
> individual units at the
> factory. The larger the
> mullion window, the
> harder it is to handle
> during installation."

shape; simple ones can be specified with a drawing. When ordering more complicated polygons,
however, it's easier and safer to provide a template. In either case, be sure to state whether the
measurements or templates refer to the rough
opening or the unit size. A clearance of ½ in.
between the perimeters of the rough opening
and the unit makes for a comfortable fit.

Transoms are small windows mounted directly
above large ones. They can be rectangular, semi-
circular, or elliptical. Usually they're fixed, but

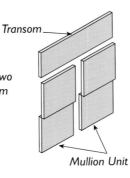

Mullion/transom
*A mullion unit consists of two
or more windows. A transom
is a sash located above a
window or door.*

Transom

Mullion Unit

they can be operable. Fastening windows side by
side, called *mulling,* produces less visual obstruc-
tion than having studs in between. Mullion windows are multiple-window units assembled from
individual units at the factory. The larger the mullion window, the harder it is to handle during
installation.

Bay windows and bow windows

The sunny microclimate created by a *bay window*
acts as a room within a room and is the perfect
spot for a kitchen table or a cozy wing chair. Bay
windows, along with their shallower cousins, *bow
windows,* come in all shapes and sizes. The typical
bay window has three sides. The middle window
usually has fixed glass, and the side windows,
called *flankers,* are operable. Bow windows feature
narrow windows arranged along a shallow arc.
They don't add much space, but they create a
feeling of expansiveness.

**This gable wall features
three types of fixed-glass
polygons: a pentagon in
the center, right
triangles that flank the
pentagon, and a
trapezoid above the
roofline.**

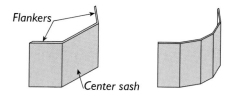

Flankers

Center sash

Bay

A bay window is a three-sided unit that usually has a fixed center sash and operable flankers. The flankers may be double-hung windows or casements.

Bow

A bow window is a multisided unit that usually has some fixed sashes and some operable sashes.

This 90-degree bay creates a sunny nook overlooking a garden.

Bay and bow windows can be built at the factory or on site. Factory-built units are usually assembled with a plywood seatboard and headboard to tie the unit together. They mount in a rectangular opening like other windows, but the

The walls of this large walkout bay are supported by a masonry foundation.

Framing a bay roof

A bay roof is framed in three phases from the bottom up. In the first phase, the plates are attached to the headboard of a factory-built bay. (A site-built bay already has plates at the tops of the walls.) In the second phase, a horizontal framework, called the cornice, is built over the plates. The cornice usually overhangs the bay for style considerations and weather protection. Finally, a small hip roof is constructed atop the cornice.

Cornice

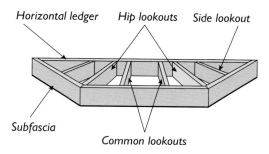

Horizontal ledger   Hip lookouts   Side lookout

Subfascia

Common lookouts

Bay

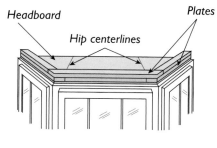

Headboard   Plates

Hip centerlines

Rafters

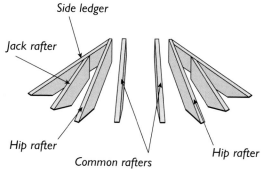

Side ledger

Jack rafter

Hip rafter

Common rafters

Hip rafter

IN DETAIL

Bow Windows

Manufacturers typically combine individual windows of only one width to make the different configurations in a bow window series. For instance, a three-panel bow may be 6 ft. wide. A different multiple of the same window may result in a seven-panel bow that is over 13 ft. wide. The wider the bow, the farther it projects from the building. An interesting variation of the bow window is the 2-sided prow window.

This prow window is comprised of two triple-mullion units set at shallow angles to the main wall.

Choosing a Window

- **Wood**—Attractive and thermally efficient, but needs regular maintenance and is prone to decay.
- **Clad** (either vinyl or aluminum)—Most of the advantages of wood, but with lower maintenance. Color choices are more limited.
- **Extruded vinyl**—Low cost, low maintenance, and nearly as energy efficient as wood. Large windows may bow or warp in hot weather.
- **Extruded Aluminum**—Durable and low maintenance, but will transfer heat and cold without an effective thermal break.
- **Fiberglass**—Stronger than vinyl, thermally efficient. Must be painted on both the interior and exterior.

seatboard becomes a seat or a counter. Site-built bays and bows can have window seats, but more often they're simply built as extensions to the room. The floor and separate walls are framed for the bay, with a window in each wall. This is called a *walkout bay* or *bow*. The bay's floor framing may cantilever out from the main foundation, or the foundation itself may follow the line of the bay.

Bays can be capped in different ways. Factory-built bays are available with prefabricated roofs that are attached as a single piece. Roofs can also be custom-framed. This is the most flexible option, since you can create any roof *pitch* (steepness) and use any type of roofing materials to match the main roof. Yet a third way to cap a bay is to let it die into a broad overhang of the main roof.

Material Options

Technology has transformed our homes from simple domiciles into complex "machines for living," and windows have evolved to keep pace. Today it's easy to become swamped by choices in glass, weatherstripping, exterior cladding, and other features.

Wood and clad windows

Wood remains a popular choice for window construction because it combines attractiveness with thermal efficiency. To circumvent wood's major liability—decay—wood windows can be *clad* on the exterior. Most manufacturers clad with aluminum, though the largest wood window manufacturer, Andersen, clads with vinyl. Recently, Marvin Windows introduced Ultrex, a fiberglass cladding.

Window Performance Factors

Heat transfer is expressed as U-value. The lower the U-value, the more energy-efficient the window.

- **Solar gain** is an asset in cold climates but a liability in hot ones. Solar gain is measured on a scale of 0 to 1, which is called the solar heat gain coefficient (SHGC). A higher number indicates more solar gain. Suggested ratings are as follows: Northern U.S.—.55 or above; Southern U.S.—.40 or below; temperate climates—.40 to .55.

- **Air leakage** is measured in cubic feet per minute (cfm) per square foot of glass. The higher the number, the leakier the window. A rate of less than .30 indicates a good seal.

- **Visible transmittance** (VT) is the amount of light that comes through a window. This is one factor you can judge yourself simply by comparing the views through different windows.

"Today's glass is two to five times more efficient than the single-pane glass of yesteryear. That's good for the environment and good for the pocketbook."

IN DETAIL

U-Value vs. R-Value

U-value and R-value measure the same thing from opposite directions. When applied to windows, the U-value is the window's tendency to *transfer* heat, whereas the R-value is the window's tendency to *insulate*, or prevent heat transfer. Thus, an energy-efficient window has a low U-value and a high R-value because it transfers *less* heat and it insulates *more*.

IN DETAIL

Why Old Glass Is Wavy

Surprisingly, that pane of wavy glass in your attic started its life as ordinary smooth glass. Glass is a super-cooled liquid, not a solid. Glass molecules gradually slump and, after 100 years or so, a pane of glass will be thicker at the bottom than at the top.

Aluminum cladding is available in a limited range of colors and vinyl is usually limited to white and brown. Aluminum cladding can be painted if you ever want to change the color, but special surface preparation is required. You can paint dark vinyl cladding but not white vinyl cladding, which has a different composition. Unclad *primed* wood windows can of course be painted any color, but they need frequent repainting. A compromise between clad and primed windows are windows with a baked-on automotive-type finish.

Extruded aluminum and vinyl

Extruded aluminum windows without a wood core are durable and appropriate for sleek, modern interiors. However, metal windows transfer heat and cold readily. To prevent this, manufacturers incorporate *thermal breaks* (vinyl or foam inserts that block conduction) into metal windows. Since the effectiveness of thermal breaks varies widely according to the quality of the window, it's especially important to look at performance ratings for metal windows.

Extruded vinyl windows combine low maintenance with low cost, so they comprise the fastest-growing segment of the market. Vinyl doesn't insulate quite as well as wood, but it does insulate much better than metal. A liability of vinyl is its high rate of expansion and contraction, which can make vinyl windows bow under hot conditions. Large windows are most susceptible to this problem.

Glazing options
Single-glazed windows are suitable for outbuildings and mild climates. Double-glazed units are the norm, and their efficiency can be boosted with various options, such as low-e film. Triple-glazed units provide maximum efficiency in extreme environments.

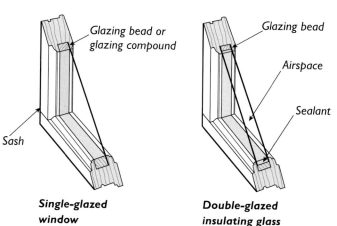

Single-glazed window · **Double-glazed insulating glass** · **Triple-glazed insulating glass**

Fiberglass

Fiberglass windows are a recent innovation. Fiberglass is stronger than vinyl and doesn't rot. It requires paint to protect it from sunlight, but the finish is applied at the factory. The components used in fiberglass windows are *pultruded*, or drawn through a resin bath.

Glazing Options

Once upon a time, glass was glass. Then the energy crisis struck in the 1970s and the millwork industry scrambled to find ways to save fuel. The good news is that today's glass is two to five times more efficient than the single-pane glass of yesteryear. That's good for the environment and good for the pocketbook. The bad news is that trying to make an intelligent choice about glass options requires some serious homework.

TOOLS AND MATERIALS

Sealing an IG Unit

The sealant around the edges of an IG unit can be damaged by solvents, including the solvents found in glazing compound. Therefore, *never* use glazing compound to hold an IG unit in its sash. Wood moldings are typically used for custom work, while door and window manufacturers use extruded vinyl or aluminum glazing beads.

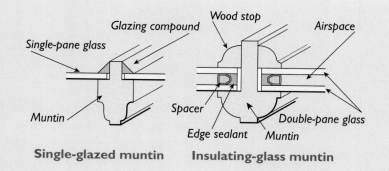

Single-glazed muntin · **Insulating-glass muntin**

IN DETAIL

Safety Glass

Safety glazing is a generic term that includes two types of glass: *laminated* glass and *tempered* glass. Laminated glass is comprised of two panes of glass with an adhesive film sandwiched between the panes. When laminated glass shatters, the film holds the shards together. Laminated glass is thicker than normal, so it may push the moldings out too far. It also adds considerable weight. Tempered glass is a single pane of glass that's been heat-treated. When tempered glass breaks, it crumbles into little cubes that aren't dangerous.

WHAT CAN GO WRONG

Seal Failure

When the seal of an IG unit fails, moisture leaks inside, inevitably condensing and fogging up the unit. Local glass shops usually order custom IG units from wholesale fabricators. The quality of these units is often poor, and the warranty period is typically only five years. Before taking delivery of custom IG units, inspect them carefully. Skewed spacer bars and messy, blistered seals are signs of poor workmanship that may lead to early seal failure. If you find these defects, return the units immediately.

"The wider the airspace, the greater the window's resistance to heat conduction, which is also expressed as R-value."

Specialty Glazing

The most familiar specialty glazing is stained glass, which features many smaller pieces of glass joined by metal bars called cames. Cames, which come in brass, copper, lead, and zinc, are also used to join clear glass in special ways, such as in medieval-looking diamond panes. A multicolored cousin of stained glass is iridized glass. In addition to variations in color, stained and iridized glass comes in various surface textures such as crackle, reeded, and water glass. Although stained and iridized glass are usually segmented, they can also be used in large sheets. For the budget-conscious, stained glass can be simulated with translucent overlays.

Beveled glass acts as a prism to throw light in dramatic ways. Glass can also be etched and sand blasted. Restoration glass simulates the wavy glass found in old houses. Another type of glass found in old houses is bull's-eye glass, originally a by-product made while spinning flat glass, which colonial builders recycled into door transoms.

Iridized glass creates a dramatic effect in these dormer windows.

This whimsical bathroom door features an etched-glass design with a nautical theme.

The diamond-shaped panes in these casement windows are joined by lead cames.

Single-glazed windows

Each lite in a single-glazed window consists of a single pane of glass. Traditionally, *glazing compound*, also called putty, held the glass in the sash. Now, most window manufacturers use snap-in vinyl glazing beads instead of putty because they last longer. Glass for single-glazed windows comes in two thicknesses: single strength (abbreviated as SSB), which is 3⁄32 in. thick, and double strength (abbreviated as DSB), which is 1⁄8 in. thick. SSB is fine for small panes, but DSB makes large panes sturdier.

The muntins in single-glazed windows can be very thin (as little as 5⁄8 in. wide) because the glass is light and thin. Insulating glass, on the other hand, requires heavy muntins. For this reason, single-glazed windows are still used for remodeling older homes and for achieving a "cottage" look, especially in mild climates. Storm windows can be added to single-glazed windows to boost their efficiency in severe climates while retaining the look of true divided lites.

Insulating windows

To better insulate glass, you can combine multiple panes of glass into *insulating glass* (IG) units. The simplest type of IG unit is a *double-glazed* window, which has two panes of glass with an airspace between them. It's the airspace that provides the insulation, not the additional glass. Spacers around the edge keep the panes a set distance apart and sealant keeps moisture from contaminating the airspace. The wider the airspace, the greater the window's resistance to heat con-

duction, which is also expressed as R-value. The typical thickness for IG units used in residential construction range from 1⁄2 in. to 1 in. That's the overall thickness of the unit—the airspace is less.

Triple-glazed units have a third pane of glass spaced equidistant between the two outer panes. This improves the window's performance, but it also adds weight and substantially increases the

Low-e glass
Low-e glass reflects heat while admitting light. This keeps heat out during the summer and in during the winter. In the winter, low-angle light passes into the house and is absorbed by the interior.

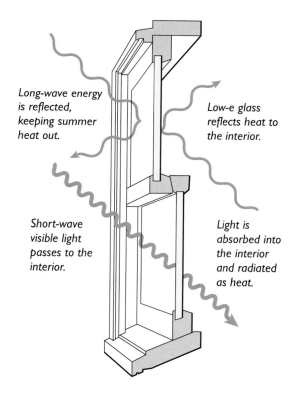

Long-wave energy is reflected, keeping summer heat out.

Low-e glass reflects heat to the interior.

Short-wave visible light passes to the interior.

Light is absorbed into the interior and radiated as heat.

 According to Code

Windows require safety glazing if *all four* of the following conditions exist: 1) The exposed area of an individual pane is greater than 9 sq. ft.; 2) the bottom edge is less than 18 in. above the floor; 3) the top edge is greater than 36 in. above the floor; *and* 4) there is a walking surface (such as a sidewalk) within 36 in. Such windows can be exempted from the safety-glazing requirement if they're equipped with a sturdy guardrail no less than 1 1⁄2 in. wide placed at 35 in. to 37 in. above the walking surface or the floor.

IN DETAIL
The Pane Spacer in an IG Unit

The spacer that separates the panes is the "Achilles' heel" of an IG unit because it acts as a thermal bridge. Quality units have *warm-edge* spacers instead of aluminum spacers. These improve the U-value of a window by as much as 10% and reduce the likelihood of condensation around the edges of the glass.

TOOLS AND MATERIALS
Energy Panels Must Be Cleaned

An energy panel isn't sealed to the sash, so you must remove it every few years to clean the sash and the back of the panel. This is somewhat less convenient than insulating glass, but the advantage is that you don't ever have to worry about seal failure.

TRADE SECRET

Like doors, the size of windows is *always* expressed with the width preceding the height. Some manufacturers use feet and inches, whereas others use only inches. Get it straight when you order, or you may receive a 2-ft., 4-in.-wide window for a 24-in.-wide opening.

TAKE YOUR PICK
Energy-Efficient Glazing with a Divided-Lite Look

- IG with snap-on grilles
- IG with grilles between the panes
- IG true divided lites (or "actual divided lites")
- Single-glazed with energy panel

"A sash with an energy panel has an R-value that's almost as good as an IG unit, and it costs less."

cost of the glass. Fortunately, there are other options for increasing the efficiency of double-glazed units that are more cost-effective.

Low-e coatings, invisible films applied to IG units, admit light while reflecting heat and ultraviolet rays (UV), which can fade fabrics and furniture. The location of the low-e within the unit depends on whether the glass is being used in a cold climate or a hot one. The primary job of a low-e coating in cold climates is to reflect heat back to the interior, so the coating is placed on the inner pane of glass. In hot climates, the low-e works primarily by reflecting the heat in sunlight back to the exterior. Therefore, the coating is applied to the outer pane. In both cases, the coating is between the panes, so it doesn't get scratched.

An alternative to low-e coatings is *interpane low-e films.* These are positioned in the middle of the airspace, similar to a middle pane in a triple-glazed unit. Another way to boost the R-value of IG is to replace the air inside with *argon* or *krypton.* These low-conductance gases eventually leak out, but the loss is only about 10% after 20 years. Meanwhile, they save energy costs.

Muntin options for insulating glass

IG glass is problematic for traditional styles of architecture where multiple-lite windows are used. That's because the thin muntins used in single-glazed windows aren't heavy enough to support IG units. To circumvent this problem, manufacturers have come up with different solutions.

Energy panels on these true divided-lite French doors provide the energy efficiency of insulating glass without the risk of seal failure. Turn buttons permit easy removal for occasional cleaning.

Snap-in grilles usually mount on the inside and can be removed for easy cleaning. In addition to having the lowest initial cost, this option is the most energy-efficient. It eliminates the conduction losses that result from having numerous muntins and spacers. The drawback of grilles is that they are less than convincing. A similar option—grilles between the glass panes—is even worse. Not only do they look as bad as snap-in grilles, but they also conduct heat. Their only advantage is ease of cleaning.

To achieve a three-dimensional look, manufacturers offer *true divided lite* (TDL) units, also referred to as *actual divided lite* (ADL) units. The narrowest muntin available is 1⅛ in. wide, which looks pretty good. Wider muntins start to spoil the view. TDL windows are more expensive than the other muntin options and they're also less energy-efficient because the additional muntins and spacers conduct heat and because thinner IG units with a lower R-value are used. The multiple lites create potential air leaks, too.

To achieve better energy efficiency with an even narrower muntin, some manufacturers offer *simulated divided lites* (SDL). In this system, false ⅞-in.-wide muntins are glued to the inside and outside of a large IG unit, with spacers between the glass. The look is almost identical to a single-glazed window, but it uses insulating glass and doesn't have the air leakage problems associated with TDL windows and doors. The main disadvantage of SDL units is their high initial cost.

Muntin Configurations

Glass panes are arranged in different configurations that reflect different architectural styles. For instance, the sashes in old New England houses have many small lites, whereas the sashes in Victorian houses usually have just one or two large lites. The configuration is expressed as the number of lites in the top sash "over" the number of lites in the bottom sash, such as 6 over 6. The upper and lower sashes usually have the same number of lites, but not always. For instance, 6-over-1 sashes are typical of the shingle style.

Another variation is the proportion of the sashes. The upper and lower sashes are usually the same height but, again, there are exceptions. When the lower sash is taller than the upper sash, the window is referred to as a cottage sash window. When the upper sash is taller, it's referred to as a reverse cottage window.

Muntin configurations
A muntin configuration is expressed as the number of lites in the upper sash "over" the number of lites in the lower sash.

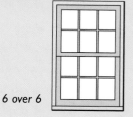

6 over 6

4 over 1

Energy panels

Energy panels are large panes of glass that mount on the outside of a single-glazed, divided-lite sash or door. The panel is mounted directly to the sash or door, as opposed to a storm panel that slides in a separate frame. Clips hold the energy panel in place. A sash with an energy panel has an R-value that's almost as good as an IG unit, and it costs less. Also, narrow muntins aren't a problem when you use an energy panel. Purists may object to the flat look of an energy panel on the outside of the house because it's a departure from the look of traditional exterior glazing.

TOOLS AND MATERIALS
Folding Rule

A folding rule with a slide extension is the most accurate tool for taking inside measurements, such as the width of a door opening. Fold the rule out as far as possible, and then extend the slide to measure the remainder. The remainder is added to the last number on the rule to calculate the total measurement. Folding rules measure only in inches (not feet and inches), with multiples of 16 in. highlighted in red.

A folding rule is ideal for inside measurements. The unfolded length of the rule (7 in.) is added to the remainder on the brass extension (1⅜ in.) for a total measurement of 8⅜ in.

Condensation leads to paint failure and decay. It occurs when moist, hot air contacts cool glass. Storm windows and insulating glass reduce condensation in cold climates by raising the temperature of the inner pane of glass.

"The insulation value of an airspace increases with its width, so a well-made primary window with a storm window over it has a higher R-value than a sole double-pane window."

Ordering Windows

So, you've decided on the type, material, and glazing of your windows. Is that it? Not by a long shot. First, you need to specify the width of the jamb and the type (or lack) of exterior casing. In some cases, you also need to specify whether or not the window will require sill extensions, called *horns*. These options apply to windows just as they do to exterior doors.

You also need to specify the color of the window if it's clad or painted. If you plan to paint the window's interior instead of staining it, you can order a primed interior. The color or finish of the hardware needs to be specified, as well. For double-hung windows, be sure the sash locks are included—sometimes they're not. Do you want

Wood storm windows hang between a window's exterior casings.

screens? If so, state the color. Interior casing is usually ordered later, but if you think your lumberyard will just happen to have a piece of colonial casing laying around with an exact 2-ft., 3-in. radius for a half-round transom, think again. It needs to be ordered with the window.

Sizing windows

Window sashes are typically 1⅜ in. thick, though 1¾-in. sashes are used for exceptionally large windows and for high-end jobs. Window catalogs list several dimensions for each window size. Working from the inside out, the first dimension is the *glass size*. This is the clear opening of the sash from rail to rail and from stile to stile (don't confuse this with the lite size, which is measured between the muntins). On a two-sash window, the glass size refers to each sash.

The next dimension is the frame size, or *unit size*. This refers to the outside width and height of the window frame. Next comes the *rough opening (R.O.) size*, which is the required clearance for openings in wood-framed walls. The last dimension is the *masonry opening size*, which applies only to masonry buildings.

Most window manufacturers use the glass size to identify a particular window size. This is straightforward with casements but confusing with double-hung windows, where the glass height is only half of the window height. Other manufacturers use the unit size, which I think makes the most sense. Still others use the R.O. size, particularly makers of aluminum sliding windows.

TAKE YOUR PICK

Triple-Track vs. Double-Track Storm Windows

Triple-track storm windows have separate tracks for both storm panels and the screen. In the summer, this allows you to have ventilation at either the top or the bottom of the window. On double-track windows, the upper storm panel and the screen share the outermost track; the screen snaps in place under the upper storm panel. Double-track storm windows allow you to ventilate only the bottom half of the window, but they have a lower profile.

Alternating Aluminum Storm and Screen Sashes

Instead of self-storing multitrack aluminum storms, you can buy separate aluminum storm sashes and screens that alternate with the season. Or, if you have insulating glass in your primary window, you may need the screen but not the storm. A third case is fixed, single-glazed windows, including stained glass and other types of accent windows. For those you may want a storm but not a screen.

A plain aluminum storm sash is called a C-sash in the glass trade. The extrusion used for the stiles and rails is only ⅜ in. by ¾ in., so a C-sash doesn't detract from the look of an old window as much as a multitrack storm or sash does. In fact, you could argue that a C-sash is less conspicuous on an old window than a wooden storm. C-sashes are secured in place with turn buttons or aluminum round-head screws.

When ordering C-sashes and aluminum screens, remember that they can't be trimmed, so measure carefully. Make sure you specify the height of the cross rail so that it aligns with the meeting rails of the primary window.

A C-sash is mounted year-round on this inoperable window. Turn buttons permit occasional removal for cleaning.

Ordering Storm Windows and Screens

The airspace between a storm window and a primary window acts as an insulator like the airspace between the panes of an IG unit. In fact, the insulation value of an airspace increases with its width, so a well-made primary window with a storm window over it has a higher R-value than a sole double-pane window.

Aluminum is an obvious choice for storm windows because it requires so little maintenance. Aluminum combination windows are also self-storing. In contrast, wooden storm and screen windows require periodic maintenance and must be changed from season to season. Wood has more esthetic appeal, however, especially on vintage homes. A wooden frame is also a better insulator than an aluminum frame.

Shopping for aluminum storm windows

Aluminum storm windows can be ordered from glass shops, home-improvement centers, and storm-window contractors. In many cases, the glass supplier measures the windows, which is a

TOOLS AND MATERIALS
Tape Measures

Tape measures are ideal for taking outside measurements, such as the length of a door. Most tapes have two sets of scales. One measures in inches only (73 in., for example), while the other measures in feet and inches (6 ft., 1 in.). Multiples of 16 (16 in., 32 in., 48 in., etc.) are usually highlighted in red for easy layout. Most tapes divide inches into sixteenths, with subdivisions at the half, quarters, and eighths.

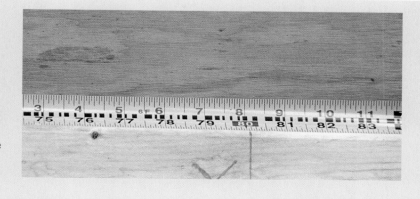

Rating Windows

The National Fenestration Rating Council (NFRC) was established to rate windows, and participating manufacturers apply the NFRC label to their products. The label must include the window's U-value, but other values are optional. As a shortcut through these numbers you can just look for the *Energy Star*. This label represents a certification program started by the U.S. Department of Energy. The program evaluates test data to see if windows meet certain minimum requirements for energy efficiency. The program recognizes three distinct climatic zones and may grant the star for use in one zone but not in another.

Storm windows are measured to fit between the exterior casings. Here the width measurement would be 36 in., less ⅛ in. for clearance. The storm window flange mounts on the blind stop (the narrow strip adjacent to the casing).

good idea in case there's a mistake. Inspect a sample of the window—preferably a stock rather than a showroom sample. The extrusions for the frames and sashes should be heavy and fit well at the corners. The retaining pins should work smoothly, and the sashes should raise and lower easily. If it is painted, the finish should cover it completely, with no bare metal showing. The fiber weatherstripping on the sashes should have a dense pile and be secure. Note whether the window is a double-track or triple-track unit.

Paint color is usually limited to white, but you may be able to special-order a custom color if your order is large enough. Anodized aluminum is a good choice if you want a dark bronze color because it won't corrode and there's no paint to chip off. *Mill-finished* raw, unpainted aluminum should be avoided because it pits and oxidizes.

Measuring for aluminum storm windows

Aluminum storm windows have a flange that mounts on the primary window's blind stop.

> "Some trimming is expected with wooden storms, so measure several locations and go with the largest measurement."

Wooden screens are right at home on this seaside cottage.

Measure the width between the exterior casing legs and the height from the exterior casing head to the sill. The width you supply will be the exact width of the unit, so deduct ⅛ in. from the opening for some wiggle room. The height is less critical because an expander at the bottom of the unit gives you some flexibility. Also, check the width at the top, bottom, and middle. If the discrepancy is less than ³⁄₁₆ in., use the narrowest dimension. If the discrepancy is greater than ³⁄₁₆ in., use the widest dimension and figure on trimming the side flanges with tin-snips. The blind stops are only about ½ in. wide, so if the width you order is too narrow, the mounting screws won't catch them.

Check the diagonals to make sure the window is reasonably square. If not, the head and sill are probably sloped from one side to the other, so use a level to determine the overall drop. Again, if the error is less than ³⁄₁₆ in., deduct it from the height. If it's more than ³⁄₁₆ in., you'll need to trim the flange. The cost of aluminum storm windows is based on *united inches,* which refers to the combined width and height. For instance, a 30-in. by 60-in. unit contains 90 united in.

Measuring for wooden storm windows and screens

Wooden storm and screen sashes close against the blind stop, and they're hung from the top. Some trimming is expected with wooden storms, so measure several locations and go with the largest measurement. For wooden storms, measure the height of the middle cross rail so it will align

The placement of the off-center rail on this wooden storm sash matches the cottage sash primary window behind it. Ventilation holes at the bottom of the storm sash dry condensation. An adjustable cover on the inside of the storm sash regulates the airflow through the ventilation holes.

with the meeting rails of the primary window. This is especially important for cottage and reverse-cottage windows that have unequal upper and lower sash heights. Measure from the head casing to the center of the meeting rails to establish the exact center of the cross rail, even if the primary sashes are equal in height.

The height of a storm/screen sash is affected by the slope of the sill. Assuming that the thickness of the sash is the same as the thickness of the exterior casing, measure the sash's height at the outside face of the casing. The lower edge of the sash will have to be beveled to fit the sill. Alternatively, you can measure the height at the *inside* of the casing and leave the lower edge of the sash square, which prevents the stiles of the sash from wicking up water and subsequently rotting.

CHAPTER NINE

Windows

1 Framing a Window Opening, p. 132

You're probably wondering what I mean by a basic window. Let's define it as a window that fits in a relatively narrow or short rectangular opening. That means casement windows and their cousins, awning and hopper windows, double-hung windows, and sliders.

Installing a simple window is very similar to the process of installing a hinged single prehung exterior door. The rough opening is framed essentially the same, except that it doesn't extend all the way to the floor. After that, it's a matter of paying attention to the window's particular needs for prep work and exterior finishing. As with exterior doors, the goal is to make the installation as weatherproof and water-resistant as possible.

2 Prepping a Rough Opening for a Window, p.134

3 Installing a Wooden Casement, p.137

4 Installing a Clad Double-Hung Window, p. 139

5 Installing a Sliding Window, p. 142

Framing a Window Opening

Window openings are just like door openings with some additional in-fill below (see p. 20 to see how door openings are framed). Once the header is in place and the studs on both sides of the opening have been doubled, it's simply a matter of adding a rough sill and a few bottom cripples. This can be done before or after the wall is raised. If you sheath the wall before raising it, you'll have to complete the windows first, but if you sheath the building later, you can postpone framing the windows until after the roof is on. I often take this approach so I can come back on rainy days and frame the windows and do other miscellaneous tasks.

Laying out the sill and cripples

Hold the end of your tape against the underside of the header and measure and mark the window's R.O. height. Then make another mark 1½ in. below that to allow for the thickness of the sill (you can simply use the edge of a short block of 2×4 to locate the second mark). To determine the length of the bottom cripples, measure from the bottom plate to the second mark.

To lay out the position of the cripples on the bottom plate, hook your tape on one of the regularly spaced studs in the adjoining wall and then position the cripples at regular 16-in. intervals. This is called staying *on the module* or *on layout* and is done so that if a sheet of drywall or plywood ends below the window, there will be a stud in the right place to support its edge.

Measure at floor level between the jacks to find the length of the sill. The dimension is locked in at these two points, whereas a bowed stud may throw off the measurement at mid-height. Installing a sill of the right length will push or pull the bowed stud to where it needs to be. After cutting the sill, lay it on top of the bottom plate and transfer the stud layout directly onto it.

Lay out the locations of the cripple studs on the bottom plate first. Then transfer the layout directly to the rough sill before installing it.

WHAT CAN GO WRONG
Rounding Off R.O. Dimensions

The R.O. dimensions in catalogs are typically awkward, such as 38 7/16 in., and they leave you with enough room to squeeze in the window *if* the framing is totally dry, straight, and plumb. Don't count on it. If the window arrives on the job, I measure it and add ½ in. to both sides and the top. If I'm working from a catalog, I round up to the nearest ¼ in. and then add ¼ in. Framing a rough opening a bit too large is rarely a problem, but if it's too small, you're in for some nasty hatchet work.

Assembling the frame

Begin the assembly by nailing the cripples to the bottom plate. Use toenails if the wall is already standing. If the wall is still flat on the deck, nail through the bottom plate into the cripples. In that case, start two nails in the underside of the plate at each stud location, with the point of the nail just poking through. Hold the cripple in position and then wallop the nails home. The protruding points of the nails will keep the cripple from skittering around.

Knock the sill into place and nail through it into the tops of the cripples. Then toenail the sill to the jacks. Sometimes there's a cripple very close to a jack, which makes it tough to toenail the underside of the sill. A heavy punch is handy for driving nails in awkward positions.

Use a punch to drive toenails in tight spots.

Toenailing

The secret to toenailing is starting the nails correctly. Rest the end to be toenailed on something solid. For instance, if you're toenailing a stud to a plate, rest the end of the stud on the plate. Elevating the end keeps it from bouncing as you start the nails. Hold a nail perpendicular to the stud about 1¼ in. from the end and tap it with your hammer to set the point in the wood. Then re-position the nail at a 45-degree angle and drive it until it just pokes through the end of the stud. Start other toenails in the same way. Then hold the stud in position slightly off the mark and give one of the toenails a good swat. The piece will drift slightly as you nail it, hopefully coming to rest in just the right spot.

Always finish toenailing one side before moving on to the other side, even if you see that you are going to be off the mark. Don't worry—you can pound the stud to the mark after it's drawn up tight. However, if you start toenailing from the opposite face before the stud meets the plate, the nails will cross. When that happens, there's no way to drive the stud home, so pull it out and start over.

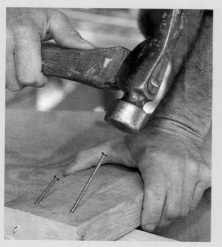

The secret to toenailing is to start your nails first. The point should just peek through the end grain of the wood.

Making an opening in an existing wall

Cutting an opening in an existing wall for a window is almost identical to the procedure for cutting an exterior door opening (see p. 48). We'll discuss wide openings that require shoring in Chapter 10.

SAFETY FIRST

When fastening studs to a plate with an air nailer, hold them at least 4 in. from the end. Otherwise, a misplaced nail can skewer your hand.

WHAT CAN GO WRONG
Measure from the Right Stud

When laying out window cripples, stay on the module by making sure your tape isn't hooked on a special off-layout stud. Special studs may be present for various reasons, such as support for an intersecting wall. It's easy to tell which studs are "specials" and which ones are 16 in. on center just by stretching a tape on the wall.

Flexible Membranes and Housewrap

- *Builder's felt*, commonly called tar paper, is inexpensive but is more brittle and less durable than the newer membranes.

- *Housewrap* has largely replaced felt. Some brands are water-repellent rather than waterproof so housewrap is not ideal for horizontal flashing, where water often lingers.

- *Bituminous membranes* combine a polyethylene film with asphalt mastic. They are self-adhering and *self-healing*, which means that a nail penetrating the membrane won't create a leak.

- *Waterproof paper*, which is adhered with caulk or staples, is available in narrow rolls made specifically for flashing doors and windows.

TRADE SECRET

You can use housewrap to make patches for window openings, but 15-lb. asphalt felt paper is stiffer and easier to shape.

> *"Windows (and doors) can be installed either before or after a housewrap has been applied to the sheathing."*

Prepping a Rough Opening for a Window

Window installation is a happy milestone for any building project. Suddenly your ugly plywood box starts to feel like a room. It's tempting to slap in the windows and move on to the next phase—but wait! Now is your best shot to provide permanent protection from the elements. Flash now, or forever hold your peace…

Prepping an opening after housewrap has been applied

Windows (and doors) can be installed either before or after a housewrap has been applied to the sheathing. I use the term *housewrap* loosely here. Other types of moisture barriers, such as felt paper and kraft paper, are handled in the same manner.

When wrapping before window installation, first slit the wrap diagonally at the corners of the opening. Fold it in, staple it lightly to the jambs, and trim off the excess flush with the inside (photo 1). This leaves the rough sill exposed at the corners, so you'll need patches. Cut the patches about 8 in. by 8 in. and fold them into

each corner so that 4 in. extends up the side of the opening and 4 in. lies on the rough sill. Make a slit on the overhanging portion of the patch along its crease, dividing it into an upper ear and a lower ear (photo 2). Fold the lower ear down over the wall, fold back the upper ear so it is flush with the sheathing (photo 3), and then place the housewrap *over* the patch where it turns up the side of the opening (photo 4).

Now lift the edge of the patch that's lying flat on the sill and shoot a bead of caulk underneath it to seal it to the housewrap. As an alternative to caulk, tape over the joint with flashing tape (photo 5). In addition, squirt a dab of caulk at the extreme outside corner and work it in with your finger. When it is time to install the window, just slit the housewrap at the top of the opening and guide the top flange under it. (To prep windows that will be exposed to severe wind-driven rain, see sidebar, p. 136.)

Prepping an opening before housewrap has been applied

When windows are installed before housewrap, use splines (strips of 15-lb. felt paper about 6 in. wide) to prep the opening. Start with the sill piece, slitting it horizontally so you can turn an

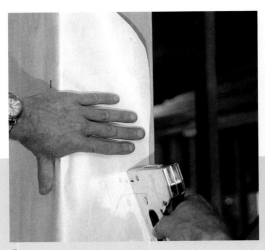

1. Use the housewrap rolled over the wall to flash the rough sill and seal the corners with patches. To do this, slit the housewrap at the corners, fold it back over the framing, and trim it flush with the interior.

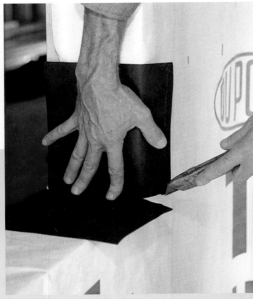

2. Fold a patch into the corner and slit the overhanging portion along the crease.

ear up at each end. Next apply the side splines (see the bottom photo, p. 136). A top spline isn't necessary at this point. Mount the window over the bottom and side splines with a bead of caulk between the splines and the exterior casing or nailing fin. (The head casing or head-nailing fin is caulked to the sheathing.) Then install the head flashing (see p. 60).

When it's time to apply the housewrap, roll it right over the window. Then cut away the portion that covers the windows, trimming it with a sharp utility knife about ½ in. away from the window. Extend the cut at the bottom of the opening in both directions by making a slit that reaches a few inches past the side splines. Reach behind the housewrap below the window and pull out the bottom spline so it overlaps the housewrap.

Slip patches into the slits as if you were adding a playing card to a poker hand. They should tuck *under* the housewrap above the slit and lap *over* the housewrap below the slit (see photo, p. 137). If the housewrap above the window has been successfully trimmed to overlap the head flashing, then a head spline isn't required. If the housewrap has been accidentally trimmed too high, then add a head spline.

Housewrap and Window Flashing Details

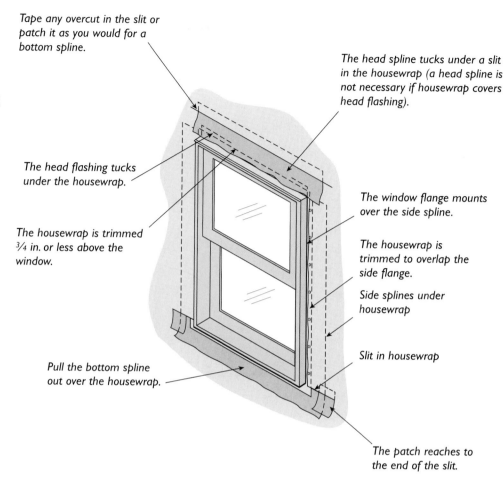

Tape any overcut in the slit or patch it as you would for a bottom spline.

The head spline tucks under a slit in the housewrap (a head spline is not necessary if housewrap covers head flashing).

The head flashing tucks under the housewrap.

The window flange mounts over the side spline.

The housewrap is trimmed ¾ in. or less above the window.

The housewrap is trimmed to overlap the side flange.

Side splines under housewrap

Slit in housewrap

Pull the bottom spline out over the housewrap.

The patch reaches to the end of the slit.

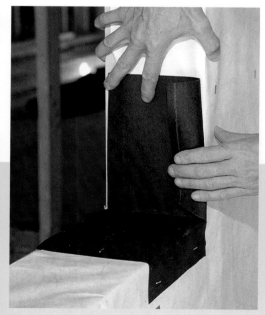

3. Secure the patch with a few staples, then fold back the upper leg's overhang.

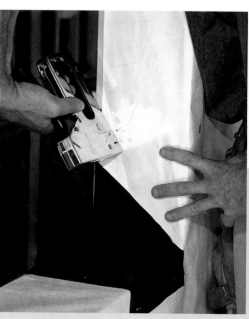

4. Staple the housewrap over the upper leg.

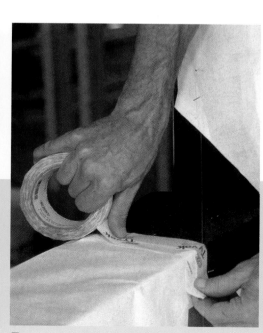

5. Tape the horizontal joint between the housewrap and the patch.

135

TOOLS AND MATERIALS

Flashing Tape

Flashing tape is self-adhering. It was originally made to seal vertical joints in housewrap, but it's also used as an extra sealant over nailing fins in severe-weather environments.

TRADE SECRET

If double-hung windows have a piece of tape across the middle to keep the jambs from spreading, don't remove it until after the window is installed. Similarly, casement windows are packed with self-stick shims between the sash and the frame to regulate clearance. Leave them in place until installation is complete.

TRADE SECRET

When flashing a window opening, you work with many layers, corners, slits, and patches. It's easy to get confused about what goes where. If you lose track, always remember the first rule of flashing: *That which is above overlaps that which is below.*

"If you're working above the ground, it's usually easier to carry the window through the house and pass it through the opening."

Window Prep for Severe Environments

A piece of bevel siding is applied to the rough sill to create an outward pitch (left), and a self-adhering bituminous membrane is used to flash it (middle). Strips of membrane are also applied to the sides and top to prevent water infiltration (right).

It pays to take extra precautions in areas where wind-driven rain is prevalent. Nail a strip of ½-in. by 6-in. cedar bevel siding to the sill with its thin edge facing out. This pitches the rough sill so that any water that seeps in will flow back out. Remember to add an extra ½ in. to the R.O. height when you frame the window to compensate for the thickness of the siding. When you set the window, add some shims under the front of the sill for support.

Flash over the sill with a bituminous membrane. These membranes are more waterproof than housewrap or felt and have an adhesive backing to fuse corner patches to the main part of the membrane. Finally, add strips of membrane over the nailing flanges for extra protection.

Prep a window opening with felt splines before applying housewrap. Turn up the bottom spline at the corners to form a partial pan, then lap the side splines over the bottom spline.

Prepping window units

Windows need some prep work before they can be installed in the wall. Remove screens and storm windows and store them in a safe place. Attach the cranks for casement windows right away, if possible. Windows with rigid nailing fins have shipping blocks on the corners to protect the fins. These have to be removed, along with any other packaging materials. Some windows have collapsible nailing fins to make shipping easier. They're furnished with self-stick L-shaped patches to complete the nailing flange at the corners. Apply the patches after the window is installed.

Installing a Wooden Casement

The process for installing a casement window with exterior trim is very similar to the process for installing a prehung exterior door. The most important thing is to make sure that the frame isn't racked. A racked frame will compromise the weather seal and, in extreme cases, can make the sash rub against the frame. As with exterior doors, it's best to have one installer working on the outside and one on the inside.

Setting the unit

Check the rough sill to see if it's level. If not, shim at one side or the other so the unit is level. If

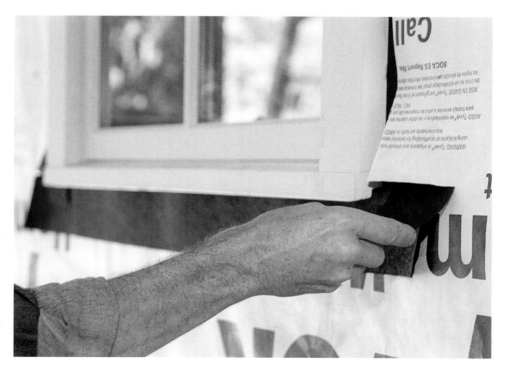

The housewrap has been slit at the sides of the window, thereby allowing the installer to reach through and pull out the felt apron spline.

IN DETAIL
Installing a Head Spline

Make a slit in the housewrap about 4 in. above the window and 2 in. past the side splines. Then slip a head spline under the housewrap, lapping the spline's lower edge over the head flashing. The head spline must extend to the very ends of the slit. If it comes up shy, add a patch. The patch and the head spline should overlap sideways about 2 in.

TOOLS AND MATERIALS
Housewrap

Housewrap is amazingly strong in spite of its light weight. It must be cut cleanly because it doesn't tear. Keep your utility knife razor sharp by changing blades often. I also use large sewing shears to cut housewrap.

Prevent Wind Damage to Window Units

Windows stored on site before installation can be blown over unless they are secure. An $800 picture window in shards is not a pretty sight. Use ropes to tie them up or brace them with 2×4s.

TRADE SECRET

The less you have to caulk the better. Never caulk the top of a window before installation, or it will be difficult to slide the top flange under the housewrap. If you tape the sides, you don't have to caulk them. This is a good method, since caulk has a way of getting on your hammer and fingers as you nail flanges. It's tempting to tape over the top and bottom flanges, as well, but I don't recommend it. It's more important to let infiltrated water weep freely to the outside.

"The main thing is keeping the frame square and the jambs straight."

you're working on the ground, you can set the window from outside. If you're working above the ground, it's usually easier to carry the window through the house and pass it through the opening. Turn the window on its side or twist it so that the exterior casing can clear the opening. If the window is large, it may take two people (or more).

As the outside person lifts the window, the inside person guides the bottom into the opening and stands the window upright. Next, the inside person centers the window in the opening by prying it to the left or the right with a flat bar.

The outside person carries most of the window's weight while the inside person guides the window into the opening.

Use extra caution when setting ladders or scaffolds on frozen ground. As the ground thaws it can give way, so make sure you distribute the weight of the scaffolds with planks or wide blocks. Dig shallow depressions for ladder feet so they won't slip, and check them for settlement as the day warms up.

Meanwhile, the outside person checks the sill and the head for level. If the window is out of level, the inside person adds more shims underneath the jambs to bring it to level.

When the window is centered and leveled, the outside person nails each leg casing at the bottom to hold the unit side to side, then checks the sides of the unit for plumb and inspects the margins all around the sash. If the unit is level and plumb, the margins should be perfect, because plumb is perpendicular to level. At that point, the exterior casing can be nailed at the top corners. The inside person checks the operation of the window. If it opens and closes smoothly, the leg casings and head casings can be straightened and nailed off.

Flashing the head

Install a wooden drip cap on top of the exterior head casing. Then cut a piece of metal head flashing to go on top of the drip cap. Slit the housewrap about ½ in. above the wooden drip cap, then slip the vertical fin of the head flashing under the housewrap. Fasten the head flashing with a few roofing nails along the top edge, hiding them under the housewrap. The nails should be made of the same metal as the flashing to prevent galvanic corrosion.

Shimming the unit

Before shimming the jambs, remove the stops from inside the unit so you can drive large finish nails through the jambs. When you reinstall the stops, the nail heads will be hidden. The stops are

Cross-Legged Casements

As with exterior doors, large casements can be affected by cross-legging, which impairs the weatherstripping seal and makes locking the sash difficult. To compensate for it, pull the exterior casing away from the wall at one corner. When the leg jambs are parallel, nail them to the framing.

usually held by just one little brad and can be removed by carefully prying them loose with a putty knife. The sill stop is especially delicate, because it is hollow underneath to make room for the connecting arm of the *casement operator*.

Shim the jambs with tapered wedges as you would for a door. Shim the sides 4 in. from the top and the bottom and every 16 in. in between. For units that are less than 3 ft. wide, shim the head jamb with one shim in the middle. For wider units, shim the head jamb every 16 in. Drive two nails through each set of shims so they won't rotate when you trim them.

If you leveled the window by shimming it under one of the leg jambs, place intermediate shims underneath the sill every 12 in. or so. If the window sill is uniformly supported by the rough sill, you don't have to shim. To avoid leakage, glue any shims under the sill rather than nailing them. Place a level underneath the sill to check for straightness as you shim, or simply use the edge of the sash as a straightedge.

Installing a Clad Double-Hung Window

Installing a double-hung window isn't much different than installing a casement. In both cases, the main thing is keeping the frame square and the jambs straight. Double-hung jambs are thinner than casement jambs, so straightening the jambs is more likely to require some persuasion. Unlike a casement, a double-hung window is not nailed through the jambs. The previous section dealt with a *wood-cased* casement window, while this section deals with a *flanged and clad* double-hung window. Keep in mind that both types of windows can have both types of exterior trim options and should be installed accordingly.

Setting the unit

Before mounting the window, apply a bead of caulk around the opening where the flanges will be mounted. Caulk at the bottom and the sides,

A prybar is used to lift the unit slightly so a shim can be added to level the unit (above). After leveling the sill, nail the bottoms of the leg casings (below).

The inside person guides the window into the opening while the outside person stands the window up.

The outside person checks for level while the inside person makes adjustments with a prybar.

IN DETAIL

Don't Nail through Double-Hung Jambs

Double-hung jambs are lined with vinyl tracks that guide the sashes; nailing through the tracks damages them. Instead, the interior and exterior casings hold double-hung jambs rigid. This arrangement is adequate because the side jambs of a double-hung window aren't subject to sideways strain. Casement jambs, on the other hand, must withstand the lateral pull of the sash as the window is opened.

"If there's a slight discrepancy, the diagonals should have priority over the level to ensure a tight-fitting sash."

but not at the top. If you intend to tape the flanges, you can forgo caulking the sides.

When working at grade level, set the window from the outside. For any installation above grade level, a two-person team is once again the best formula. The outside person slits the housewrap at the top of the opening so that

the window's top flange can tuck under the housewrap. The inside person raises the lower sash to make the unit easier to handle and hands it through the opening to the outside person. As the inside person supports the weight of the window, the outside person guides the top flange under the housewrap.

Casement stops are removed (left) before nailing through the jambs (right). When the stops are reinstalled, they will hide the nail heads.

Troubleshooting the Installation

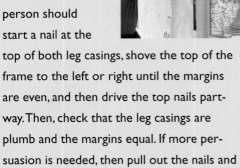

If the sides are out of plumb, the frame is racked and the margins are tapered. In that case, the outside person should start a nail at the top of both leg casings, shove the top of the frame to the left or right until the margins are even, and then drive the top nails partway. Then, check that the leg casings are plumb and the margins equal. If more persuasion is needed, then pull out the nails and try again. Apply extra pressure by prying between the jamb and the framing, if necessary.

Squaring a Window

An out-of-square window frame won't fit evenly around the sash. First, level the sill and secure the bottom of the window. Then push the top of the window to the left or the right until it's both plumb and square.

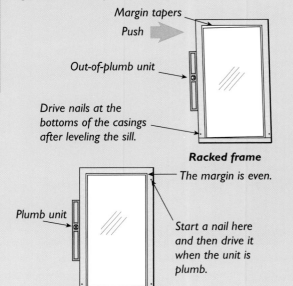

Margin tapers
Push
Out-of-plumb unit
Drive nails at the bottoms of the casings after leveling the sill.
Racked frame

The margin is even.
Plumb unit
Start a nail here and then drive it when the unit is plumb.
Squared frame

The inside person then pries the unit from side to side with a flat bar to center it.

Leveling and squaring the unit

The inside person shims the window under one of the side jambs to level the unit (if necessary) while the outside person reads the level. When the unit is level, the outside person drives one galvanized roofing nail at the top of each side flange and reads the level vertically to instruct the inside person to move the bottom of the unit left or right to plumb the side jambs.

When the sides are plumb and the top is level, the unit should be square. Double check by measuring the diagonals. If there's a slight discrepancy, the diagonals should have priority over the level to ensure a tight-fitting sash. When the diagonals agree, drive a nail at the bottom of each side flange.

Straightening the jambs

Straightening the jambs is very important to achieve a proper seal between the sashes and the *jamb liners* (vinyl tracks). The outside person uses a level or straightedge to check the jamb while the inside person either pushes the jamb toward the jack-stud or pries the jamb away from the jack. As you straighten each jamb, drive one nail through its side flange at mid-height to hold it. Before driving any more nails, check the operation of the sashes and make sure they lock properly. The lower sash should meet the sill evenly and the meeting

The housewrap is slit at the top of R.O. to slip the window's head flange underneath.

The outside person guides the top flange under the housewrap while the inside person carries most of the window's weight.

TOOLS AND MATERIALS
Aluminum vs. Vinyl Nailing Flanges

On vinyl-clad windows, the nailing flange is a rigid extension of the cladding. This creates an excellent seal between the cladding and the flange. The flange doesn't fold down however, so these units are susceptible to flange breakage during shipment. Some windows have flanges that fold down or snap into grooves on the frame, making them easier to handle. Windows with fold-down flanges require self-sticking L-patches at the corners. The heavy thickness of these patches can be a nuisance, however, and you may need to chisel out the back of the trim to accommodate the patches.

IN DETAIL

Resting the Frame While Checking for Level

Some slider frames extend 1 in. or so into the rough opening. When that's the case, rest the frame on the rough sill while you level it. Other slider frames hang entirely on the outside, so drive a couple of nails halfway into the sheathing below the opening to rest the window while you level it. The nails should be set at such a height that the top and bottom nailing flanges overhang the sheathing equally. Whether you rest the unit on nails or on the sill, make sure you slip the head flange under the housewrap.

WHAT CAN GO WRONG

Condensation on Drywall Window Jambs

Condensation can rot the drywall window jambs sometimes used with sliding windows. For jambs, use *green board* (water-resistant drywall) or, better yet, *cement-based backer-board* (tile backer). If you use backer board, cover it with joint compound for an even finish. In bathrooms, avoid drywall jambs altogether, because high humidity causes condensation.

> *"Aluminum sliders are somewhat different from wood or vinyl sliders. The frame— which is really more of a track—is mounted on the outside of the wall."*

rails should be flush where they meet. None of these requirements should be a problem if the frame is square.

When everything looks good, it's time to nail off the flanges. Nail through the prepunched holes in the flanges about every 8 in. At the top of the window, lift the housewrap above the flange as you nail the head flange.

To deflect runoff, slip a metal head flashing under the housewrap at the top of the window. Nail the flashing with a few nails along its top edge.

The side flanges should be taped to seal out drafts and moisture. You can use lightweight housewrap tape or a heavier bituminous membrane.

Installing a Sliding Window

Installing a wooden or vinyl slider isn't much different than installing a wooden or vinyl double-hung window. The main thing is to keep the frame square and straight. The only difference is that you should pay special attention to shimming the sill if the rough sill isn't level. A slider sill carries the weight of the sashes, so shim under the center of the unit and at least every 8 in. elsewhere. Aluminum sliders are somewhat different from wood or vinyl sliders. The frame— which is really more of a track—is mounted on the outside of the wall.

The outside person reads a level while the inside person shims under one of the leg jambs (if necessary).

After tacking the top of the window, pry the bottom to the left or right to plumb the unit. (Alternatively, tack the bottom and pry the top.)

Compare the diagonals to make sure the unit is a perfect rectangle, not a parallelogram.

Adding Trim Around Flanged Windows

You can add custom wood trim around flanged windows to spruce them up. The sill is the hardest part. It must be wide enough to extend past the casings and can be tricky to fasten. One solution is a two-piece sill with a tongue-and-groove joint connecting the two halves. Screw the inner half to the wall through the bottom of the nailing flange, and then attach the outer half to the inner half with finish nails. Apply a bead of caulk to the joint during assembly to seal it.

Wrap a wide 5/4 ×4 casing around the sides and top of the opening, with a shallow rabbet in back to accommodate the thickness of the nailing flanges. Attach back band molding around the outside edges of the casing, and then attach flashing at the top of the window to cover both the head casing and the back band.

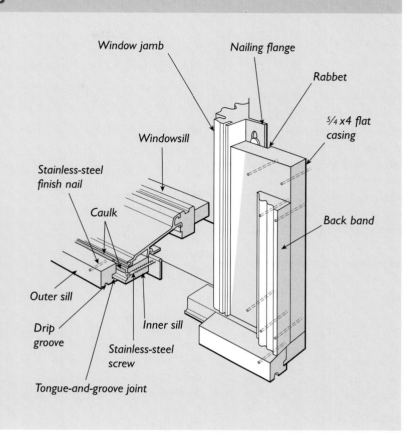

Window jamb

Nailing flange

Rabbet

⁵⁄₄ x4 flat casing

Windowsill

Stainless-steel finish nail

Caulk

Back band

Outer sill

Inner sill

Drip groove

Stainless-steel screw

Tongue-and-groove joint

After making sure that the jamb is straight from top to bottom, start a nail through the side flange at mid-height. Before driving the nail home, check the sashes for smooth operation.

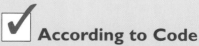

Housewrap is lifted while nailing the window's top flange. This waterproofs the nail heads and the top edge of the flange.

✓ According to Code

A small logo etched in one corner of the window lets the building official verify the use of safety glazing. This logo should remain visible after the glass is installed.

143

TOOLS AND MATERIALS
A Double Slider

Most sliding windows, also known as *sliders*, *gliders*, and *slide-by* windows, have one fixed panel on the outside and one operable panel on the inside. When the window is closed, a sash lock clamps the operable sash and the fixed sash together at the meeting rail. A notable exception is the Andersen slider, which has two operable sashes. A locking handle controls a three-point lock that bolts one sash to the top and bottom of the frame while simultaneously drawing the sashes tightly together.

Hanging a nail-on aluminum slider

Begin the installation by removing the operable sash and the screen (simply lift them up and out). This makes the unit lighter and easier to handle. Prep the opening as you would for other types of windows. If you have already installed housewrap, slit it horizontally at the upper corners so you can slip the window's head flange underneath. If the house hasn't been wrapped yet, install bottom and side splines but not a top spline. A top spline is necessary only if the subsequent housewrap is accidentally cut above the head flange, in which case a head spline should tuck under the housewrap and over the head flange.

Sliding Windows

Wooden and vinyl sliders have jambs as deep as the opening (left). Aluminum sliders have tracks that extend only partway into the rough opening (right), so the sides of the opening are finished with wood or drywall.

The screen on most sliders shares the outside track with a fixed sash, so only the inner sash operates (right). The Andersen slider (left) has a third track for a screen, allowing both sashes to operate. This facilitates cleaning from the inside.

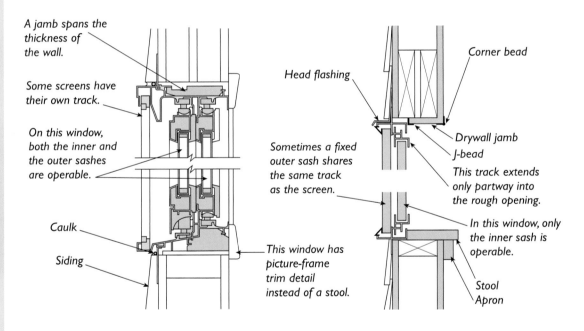

A jamb spans the thickness of the wall.

Some screens have their own track.

On this window, both the inner and the outer sashes are operable.

Caulk

Siding

This window has picture-frame trim detail instead of a stool.

Head flashing

Sometimes a fixed outer sash shares the same track as the screen.

Corner bead

Drywall jamb

J-bead

This track extends only partway into the rough opening.

In this window, only the inner sash is operable.

Stool

Apron

Clad-wood slider

Aluminum slider

WHAT CAN GO WRONG

A Slider That Doesn't Slide

There's no tilt adjustment for sliding sashes as there is for sliding patio doors, so if the sash and frame don't meet evenly, remove the nails in the upper corners and rack the frame until they do. If the sashes still don't glide easily, sight the opening for cross-legging. Since nail-on windows are entirely dependent on the nailing flange, they should remain tight against the sheathing. Try some silicone spray to loosen them up. The only alternative is to move the flange away from the sheathing at one corner. The tapering gaps left between the flange and the sheathing will then need to be filled with special shims or a heavy bead of caulk.

Seal the window's side and bottom flanges with a bead of caulk around the opening before mounting the unit. If the house hasn't been wrapped, shoot a bead of caulk on the bare sheathing above the opening to seal the head flange.

After you've placed the unit, check the top of the frame for level. If it is level, drive a nail at each of the corners. Leave the nail heads loose, just in case. If the frame isn't level, drive one nail at the upper corner on the high side. Then lift the lower side until the frame is level and drive nails at the remaining three corners. Check the straightness of the bottom track with a level. If it's straight, drive one nail through the flange at the middle of the window. If the bottom track sags, push it up while you nail it. The sash should roll easily and meet evenly with the side of the frame as it closes.

Nail-on windows don't have jambs, so drywall is often used instead of wood to finish off the sides of the opening. Drywall is applied to the top and sides of the opening, and a wooden stool is installed on the bottom. Drywall can't be used for the stool, because it won't fare well when junior tosses his ice skates on the windowsill. To protect the corners of the drywall, apply metal corner bead around the opening. The corner bead also guides the drywall finisher's knife as he or she smoothes joint compound. Nail the corner bead every 4 in. with drywall nails. Trim the ends of the beads to meet perfectly, or finishing will be a difficult task. Set all the nails before applying joint compound.

A drywall window jamb is finished with joint compound (mud). The finisher's putty knife runs along a metal L-bead applied to the corner. The right side of the finisher's knife travels against a J-bead that caps the edge of the drywall where it meets the window.

IN DETAIL
The Importance of Head Flashing

Some installers skip the head flashing over flanged windows, believing that the nailing flange will effectively double as flashing. I'm skeptical of this, so I always add the flashing. In addition to providing double protection, head flashing encourages runoff to drip freely instead of being drawn under the head jamb by capillary action.

TOOLS AND MATERIALS
J-Bead and Corner Beads for Drywall Jambs

Cap drywall edges that fit against the window with J-bead to keep the drywall from absorbing condensation that forms on a cold window frame. In this instance, vinyl J-bead is preferable to metal J-bead because it's a better thermal insulator. J-bead can be covered with joint compound to disguise its presence.

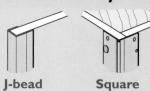

J-bead   **Square corner bead**   **Bullnose corner bead**

CHAPTER TEN
Windows

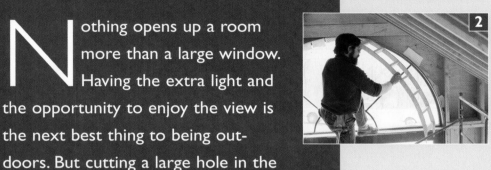

Nothing opens up a room more than a large window. Having the extra light and the opportunity to enjoy the view is the next best thing to being outdoors. But cutting a large hole in the exterior of your house presents a few challenges. You need to provide temporary support while you do the demolition and framing or you could severely weaken the wall. Round tops and other unusually shaped windows will keep you busy figuring out the angles, but they give you wonderful design possibilities. Here's a chance to put your high school geometry to work and make your house look distinctive. As in all complex installation or renovation projects, make sure you know the drill before you start. If you work methodically, even the most complex window won't daunt you.

WHAT CAN GO WRONG

Roadblocks

Once you have identified the location for your new window, determine whether there are any obvious obstructions in the way, such as pipes, wires, or ducts. Look for them in the basement and the attic. If they turn up, do as much rerouting as possible (or consult the appropriate tradesperson) before installation, and work out a game plan with your subcontractor (if necessary) for removing the items that can't be changed until the wall is breached. You don't want to be talking to an answering machine when you've got a 12-ft. hole in the side of your kitchen.

TAKE YOUR PICK

Bay and Bow Window Shapes

Bay (3-sided)
- 45 degrees (medium depth)
- 90 degrees (deep)
- 30 degrees (shallow)

Bow (multisided)
- 3, 4, 5, 6, or 7 sides

Prow (2-sided)

"Removing a large chunk of wall without taking the proper precautions can lead to structural damage above the opening."

Installing Bays and Bows

A smooth installation starts when you place your window order. Make sure you correctly specify the thickness of your wall so that the unit's headboard and seatboard will be wide enough to reach the inside wall surface. Otherwise, you may need jamb extensions, and a crack may eventually show at the joint. Depending on the stud width, the standard wall thickness for a wood-framed house is either 4⁹⁄₁₆ in. or 6⁹⁄₁₆ in. (These dimensions include ½ in. plywood or OSB sheathing, 2×4 or 2×6 studs, ½-in. drywall, and an extra ¹⁄₁₆ in. for good measure.) The height of your window should allow the top of the unit to align with nearby windows and doors. If the seatboard will be used for seating, it should be situated about 18 in. above the floor.

Locating and laying out the opening

Once you've narrowed down the location of the new unit, locate the studs in that vicinity. The interior will need repainting (at the least), so don't worry about marking the walls. Once you determine a precise centerline, establish the sides of the new opening in relation to it. If you have some flexibility in the side to side placement, you may opt to use an existing stud as one of your king studs.

Locating a Retrofit

In most cases, the tops of doors and windows should be aligned. Therefore, when retrofitting a window, the head jamb of an existing door often becomes the starting point for laying out the new opening.

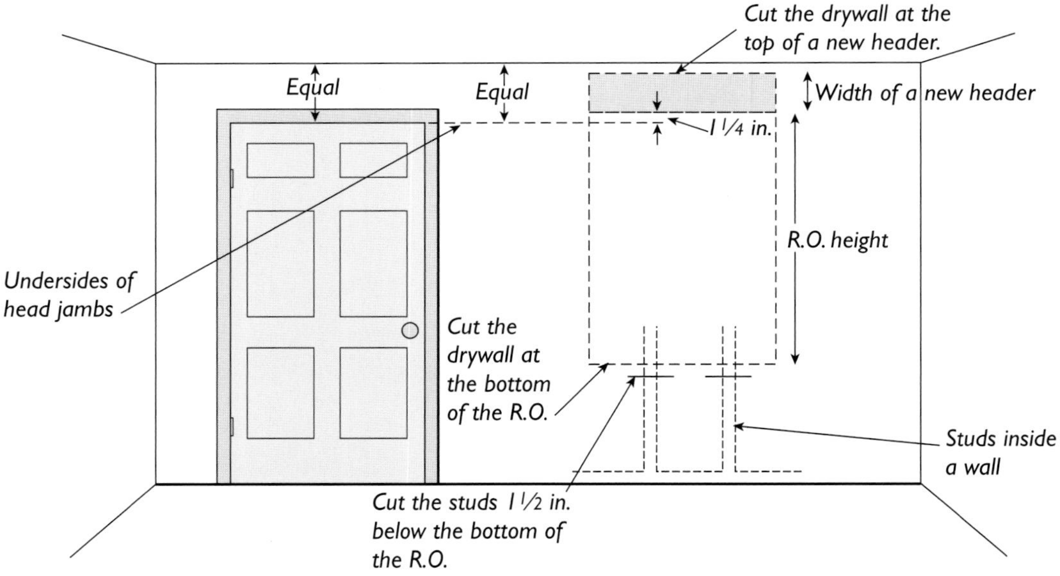

SAFETY FIRST

If you have a cathedral ceiling don't cut an opening in the gable wall without first consulting an engineer or architect. In a gable roof with a structural ridge, a heavy beam runs just below the peak of the roof from one gable wall to the other. The structural ridge carries the tops of the rafters in lieu of ceiling joists so the rafters won't spread. In so doing, the ridge collects half the weight of the roof, and this weight is delivered to the foundation through posts in the gable wall. Supporting this kind of wall while making an opening takes a different strategy. Consult a professional.

The top of a new window should align with nearby windows and doors to fit into the room. The exception is a feature window that rises dramatically above its neighbors, but that's a rarity. To align the top of the new window with the others, measure from the ceiling to the underside of the head jamb on an existing window or door. Measure down the same distance from the ceiling to the new opening, and then back up 1¼ in. to allow for the thickness of the jamb and the shim space. This will be the top of the new opening.

Starting at the top, measure the height of the window's R.O. to establish the bottom of the opening, then add another 1½ in. to locate the underside of the rough sill. This is where you'll cut the studs. From the top of the opening, measure the width of the new header. This is where you'll cut the drywall. If the ceiling is high you may be left with cripple studs above the header, in which case you'll cut the studs there as well. With a standard 8-ft. ceiling, however, there won't be any room above the header for cripples. The new header will just fit directly under the top plate.

Providing temporary structural support

The procedure for cutting a wide opening isn't that different than cutting a narrow opening, except for the fact that you *must* provide temporary structural support. Removing a large chunk of wall without taking the proper precautions can lead to structural damage above the opening. The

best type of temporary support depends on the nature of the wall.

Eaves walls are a little more complicated than gable walls. The first step is to shore up the ceiling 2 ft. back from the existing wall. The shoring can be

Shoring Exterior Walls

Ahouse with a gable roof has two kinds of exterior walls. *Eaves walls* are the low walls that *rafters* (roof beams) stand on. In a simple Cape-style house, the front and back walls are the eaves walls. Eaves walls usually carry all the weight of the roof. They also carry the weight of ceilings and floors in 9 cases out of 10. *Gable walls* (also called *rake walls*), the higher A-shaped walls at the ends of a simple house, carry only their own weight—in most cases. The load-bearing difference between eaves walls and gable walls requires different shoring methods.

Shoring
Shoring provides temporary support for the load above while a new opening is cut. The type of shoring depends on whether the wall in question is an eaves wall or a gable wall. Eaves walls carry most of the weight of the building, so they're typically supported by a temporary wall set in from the wall to be modified. The uprights in the temporary wall can be wooden props or steel jack posts.

Gable walls don't usually carry any roof loads or floor loads, so they're typically supported by a temporary ledger board bolted to the studs.

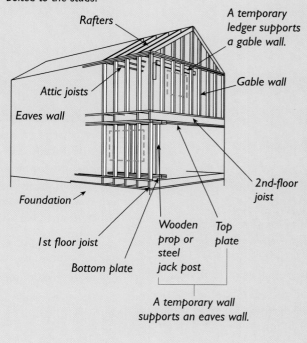

Rafters

A temporary ledger supports a gable wall.

Attic joists

Gable wall

Eaves wall

2nd-floor joist

Foundation

1st floor joist

Wooden prop or steel jack post

Top plate

Bottom plate

A temporary wall supports an eaves wall.

TRADE SECRET

To retrofit a wide header without shoring, first determine which studs need to be removed. Cut between the ends of each stud and the top and bottom plates using a metal cutting blade to sever the nails. As each stud is freed, twist it 90 degrees and bump it flush with the outside of the wall. Suppose the wall in question is a 2×4 wall. Once all the studs are twisted, there will be enough room to get half of the header (a single 2×) into position. Meanwhile, the studs will still be supporting the opening. In a 2×6 wall, you'll have enough space at this point to insert a double 2× header.

Shoring Options

The type of temporary support you use depends on the width of the opening and the type of wall:

- **Narrow opening**—no shoring is necessary, because the structure supports itself.
- **Wide opening in an eaves wall**—shore the ceiling with 2×6 props offset from the wall.
- **Wide opening in a gable wall**—support the wall above by bolting a 2×10 ledger to the framing.

IN DETAIL

How Weight Is Transferred by Shoring

On a second floor, the combined weight of the roof, attic joists, and second-story wall bears on the second floor joists, which normally bear directly on the first-story wall. While you install a window on the first floor, however, the second floor joists will bear on the shoring instead. The shoring bears on the first floor joists or on a slab, which will transfer the weight to the foundation.

> *"It's okay if the prop is a bit too long and therefore stands slightly out of plumb. The main thing is that it's holding the weight."*

Before enlarging a window, use steel jack posts to shore up the structure above. A double 2×6 top plate transfers the load from several overhead joists to each post. If the floor were wood instead of concrete, a similar plate would be placed under the posts to distribute the load over the floor.

either a temporary stud wall with wooden props or a wooden beam supported by steel jack posts.

Begin by locating the ceiling joists, marking them with tape so you won't have to erase pencil marks later. Place a wooden prop or a steel jack post under every other ceiling joist (32 in. on center). Put the outermost prop or post 16 in. or less from the sides of the opening. You may have to add extra posts or props. The idea is to support all of the ceiling joists that terminate over the opening.

Lay four 2×6s on the floor where the shoring will stand. Two of these will be a double top plate; the other two will be a double bottom plate to distribute weight evenly over the floor. The plates should extend 3 in. past the last prop on each end. Make sure that the joists in the floor below are running perpendicular to the wall.

The wood props should fit snugly, so they'll need to be marked individually because they will probably vary slightly in height. Cut the props ⅛ in. *heavy,* or beyond the cutline, to ensure a snug fit.

To install the props, have a helper hold the top plate against the ceiling while you jam a prop into position. It's okay if the prop is a bit too long and therefore stands slightly out of plumb. The main thing is that it's holding the weight. Toenail the prop into the top and bottom plate, and then install the rest of the props the same way, nailing the props as you go. If you're using steel posts, simply crank them up until they're nice and tight.

Gable walls are easier to support than eaves walls. A simple gable wall doesn't involve much weight; if the building has plywood sheathing, it will provide a lot of temporary support, as well. All you have to do is fasten a temporary 2×10 ledger to the wall above the opening. The ledger must extend past the sides of the opening and reach the first stud on each side that will remain uncut. Use two ⅜-in. by 4-in. lag bolts in each stud.

If there's plenty of room above the opening, locate the ledger below the ceiling. If not, locate the ledger in the room or attic above the opening. The idea is simply to collect the load

TRADE SECRET

The props fit between the top plate and the bottom plate. Use the following trick to measure the props, and you won't have to hold the top plate against the ceiling while you measure. First, cut the props to about 1 in. less than the floor-to-ceiling height. Then hold each prop against the ceiling where it will be placed and mark the bottom of the prop where it crosses the top of the stack of 2×6s. This is easier and more accurate than trying to obtain an exact vertical measurement with a tape measure.

that's coming down from above and to divert it to the sides of the opening. *Do not cut an opening in a gable wall with a structural ridge* (as in a cathedral ceiling) without first consulting an engineer.

Doing demolition work

Once you've provided temporary support for the structure above the new opening you're ready to start demolition work. Set up a dust-control curtain using the shoring as a framework.

1. Remove the drywall (or other interior finish) from the top of the new header to the bottom of the new rough opening. Depending on the layout, you may have to remove the drywall past the sides of the R.O. to the first remaining stud on each side so that you can install the new jacks.

2. Before you cut, make an exploratory opening 3 in. shy of your final cutline by punching a line of overlapping holes in the drywall with a hammer. Remove the bulk of the drywall and insulation, and then trim back the drywall to the cutline with a reciprocating saw.

3. Cut the studs with a small chainsaw or a reciprocating saw, but stop when you reach the sheathing. If the stud will be removed all the way to the top plate, then just use a reciprocating saw to cut through the nails holding the top of the stud. Pry the studs slightly away from the sheathing and cut the sheathing nails by sliding the reciprocating sawblade between the stud and the sheathing.

To remove a stud all the way up to the plate, simply cut the nails with a reciprocating saw. A metal cutting blade works best.

A reciprocating saw can reach behind a stud to cut sheathing nails. A few whacks with a hammer will loosen the sheathing enough to slip the blade behind the stud.

| WHAT CAN GO WRONG |

When Joists Are Not Parallel to the Eaves Wall

When breaching an eaves wall, make sure that the joists in the floor below run *perpendicular* to the wall. If not, your shoring may bear on nothing more than the subfloor between two joists. In a similar vein, the ceiling joists should run perpendicular to the wall. Otherwise, there's nothing to transfer the load from the outside wall to the shoring. If you find that either the floor joists or the ceiling joists run *parallel* to the eaves wall, consult a professional about alternative shoring strategies.

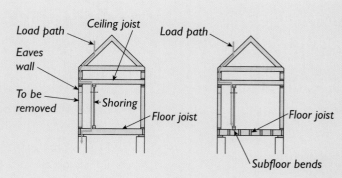

Window-Framing Math

Jack length =
king length − header width

Header length =
R.O. width +
combined thickness of the jacks

TRADE SECRET

A centerline is often used as the starting point for laying out the width of a rough opening. In that case, you need to divide the specified R.O. measurement in half to locate the sides of the opening. This may seem difficult when the R.O. width contains a fraction, such as ⅝ in. In fact, to divide the fraction in half all you need to do is double the denominator. For example, half of ⅝ in. is ⁵⁄₁₆ in. If a total R.O. width is 42¾ in., half the width is 21⅜ in.

A new king and jack stud combination is installed in preparation for the new header.

Framing the new opening

Frame the rough opening using the window manufacturer's R.O. size. Take the time to make the rough sill perfectly straight and level, because that will be easier than shimming the seatboard later. For a bay or bow window, double the rough sill so it will be strong enough to support the brackets that buttress the bay.

Prepare a king and jack stud assembly for one side of the opening, either by adding a new jack to an existing stud or by assembling and installing a new unit. The jack's length equals the king's length minus the header's width. If you're framing a window, it may be difficult to fasten the bottoms of the new studs inside the wall. In that case, use screws or remove the remaining drywall below the window.

Cut and assemble the header. The header's length equals the R.O.'s width plus the combined thickness of the jacks (remember, for openings 6 ft. wide or more, you need to install double jacks on each side). The length of the header indicates where to place the second king stud in relation to the king and jack stud assembly already installed. Leave the second jack loose for now, though, to make the header easier to install. Seat one end of the header on the first jack, and then lift the other end of the header by driving in the bottom of the second jack.

A jack stud is slammed into position under a new header. This header is light, so it is simply nailed in place until the jacks are installed. A heavier beam may require a scab block to hold one end temporarily.

> *"The length of the header indicates where to place the second king stud in relation to the king and jack stud assembly already installed."*

SAFETY FIRST

When setting props for shoring, tack each prop immediately with a nail—even if it seems tight. When the next prop is installed, it may lift the ceiling slightly, causing the first prop to come loose. A falling prop has clobbered more than one carpenter.

TRADE SECRET

When parts need to be snug, it's always better to cut a little heavy. If the line is right on the mark, then cut on the waste side of the line to give yourself some breathing room. You can always cut the piece shorter, but you can't put wood back. Try to avoid the old carpenter's excuse: "I cut it twice and it's *still* too short."

A wide window opening is divided into two narrow openings by a single intermediate stud. This extra support enables the header to be much smaller than would normally be necessary for a single, wide opening. The narrow header is desirable here because of the low basement ceiling.

Complete the wall framing by installing the rough sill between the new double studs. Intermediate studs are sometimes placed between adjoining windows so that a smaller header can be used, but this method requires wider mullion posts between the windows. Once the new framing is in place, cut out the plywood from the opening and trim back the siding so that you can set the unit. You can remove the temporary shoring at this point as well.

Bisecting Angles

When framing and finishing bay windows it's often necessary to *bisect* (cut in half) an angle to obtain the correct miter angle for cutting lumber or trim. A standard 45-degree bay corner has a half-angle of 22½ degrees, but how do you find the angles when cutting the baseboard for a five-sided bow?

To determine a half-angle, use a short length of board with straight, parallel edges as a gauge to draw *offset lines* parallel to the adjoining sides of the bow. Then connect the corners where the walls meet with the intersection of the offset lines. Record the resulting half-angle on a *T-bevel* (angle gauge), and then use the T-bevel to set the correct miter angle on your chopsaw.

Half-angles
To find a half-angle, draw lines parallel to the walls, using a block of wood as a gauge. Connect the intersection of the walls with the intersection of the parallel lines. Then use a T-bevel to transfer the half-angle to the saw.

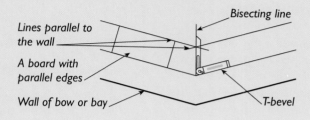

Bisecting line

Lines parallel to the wall

A board with parallel edges

Wall of bow or bay

T-bevel

Plywood sheathing is removed with a reciprocating saw after framing the new opening.

TOOLS AND MATERIALS
Chainsaws for Remodeling

You may have a mini-chainsaw in the garage that you use to trim trees. If so, you have a powerful remodeling tool. Chainsaws excel at many types of rough carpentry but especially at *blind cutting*. When retrofitting a header, for instance, you can cut through a stud and just graze the sheathing behind it. Chainsaws plunge-cut easily, so they're good for removing plywood from rough openings.

SAFETY FIRST

Chainsaws cut ferociously, so they're obviously dangerous. But one danger of chainsaws isn't so apparent. If the top-front corner of the guide bar contacts a fixed object, the saw can *kickback* toward the operator. To avoid this, always plunge-cut with the lower half of the bar nose.

IN DETAIL
Outboard Support

You must provide outboard support for bays and bows or they will sag. Sagging usually shows up as a poor fit between the flanker sash and the frame, which is caused by racking. The simplest way to support a bay window is to use sturdy brackets. Another option is to frame the walls under the front and sides of the bay, in which case there will be a dead space or storage space under the seatboard.

IN DETAIL
Supporting Bay Windows

You can support bay windows during installation with temporary posts or sawhorses. Adjust the height of the support so that the seatboard is level as it sticks out from the wall. Offset the temporary supports slightly from the outside corners where the front window meets the flankers to leave clearance for installing the support brackets.

"If the flankers work smoothly and the sashes fit properly, finish nailing the side flanges and tape them to keep out drafts."

Installing the unit

Set the unit in the opening and prop it up with a temporary support underneath the middle window. Adjust the bay's position so that the edges of the headboard and the seatboard are flush with the drywall on the inside. Nail the side flanges in a

Bay window on brackets
Sturdy 4×4 brackets can support bay windows. The three parts of the bracket—the leg, cross arm, and brace—are lag-bolted together. The bottom of the bracket is lag-bolted to the floor framing and the top of the bracket is tied to the wall framing with steel straps.

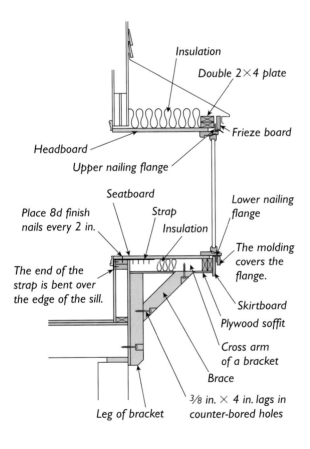

few places and check the operation of the flankers. If the flankers work smoothly and the sashes fit properly, finish nailing the side flanges and tape them to keep out drafts.

If you are supporting the bay with permanent brackets, preattach a metal strap to the top of the bracket to secure it to the rough sill. To install the bracket, pry a gap between the seatboard and the rough sill. Pass the strap through the gap from the outside, bend the end of the strap over the edge of the sill, and then pepper it with 8d common nails. Secure the bottom of the bracket to the wall with ⅜-in. by 4-in. lag bolts. Remove the temporary supports and check the seatboard with a level.

Attach double 2×4s (on edge) to the bottom of the seatboard with 4-in. screws. Nail the 2×4s to the ends of the brackets, leaving enough room between the 2×4s and the window's bottom nailing flange for a skirtboard. Nail the window's bottom nailing flanges to the skirtboard and cover the flange with molding. Add intermediate 2×4s as necessary to support the seatboard. Then insulate the cavity below the seatboard with fiberglass insulation or rigid foam, and attach a ⅜-in. plywood soffit to the undersides of the 2×4s and the cross arms of the brackets. Caulk between the trim boards and the window frame.

Pack the top of the bay with 2×4 plates and insulate it before the prefab roof goes on (see drawing on p. 119). Fasten the upper nailing flanges of the bay unit to the plates, and then wrap the framing with a frieze board. Build the roof to overhang the frieze board.

SAFETY FIRST

Lift very heavy headers one end at a time. At one side of the opening *scab* (attach) blocks onto a king stud about 2 in. below where the tops of the jacks will be. (This allows you to angle in the header.) With a helper, lift one end of the beam onto the blocks. Then lift the other end of the header and prop it in place with a jack. Lift the first end that was raised those extra inches so the entire header is tight against the cripple studs or top plate. Pry off the scab blocks. Nail a jack tight against the king stud and double the jacks on both sides of the opening.

Windows That Reach the Ceiling

A taller window means more light, and window headers can be raised above the ceiling level by incorporating them into the ceiling framing. The only problem is that the presence of a header means less bearing on the top plate for the floor joists. To compensate, use metal joist hangers to transfer the weight of the joists to the header.

A similar method can be used to frame openings for corner windows and doors with no post at the corner. The rim joist on both sides of the corner is doubled or tripled, forming heavy beams that cantilever out over the corner. To prevent a seesaw effect, the portions of the beams over the opening must be shorter than the portions *not* over the opening. Consult an engineer before tackling this project.

Header above ceiling

To allow a window to reach the ceiling, incorporate the window's header into the floor framing above it. Use joist hangers, because the joists no longer have room to bear on the top of the wall.

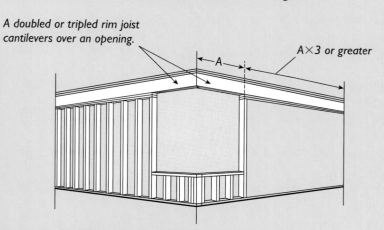

A rim joist serves as an outside layer of the header.

This triple 2×10 header has ½-in. plywood spacers in between.

Joist hangers

Corner window framing

A postless corner window can be framed with beefed-up rim joists that cantilever over the opening. As a rule, the cantilevered portion of the beam shouldn't be more than one quarter of the beam's total length.

A doubled or tripled rim joist cantilevers over an opening.

A

A×3 or greater

These corner windows have no structural posts at the corners. To frame the openings, beams cantilever over the corners.

WHAT CAN GO WRONG

Cantilevers Can Cause Floor Humps

I was once asked to fix a mysterious hump that had appeared in the floor of a new home. The header carried the inboard ends of a set of cantilever joists, and on the opposing ends of the joists was a bay window. The weight of the bay had caused a seesaw effect that lifted the header and caused the hump. The header had been installed to change the direction of the joists, thus permitting the cantilever. However, the header wasn't strong enough to counter the weight of the bay. As it turned out, we wrestled a heavy steel plate into the basement to stiffen the header.

Brackets Settle

Brackets may settle slightly under the weight of a bay, so shim as necessary directly below the outside corners of the bay between the bracket and the seatboard. To stiffen the rough sill laterally, attach it to the seatboard with plenty of finish nails.

IN DETAIL

Ordering Custom Glass for Site-Built Windows

Site-built windows are typically glazed with ⅝-in.-thick IG (insulating glass) units, though you can specify a higher r-value for thicker units. You must provide measured drawings or templates to order glass. Allow enough room at the bottom of the opening to elevate the glass on ¼-in.-thick rubber setting blocks. They cushion the glass and hold it above moisture that may seep past the exterior sill stop. You also need at least ³⁄₁₆ in. of clearance at the sides and top of the glass, because structural weight bearing on the glass may crack it.

Building a walkout bow window

This walkout bow window (see photo below) was shipped to the site of a new home as five separate windows. The windows were assembled on site as a continuous unit and placed in a wide opening in a multifaceted wall. The wall sits on floor framing that cantilevers out from the house, and each floor joist had to be trimmed in just the right place to conform to the curve of the bow.

To determine the location of the cuts for such a window, assemble the unit temporarily so you can take accurate measurements. Then make a template to transfer the measurements to the floor. After the floor overhang is constructed, build a low wall of solid lumber, then frame the wall above the window with 2×6s suspended from the roof overhang. To complete the bow, reassemble the individual units in the opening one at a time, installing a pie-shaped filler strip between each pair of adjoining windows to hold them at the right angle.

Five separate windows have been arranged along an arc to create this walkout bow window.

To build the floor of the bow, I-joists were allowed to overhang the foundation. Each joist was then trimmed in accordance with the curve.

"To determine the location of the cuts for such a window, assemble the unit temporarily so you can take accurate measurements."

Don't try to install a second-story window with nothing more than a single ladder—it isn't safe. However, you can use a pair of ladders and *ladder jacks,* or brackets that fit over ladder rungs, to make scaffolding.

Ladder jacks make a quick working platform. Note the bar clamps used to fasten the planks to the ladder jacks.

A low subwall is framed below the rough opening (above photo) and the wall above the opening is suspended from the soffit (right photo).

A pie-shaped filler strip is added between neighboring windows to join them at the correct angle.

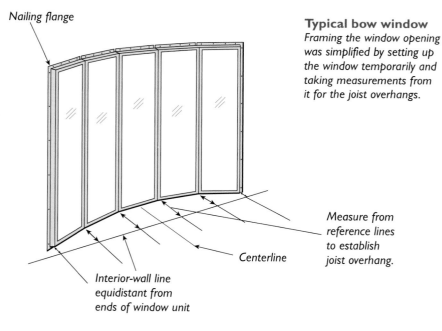

Nailing flange

Typical bow window
Framing the window opening was simplified by setting up the window temporarily and taking measurements from it for the joist overhangs.

Measure from reference lines to establish joist overhang.

Centerline

Interior-wall line equidistant from ends of window unit

WHAT CAN GO WRONG

Wood Stops vs. Putty

Single-pane glass is sealed with glazing compound, also called putty. IG glass should never be sealed with putty, because solvents in the putty adversely affect the glass unit's rubber seal. Window manufacturers seal IG units with plastic glazing beads, whereas shop-built and site-built windows employ wood stops.

TRADE SECRET

When building a temporary shoring wall on a concrete slab, skip the bottom plate, because the concrete is strong enough to withstand concentrated loads.

TRADE SECRET

For half-circle windows, the angles on the ends of the blocks should be cut at 45 degrees. For elliptical and springline windows, the angle at the top of the blocks is more than 45 degrees, while the angle that fits against the sides of the opening is less than 45 degrees. The easiest way to find these oddball angles is to simply hold an oversize block over the opening and scribe it.

> *"Round-top windows and doors bestow a touch of formal elegance and can be adapted to both traditional and contemporary styles."*

Installing Round-Top Windows

Round-top windows and doors bestow a touch of formal elegance and can be adapted to both traditional and contemporary styles. They work best when they're understated and carefully proportioned in relation to the wall in which they're situated. In the 1980s, round-top windows became something of an obsession, with builders installing them everywhere, and the results were often garish.

Framing round-top windows

Frame round-top openings in two stages. First, frame a rectangular opening using the R.O. width and height specified by the manufacturer.

An ordinary header transfers the structural loads from above to the sides of the opening. Next, fill in the corners of the rectangle to create a round opening.

After the rectangular opening is complete, trace the window on a piece of plywood sheathing, adding an extra ¼ in. for clearance. Cut the ends of the plywood to fall on the appropriate studs to the left and right of the opening. Then cut out the curve and install the sheathing on the wall *before* you install the in-fill framing.

In-fill framing can be provided in different ways. You can block narrow round-top windows with scraps of solid lumber. To do this, cut angles on the ends of the blocks to fit against the sides and top of the rectangular opening. After trimming the ends, hold the pointed blocks in

These round-top casements conform to an alcove's arched ceiling.

To cut blocking for a round top, scribe the ends of the block to fit the rough opening.

After trimming the ends of the block, transfer the curve from the sheathing.

Curved blocking is cut with a jigsaw.

position, trace the curve of the sheathing onto them, and cut the curve with a jigsaw. Then nail or screw the blocks to the rectangular opening.

Keep in mind that you need blocking behind both the exterior sheathing and the interior drywall, so build up a layer of two blocks and a scrap of ½-in. plywood for 2×4 walls. For 2×6 walls, mount one block to back up the drywall and another to provide support behind the sheathing. This leaves a cavity between the two blocks that can be filled with insulation.

Springline windows sometimes have a minimal *rise* (height of curve) that may fit within a single board positioned horizontally. The widest solid-lumber board available is a 2×12, but

IN DETAIL

The Ups and Downs of the Ladder Technique

One advantage of framing a curved opening using the ladder technique is that it maximizes insulation space. A disadvantage is that plywood doesn't hold nails well, so the window's nailing flange or exterior casing must be screwed into place. Likewise, interior trim must be screwed with small-head finish screws or glued to the drywall rather than attached with finish nails. A plywood ladder is flimsy by itself, but it will be strong enough if you nail it to the window jamb, as long as the nails penetrate the cross-blocks on the ladder.

SAFETY FIRST

Round-top windows are often featured in the center of a gable. *If the gable roof in question has a cathedral ceiling, consult an engineer before doing any demolition work.*

IN DETAIL

Installing Finned Units

Installing finned units after the housewrap is complete can be tricky, because it is often difficult to slip the top fin under the housewrap. Instead, mount the fins over the housewrap, and then slit the housewrap about 4 in. above the window. Cut a 6-in.-wide strip of felt paper and slip it under the slit in the housewrap with its lower edge over the top window fin. Tape any overcut in the slit. For extra protection, tape the bottom first and then side fins with flashing tape. The tape on the sides overlaps the bottom tape and slips under the head spline.

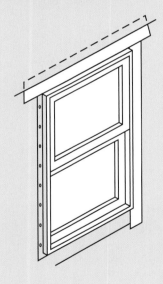

> "Flashing round tops is trickier, because the head flashing must conform to a curve (with the exception of vinyl-clad units with integral nailing flanges, which are self-flashing)."

160

greater widths are available in composite boards called *laminated veneer lumber* (LVL). When a round-top window is too big to block with boards, shape the opening with a curved ladder, using plywood rails and short cross blocks as rungs (see photo below).

LVL header for a springline window

Laminated veneer lumber (LVL) comes in wider pieces than solid lumber so it's useful for blocking round tops. The curved headers seen here give the opening its shape and the straight header above them carries the load.

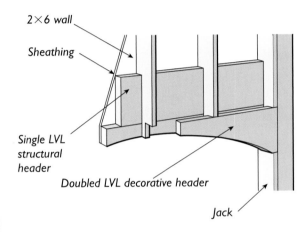

2×6 wall

Sheathing

Single LVL structural header

Doubled LVL decorative header

Jack

Large round-top windows can be framed with ladders. The curved sides of the ladder are made of plywood and the crosspieces are solid wood blocks.

Installing and flashing round tops

Round tops are installed in much the same way as other fixed windows. Shim the sill level, if necessary, and then fasten the unit to the exterior through the nailing flanges or the exterior casing. Shim between the jamb and the in-fill framing every 12 in. or so, and then nail through the jambs and the shims.

Flashing round tops is trickier, because the head flashing must conform to a curve (with the exception of vinyl-clad units with integral nailing flanges, which are self-flashing). To flash primed and aluminum-clad round tops, bend a straight Z-shaped flashing as you would for an ordinary window. Then cut intermittent slits about every 2 in. along the *upturned flange* (the flange that mounts against the wall). These slits effectively allow the upturned flange to stretch.

Meanwhile, the *down-turned flange,* which laps over the front of the window, needs to shrink. Crimp the down-turned flange with a crimping

The head flashing for a round-top window starts out as simple Z-flashing. One of the flanges is cut every 2 in.; the opposite flange is crimped to bend the flashing. Small squares of flashing will fill the V-shaped spaces left by the cuts, and caulk, solder, or tape will be used as a sealant.

tool; the more closely spaced the crimps, the tighter the curve, so practice on a scrap piece to get a feel for the correct spacing. After crimping, mount the flashing over the window by nailing through every tab on the upturned flange, and then slip flat cards of metal into the V- notches between the tabs. Each card's lower edge should overlap the tab below while its upper edge should tuck under the tab above (see top drawing, p. 162). Apply a dab of silicone caulk to hold the cards in place and seal the vulnerable spots at

Sloped Head Flashings

Fixed triangles and trapezoids often conform to a sloping roofline. These units aren't a problem when they're situated under a wide roof overhang, but without an overhang they are susceptible to water penetration. The best solution is to intercept infiltrated water with a special flashing tucked below the bottom nailing flange at the lower corner of the window. This flashing then laps over the course of siding immediately below the window to eject the water as quickly as possible. Siding without horizontal joints, such as stucco, means that infiltrated moisture has to travel all the way to the bottom of the wall before it exits, so thorough wrapping is essential before the siding or stucco is applied.

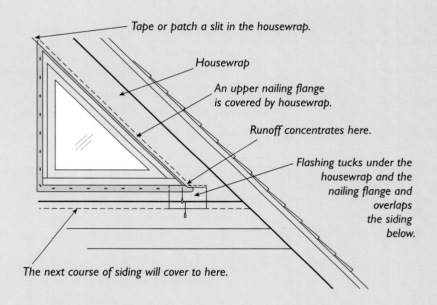

Tape or patch a slit in the housewrap.

Housewrap

An upper nailing flange is covered by housewrap.

Runoff concentrates here.

Flashing tucks under the housewrap and the nailing flange and overlaps the siding below.

The next course of siding will cover to here.

Flashing a sloped head
Sloped-head units, such as this triangle, generate concentrated runoff at their corners. Caulk may fail here, so intercept any infiltrated water with a hidden flashing. The flashing tucks under the window's nailing flange and laps over the siding below.

TOOLS AND MATERIALS
Trammel Rods

A trammel rod works like an oversize compass for laying out large circular curves. You can make a trammel rod in minutes out of any lightweight board you have on hand. Drive a nail through one end of the rod and place it at the center of the intended circle. At the other end, drill holes through the rod at the required radii, then jam pencils into the holes to draw the curves.

TOOLS & MATERIALS

Flashing for Round-Top Windows

A new flashing product makes sealing round-top windows easier than ever. It's called Tyvek® FlexWrap, manufactured by Dupont®. Unlike other flashing products, FlexWrap has a high degree of stretch. This lets it conform to irregular shapes such as round-tops without wrinkling. FlexWrap can also be used to seal the corners of a rough opening in lieu of felt patches.

"You can increase the dramatic effect of a round-top window by surrounding it with a sunburst."

Filling the V-notches in curved flashing

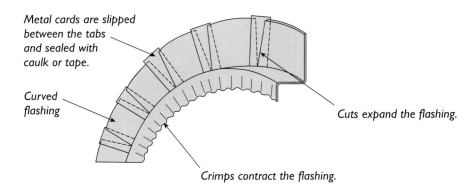

Metal cards are slipped between the tabs and sealed with caulk or tape.

Curved flashing

Cuts expand the flashing.

Crimps contract the flashing.

the points of the V-notches. Some builders use flashing tape to seal the notches.

Round-top windows are like polygons in that they divert runoff to the sides. Pay attention to where the resulting concentrated water flows when it reaches the bottom of the window on each side. The bottom nailing flange should lap over the housewrap. If you have horizontal siding around the window, it's good practice to tuck an additional flat metal flashing under the lower nailing flange at the corners of the window. The lower edge of the flashing should then lap over

the top edge of the nearest course of siding so that infiltrated water can quickly drain to the exterior (see Sloped Head Flashings, p. 161).

Finishing the exterior of round-top windows

The procedure for cutting horizontal siding to fit a round-top window depends on the type of window. Most round tops, including springline windows, have a *circular curve,* which is constant regardless of where it occurs on the window. On the other hand, an *elliptical curve* varies

Different Types of Round-Top Windows

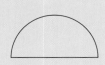

Half-circle windows and transoms are the most common type of round top.

When a half-circle is fused directly with a rectangle the result is called an arch window.

A springline window is similar to an arch window except that the curved portion constitutes somewhat less than a half-circle.

Clapboard sunburst

A clapboard sunburst mimics the rays of the sun around a gable-end round-top window. To position the clapboards, measure off equal increments along the rake board and around the circumference of the arch.

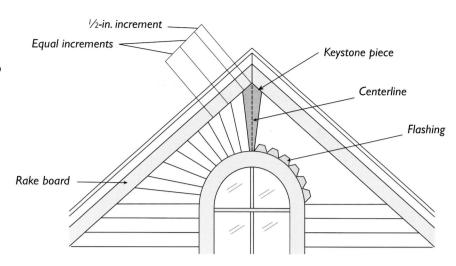

½-in. increment

Equal increments

Keystone piece

Centerline

Flashing

Rake board

throughout its length; it is tightly curved on the sides and gently curved on the top.

To fit siding against a circular curve, trace a portion of the window's outline on a piece of plywood or cardboard to use as a template. Let the siding overlap the window and mark the siding's top and bottom edges where they hit the curve. Then connect the marks with the template. The same template can be used for all of the siding courses. For an elliptical window, mark where the top and bottom edges of the given course hit the curve, and then make a

rubbing for that portion of the curve to use as a template.

You can increase the dramatic effect of a round-top window by surrounding it with a *sunburst*, an arrangement of wooden *clapboards* (beveled siding boards) that mimics the rays of the sun. Measure off equal increments along the *rake board*, or gable trim, to locate the outer ends of the clapboards, then use a compass to step off the same number of increments around the circumference of the window. Make a keystone piece at the top from a ¾-in.-thick board.

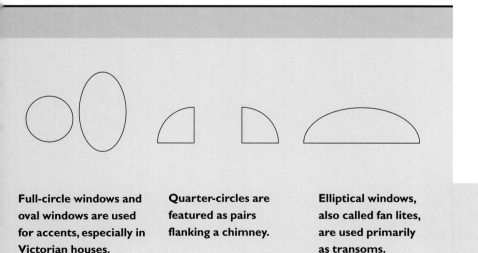

Full-circle windows and oval windows are used for accents, especially in Victorian houses.

Quarter-circles are featured as pairs flanking a chimney.

Elliptical windows, also called fan lites, are used primarily as transoms.

CHAPTER ELEVEN

Windows

Windows that don't work correctly are a constant nuisance. After years of straining to open and close them, it's probably tempting to say, "Just tear 'em out and put in new ones." But wait! The problem may be nothing more serious than a little too much paint buildup.

With some elbow grease and common sense you can fix most window problems at a fraction of the cost of new windows. This chapter will start with a look at tuning up old windows so they work better. Then I'll walk you through some common window repairs, such as fixing sash ropes and replacing broken glass. Finally, we'll look at sash replacement with jamb liners or vinyl replacement windows. These systems let you keep the old frame and trim, so they yield most of the benefits of new windows without the "radical surgery" of full replacement.

1 Tuning Up Old Windows, p. 166

2 Replacing Sash Ropes, p. 169

3 Reglazing Window Sashes, p. 172

4 Replacing Double-Hung Sashes and Tracks, p. 176

5 Installing Vinyl Replacement Windows, p. 179

TOOLS AND MATERIALS
What You'll Need: Repairing Windows

- Putty knife
- Flat prybar
- Utility knife
- Nippers
- Vise-Grip pliers
- Chisel
- Power drill
- Hook scraper

WHAT CAN GO WRONG

Don't Bludgeon the Meeting Rail

Beating or pushing too hard on the meeting rail of a stuck window can cause it to separate from the adjoining stiles. It's always better to pry up from the bottom (for lower sashes) or down from the top (for upper sashes). If you *do* damage the corner joints, the sash should be taken out, reglued, and clamped. Then attach lifting handles, called *sash lifts,* to the lower sash to prevent any further strain on the meeting rail.

> "Sometimes, a double-hung lower sash can be completely frozen by paint. To get it to move freely, remove the excess paint from the track above the sash."

Tuning Up Old Windows

Paint is essential for protecting wooden windows from the elements, but in some ways it is a window's worst enemy. In fact, the window that operates best in most old houses is that dusty double-hung window up in the attic that was never painted in the first place.

Getting sashes to move freely

Sometimes, a double-hung lower sash can be completely frozen by paint. To get it to move freely, remove the excess paint from the track above the sash. The most effective tool for this is a small, sharp hook scraper. Scrape excess paint from the *parting bead* (the rail between the upper and lower sashes) and from the edge of the interior stop. Remember that scraping produces

A small hook scraper is effective for removing paint buildup. To keep the scraper sharp, file the edge at a 45-degree angle.

dust that may contain lead, so take proper safety precautions.

Next, score the paint around the sides and bottom of the sash with a utility knife. Drive a putty knife between the sash and the stops in several places to break the seal. Then try pushing up gently on the meeting rail. If the sash still won't budge, go outside and break the paint seal on the exterior as you did on the interior. From the outside, carefully drive a flat bar under the lower sash and pry it upward, using a soft piece of wood as a fulcrum to cushion the sill. Make sure you pry under the stiles—first one and then the other—rather than under the middle of the sash, because the lower rail could flex and break the glass.

Paint is scraped from a parting bead to restore proper clearance. When the scraper starts to cut poorly and makes a squeaking sound, it's time to sharpen it.

SAFETY FIRST

Lead paint is poisonous, especially to children. Use a respirator—not a dust mask—when sanding it. If possible, work outdoors and protect the environment by using curtains and drop cloths to retrieve dust. If you must work indoors, vacuum thoroughly afterward and wet mop all surfaces. Dispose of the dust according to local regulations for hazardous materials. Wear a disposable coverall or wash your clothes separately from the household laundry.

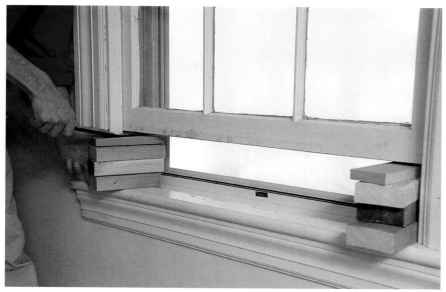

To raise a frozen sash, pry it up from the outside, using a shim to protect the sill from damage. Pry a little at a time under each stile to prevent glass breakage.

Once the bottom of the sash is raised above the stool, you can go back inside to finish prying. Keep stacking blocks on the stool to raise your fulcrum as you go. Progress will accelerate as more and more of the sash rises into the channel you already scraped. When the sash is fully raised, scrape the lower portion of the channel that was previously covered by the sash. After scraping the channels, sand them with a sheet of 50-grit sandpaper wrapped around a block that fits inside the channel. Finally, lubricate the channels with paraffin or silicone spray.

Upper sash top rail

Misaligned sash lock

Upper sash meeting rail

Head jamb

Paint buildup prevents the upper sash from going up all the way.

A gap between the meeting rails causes a draft.

Lower sash meeting rail

Paint buildup prevents the lower sash from going down all the way.

Sill

Lower sash bottom rail

Once the sash is raised above the stool you can finish prying on the inside. Stack blocks as you go to raise your fulcrum.

Paint buildup prevents locking
Excess paint can keep the upper sash from going up all the way and the lower sash from going down all the way. As a result, the sash lock doesn't close and the meeting rails don't seal against each other properly, causing a draft. Sanding or trimming the sashes solves the problem.

IN DETAIL
Casement Windows

While casement windows may have similar problems with paint, more often they are sagged and racked like hinged doors. First, try breaking the paint seal. However, the remedy may involve shimming hinges and/or planing the sash.

SAFETY FIRST

Sashes that are badly frozen with paint are easier to free if you first remove the stops and the parting beads. At that point, it's tempting to yank on one corner of the window to loosen it. If the paint suddenly lets go, however, the sash may be twisted to the point of shattering the glass, and falling shards can inflict serious injuries.

TOOLS AND MATERIALS

Supply Sources for Window Replacement Hardware

- Stry-Buc Industries: 800-352-0800
- Blaine Window Hardware: 800-678-1919
- Hope's: 716-665-5124
- Phelps Company: 802-257-4314

TRADE SECRET

A good way to remove paint from window hardware is to soak it for a day in a coffee can filled with boiling water and one cup of granulated dishwasher detergent. Use steel wool and a toothbrush to get paint out of all the nooks and crannies. A wire wheel mounted on a bench grinder speeds up the process.

"If you see or feel clearance between the meeting rails but they still won't align, the problem may be paint buildup."

Getting sashes to meet in the middle of the window

Besides being drafty, sashes that don't meet properly rattle and are difficult to lock. To fix this, first try scraping the mating edges of the meeting rails to remove paint. You'll need to lower the upper sash and raise the lower sash to access these edges, so restoring full operation of the sashes may be necessary first. If there's interlocking metal weatherstripping on the meeting rails that's hopelessly clogged with paint, you can replace it with leaf-type weatherstripping.

If you see or feel clearance between the meeting rails but they still won't align, the problem may be paint buildup on the top edge of the upper sash and the bottom edge of the lower sash. The most effective way to correct this is to remove the bottom sash and use a circular saw to shave its bottom edge, being careful to tilt the saw to the correct bevel for the sill. For example, if the sashes are ¼ in. apart at the meeting rails, shave ¼ in. off the bottom of the sash. A racked window frame can also keep the sashes from meeting properly, in which case the bottom of the lower sash should be scribed and trimmed on a taper to close against the sill.

Fixing window hardware problems

In many cases, window hardware can be restored to full function simply by removing paint. In other cases, though, the window hardware may be broken or worn out and should be replaced. Fortunately, there are a number of mail-order houses that specialize in window replacement hardware.

Weatherstripping for Windows

Metal-leaf weatherstripping can be retrofitted to double-hung windows. The flat type works well between the jambs and the stiles (left), where clearance is minimal. The V-type has more spring and works well at the top of the upper sash and the bottom of the lower sash (center). Both types can be used for the meeting rails (right), depending on the amount of clearance.

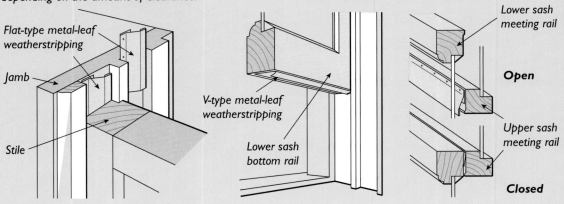

Flat-type metal-leaf weatherstripping

Jamb

Stile

V-type metal-leaf weatherstripping

Lower sash bottom rail

Lower sash meeting rail

Open

Upper sash meeting rail

Closed

Widely available foam and vinyl-tube weatherstripping looks terrible and isn't very effective. The best product for sealing both casements and double-hung windows is leaf-type metal. Use the flat type rather than the V-type on double-hung jambs, because there isn't much clearance between the sash and the jambs. The V-type works best for casements and double-hung windows at the top of the upper sash and the bottom of the lower sash. Which type you should use on the meeting rails depends on their design. You can substitute metal with vinyl V-type strips, but they are more fragile.

Sometimes, sash locks don't function correctly not because they're broken or frozen by paint, but because the meeting rails of the upper and lower sashes don't align. Getting the sashes to meet properly is the best solution, but a quicker fix is to shim the *keeper* (the female part of the lock) so that it aligns with the lock. You can use wood or cardboard to make a shim. Make it oversize to start, then trim it with a sharp chisel after it's installed. Drill clearance holes in the shim to keep it from splitting.

Casements that have just one lock in the middle may not hold the sash fully closed. Consider adding additional locks at the top and bottom, especially on tall casements.

Replacing Sash Ropes

Most older double-hung windows employ iron weights to counterbalance the sashes, making the window easier to open and close. The weights hang from cotton ropes; after a few thousand trips over the pulley, the ropes eventually break. Despite this, the simplicity of the weight-and-pulley system makes the window quite dependable. In contrast, spring-type *balances* (lifting mechanisms) eventually fail when the springs wear out. At that point, you have to find an exact replacement, which is more difficult than simply going down to the hardware store to buy new rope.

Removing the sashes

To replace a sash rope, remove the lower sash and then the upper sash. Even if only one sash rope

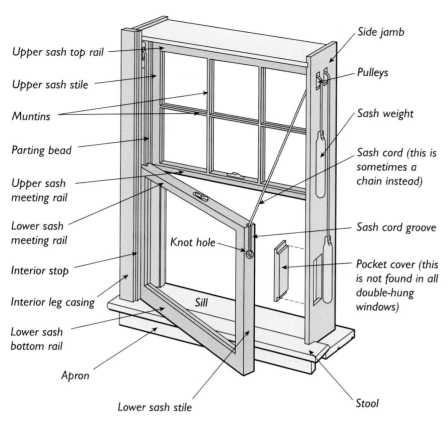

Double-hung window with sash weights
Iron weights counterbalance the sashes in this window, making the sashes easy to raise and lower.

Labels: Upper sash top rail, Upper sash stile, Muntins, Parting bead, Upper sash meeting rail, Lower sash meeting rail, Interior stop, Interior leg casing, Lower sash bottom rail, Apron, Lower sash stile, Knot hole, Sill, Side jamb, Pulleys, Sash weight, Sash cord (this is sometimes a chain instead), Sash cord groove, Pocket cover (this is not found in all double-hung windows), Stool

A sash is scribed before trimming to obtain the correct taper. After trimming, the sash will mate tightly with the sill.

IN DETAIL
Making a Homemade Sash Weight

You can make your own sash weights by pouring molten lead into a pipe. A threaded cap closes the bottom of the pipe and an eyebolt cast into the top of the weight attaches to a rope or chain. Before assembling the weight, weigh its components and adjust the amount of dry lead to achieve the correct weight. Fishing-line weights are a good source of lead. Use a plumber's ladle to melt the lead and work outdoors with a respirator, so that you don't inhale poisonous lead fumes.

Supply Sources for Weights, Pulleys, and Tape Balances

The first place to look for window weights and pulleys is at local building materials salvage yards. An excellent source guide for salvage yards and restoration products is *The Old House Journal Restoration Directory* (800-931-2931).

For weights and pulleys:
- Barry Supply Company: 212-242-5200
- JGR Enterprises, Inc.: 800-223-7112
- Van Dyke's Restorers: 800-558-1234
- Phelps Company: 802-257-4314

For tape balances:
- Pullman Manufacturing Corporation: 716-334-1350

TAKE YOUR PICK

Rope vs. Chain

- **Rope** for hanging sashes is a blend of cotton and synthetic fibers. Pure cotton rope isn't durable enough; pure synthetic rope is difficult to work with because it's slippery. Sash rope is sold by number; a #8 rope is about right for residential windows.
- **Sash chain** is more expensive than rope, but it lasts indefinitely.

"Even if only one sash rope has broken, it's wise to replace both, because they're probably brittle with age."

has broken, it's wise to replace both, because they're probably brittle with age. If the upper sash is frozen with paint, as is often the case, this is also the best time to free it.

Begin by prying off the interior stops. Drive a putty knife between the stop and the jamb at about mid-height and pry gently. As soon as a slight gap opens up, insert a flat prybar as well, then work from the middle toward the ends until the stop pops out. Cutting through the paint initially with a utility knife reduces damage to the adjoining trim. After you have removed the stops, use nippers to pull the nails through from the back.

If both ropes are broken, lift the lower sash out at this point. If one of the ropes remains intact, you'll have to cut it, but don't let the tail of this rope disappear through the pulley, as it will later help you remove the weight. Clamp Vise-Grip

Anatomy of a weight pocket

A hollow pocket between the jack stud and the side jamb accommodates a pair of weights that travel up and down.

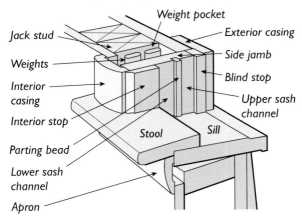

- Weight pocket
- Jack stud
- Exterior casing
- Side jamb
- Weights
- Blind stop
- Interior casing
- Upper sash channel
- Interior stop
- Stool
- Sill
- Parting bead
- Lower sash channel
- Apron

To remove a window stop, start prying in the middle and work toward each end. Score the paint first and drive in a putty knife to make room for the prybar.

pliers on the rope next to the pulley and cut the rope just above the sash. Tie a knot in the end of the rope, applying some tension. Then release the Vise-Grip pliers and lower the weight.

To remove the upper sash, remove the *parting beads*. These are the slender rails partially recessed in the vertical grooves in the window jambs. I don't even try to save the parting beads in most cases, since they're easy enough to make. Leave the upper sash where it is and chop through the parting beads just above and below the meeting rail, then break out the wood between the cuts. This way you will avoid crushing the meeting rail as you back out the parting beads. Split out the parting beads with a chisel. After everything is reinstalled, make new parting beads to replace the originals.

TRADE SECRET

To keep windows operating smoothly, paint them as seldom as possible, especially the tracks. When you do paint, always cut the brush up to the edge of the sash, rather than sloshing paint into the crack between the sash and the stop.

Tape balances

- Case
- Mortise for original pulley

Tape balances can be used to replace a weight-and-pulley system, so that the weight pockets can be insulated. The tape balance cases fit into the mortises where the original pulleys were (left). The ends of the tapes are pulled out of the cases and slipped over brackets screwed to the sash (right).

To remove a parting bead, chisel it down to the jamb above and below the meeting rail. Then split out the intervening wood. Now you can back out the remainder of the parting bead without crushing the lip of the meeting rail.

Remove the upper sash. If it's frozen, drive a putty knife between the blind stop and the sash to free it. If you free the sash and find that it's still suspended from its ropes, lower it as far as you can, then sever the ropes as you did for the lower sash. Remember to knot the ropes so that they don't slip through the pulleys. After cutting the ropes, remove the upper sash.

With the sashes removed, you have a golden opportunity to get rid of paint buildup. Remove paint from the blind stops and the interior stops with a scraper or coarse sandpaper. Remove paint from the sashes with a belt sander.

Making Parting Beads

Parting beads are usually sacrificed when fixing sash ropes, but they're easy to replace. First measure the groove in the jamb. Standard parting beads are ½ in. by ¾ in., which you can sometimes find as a stock molding. If not, rip your own beads on a table saw. Parting beads should be smooth to avoid friction, so use a fine-toothed blade. Alternatively, you can rip beads slightly oversize and then plane them to your final dimension.

You can avoid removing paint on the sashes by rabbeting the exposed part of the beads slightly. Leave the base of the parting beads at their original thickness, however, so they will fit snugly in the groove. The lower end of the beads should be beveled to fit against the sill. Prime the beads and rub them and the window jambs with paraffin for lubrication.

Rabbeting a parting bead for clearance

A slight rabbet along each side of the parting bead compensates for paint buildup on old sashes.

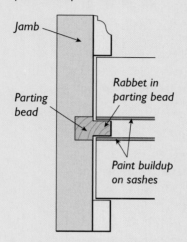

Jamb

Parting bead

Rabbet in parting bead

Paint buildup on sashes

Removing the weights

Some windows must have their interior casings removed to access their weights. Most windows, however, have narrow *pocket covers* in their jambs for this purpose. Pocket covers are located about 1 ft. above the sill in either the inner or the outer track. One type of pocket cover has a square lip at the top and bottom. Another type has a slanted top that wedges against a pair of nails driven into the jamb, with its slanted bottom held in by a screw. Locate the screw (which may be painted over) and remove it.

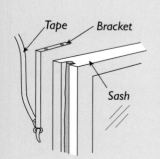

Tape   Bracket

Sash

The tape retracts to lift the sash.

The sash is then reinstalled and the tape balances help lift it.

TOOLS AND MATERIALS
Tape Balances

Tape balances can be used to replace weights and pulleys for old windows. They employ a spring-loaded tape for lifting the sash, sort of like a tape measure, and they mount in the window jamb like a regular pulley. When ordering, you'll need to specify the weight of the sash to get the right amount of tension. An advantage of tape balances is that they allow you to fill the weight pockets with insulation.

TRADE SECRET

Instead of removing paint by belt sanding, which necessitates repainting the sash, I sometimes use a carbide router bit to cut neat little rabbets along the vertical edges of the sashes. The rabbets are just deep enough to graze the original wood surface, and just wide enough to clear the parting beads or blind stops. This restores the necessary clearance and lets you avoid repainting the sash.

Fishing the weights out of their pockets is easy if you have the end of the rope to pull on. Just elevate the weight until it clears the bottom of the access door, and then guide the weight out through the door as you lower the rope. If the ropes have fallen into the pocket, you'll have to lift the weights by scooting them upward with a screwdriver or your fingers.

A rope is tied to its respective weight. First the rope was threaded over its pulley and fished out through the pocket cover. A knot keeps the upper end of the rope from disappearing into the pocket.

Rehanging the sashes

Cut an oversize length of rope for each weight and tie a knot in one end to keep the upper end of the rope from disappearing into the pocket. Then slip the unknotted end over the pulley and down into the pocket. Fish the lower ends of the ropes out through the access doors and tie them to their respective weights. Then, pull the tops of the ropes to draw the pulleys back into the pockets.

Hang the upper sash first. Pull its ropes all the way out and clamp Vise-Grip pliers on the ropes next to each pulley so they don't retract. Set the sash in the frame with its top tilted toward you, press the knots into the holes in the edges of the sash, and hold the ropes in the grooves on the sash as you guide the sash into the opening. Release the Vise-Grip pliers to tension each rope, paying the rope out gradually so it doesn't jerk.

Now lower the upper sash, install new parting beads, and reinstall the lower sash as you did the upper sash. Finally, reinstall the interior stops.

Reglazing Window Sashes

Replacing a broken window pane is a satisfying job that takes about an hour. The procedure includes removing the old glass, cutting and installing the new glass, and sealing the glass with *glazing compound* or putty. Wooden moldings are sometimes substituted for putty in glass doors.

"If the window has been neglected for a long time, the putty may chip out easily, but well-preserved putty holds tenaciously."

IN DETAIL

Setting Up Sash Chain

Sash chain is sold in a quaint little sack with some funny looking gizmos and no directions. The first gizmo is a wire helix that substitutes for the knot in a sash rope. Thread the helix onto the last link in the chain, as if you were putting a key on a key ring. The other gizmo is a little G-shaped wire clip. After looping the chain through the eye of the weight, use the clip to close the loop. Crimp the clip to keep it from coming loose.

Paint Buildup Alters the Sash's Weight

Years of paint buildup can make sashes heavier than their original weights, so the lower sash won't stay open and the upper sash droops. Compensate for this by threading a few heavy washers onto the rope or chain just above the weight.

Cutting the Ropes the Correct Length

The ends of the ropes are knotted and the knots are seated in holes in the edges of the sashes. If the ropes are cut too short, the weights will hit the pulleys before the sashes go down all the way. If the ropes are cut too long, the weights will hit the bottoms of the pockets before the sashes are fully raised. Without tension, the sashes will droop.

To cut each rope to its proper length, locate the center of the knot hole where the rope attaches to the edge of the sash and mark it on the face of the sash. With the sash in its lowered position, pull each rope down until you feel the weight hit the pulley. Transfer the center of the hole from the sash to the rope. Add an extra 3 in. for the knot, cut the rope, and tie a simple overhand knot on the end of each rope.

Correct length of sash ropes

A sash rope that's too long (left) will bottom out in the pocket before the sash is fully raised, causing the sash to droop. A rope that's too short (right) will cause the weight to strike the pulley before the sash is fully lowered.

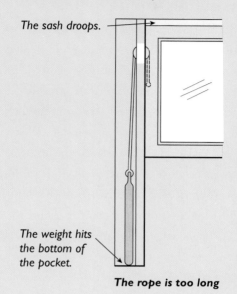

The sash droops.

The weight hits the bottom of the pocket.

The rope is too long

The weight strikes the back of the pulley.

The sash doesn't lower completely.

The rope is too short

Removing the old glass

Spread drop cloths and remove any glass shards that are already loose. To get the rest of the glass out, remove the old putty with a chisel. If the window has been neglected for a long time, the putty may chip out easily, but well-preserved putty holds tenaciously. Soften it first with an electric heat gun or a hair-dryer. If you are removing an entire sash, you can use lacquer thinner instead of heat to soften the putty.

Remove the glass with pliers. Remove and discard the little metal *diamond points,* as well. You will later replace them with *push points.* Scrape

A bottle/can opener with a sharpened point works great to scrape out the most stubborn old putty that hangs on to the wooden frame.

IN DETAIL

Sizing Sash Weights

To balance properly, each iron weight should be approximately half the weight of the sash. If the individual weights are missing, weigh the sash on a bathroom scale to find the correct replacement weight. Or measure the sash and use this formula: $\frac{1}{3} \times$ sq. ft. of sash = lb. of each iron weight. Weights are sometimes marked with Roman numerals to indicate their weight in pounds. If they are not marked, you can approximate the required length of a standard 1¾-in.-diameter iron weight with this formula: $1.5 \times$ weight of iron weight in pounds = length of iron weight in inches.

 According to Code

Always use safety glass to replace broken panes in doors, sidelites, and certain windows. (See p. 123 for specifics.)

IN DETAIL
Using Heat to Soften Putty

Intense heat may crack surrounding panes, so center the heat gun over the broken pane and direct the blast of air toward the putty at an angle. If the surrounding panes consist of valuable antique glass, shield them from heat with a piece of sheet metal, as well.

TRADE SECRET

It's always a good idea to measure the diagonals to see if the sash has racked, a problem that is more common with casement windows than with double-hung windows. If the diagonals don't agree, you will need extra clearance. If there is severe racking, you may be better off repairing or replacing the sash.

"The sound of the glass scratching should be crisp and continuous. Do not go over the cut a second time—this is a surefire way to ruin the cut."

the remaining putty from the rabbet with a hook scraper. A can opener with a sharpened point also works well.

Measuring, cutting, and installing the new glass

To find the size of the replacement pane, measure the height and width of the opening and deduct ⅛ in. from each dimension. This gives you ¹⁄₁₆ in. of clearance on each side. If you can get your glass cut to size at the hardware store, all the better, but it's not hard to do it yourself. First clean the glass and lay it on a flat surface with some type of cushion (a towel works well) underneath it for even support. You can mark your measurements with a fine-point permanent marker or position a straight edge off a ruler or tape measure.

Dip the end of the glass cutter in kerosene or light machine oil to lubricate the cutting wheel, and then brush a little kerosene or oil onto the glass and along the cutline. Hold the cutter between your index finger and ring finger, with your index finger applying firm pressure over the wheel. Start scoring at the very edge of the glass, and draw the cutter toward you with a smooth, firm stroke. The sound of the glass scratching should be crisp and continuous. *Do not* go over the cut a second time—this is a surefire way to ruin the cut. After scoring the glass, pick it up with one hand on each side of the cut and snap it. Then test the pane to see if it fits.

Methods for prepping the sash vary. Old-timers first seal the wood with a coat of raw

Use firm, steady pressure when scoring the glass.

Snap the glass along the score line.

SAFETY FIRST

Use heavy leather gloves and safety goggles to remove broken glass. A worker of mine once got a speck of glass in his eye during glass demolition. The pain in his eye was matched only by the pain in my wallet when the speck was removed.

TOOLS AND MATERIALS
Don't Use an Old Glass Cutter

Glass cutters have a hardened steel wheel that dulls quickly, like a razor, so don't use a glass cutter that's been rusting in your toolbox for several years. A new one costs only a few dollars.

Insert push points with a putty knife.

Roll the glazing compound to form a rope.

linseed oil and then *back bed* the glass into a skinny bead of putty. I prefer to prime the sash with exterior latex primer and then bed the glass in a tiny bead of latex caulk. I slice off any squished-out caulk after it dries. Secure the glass by driving push points into the sash with the end of your putty knife.

Applying new putty

Dig a wad of glazing compound out of the can and roll it between your hands to soften it, then make a rope about ¾ in. thick. Press the rope into the rabbet with your fingers, then make a series of short, hard swipes every in. or so with the corner of your putty knife to squish the putty deeply into the rabbet. If you neglect this

A series of short swipes with the corner of a putty knife ensures that the putty won't peel away as you smooth it.

TRADE SECRET

Tape measures don't work well for taking precise inside measurements, such as between two jambs. I prefer to use a folding rule with an extension slide, such as the Red End rule made by Lufkin. First, unfold the rule as far as it will fit inside the space to be measured. Then, slide out the extension to find the remain-ing distance and add it to the folded-out length of the rule. If you don't have a folding rule, use two narrow sticks held fully extended in the opening with their ends overlapping. Tilt the sticks out of the opening carefully so the overlap doesn't change and lay them against an extended tape to measure them.

Supply Sources for Jamb Liners and Spring Balances

- Stry-Buc Industries: 800-352-0800
- Blaine Window Hardware: 800-678-1919
- Adams Architectural Wood Products: 888-285-8120
- Marvin Windows and Doors: 800-346-5128

Using a Sliding Bevel Gauge

A sliding bevel gauge, also called a *T-bevel*, is used to measure and transfer angles. Unlock it (this is usually accomplished by loosening a wing nut) and set it to the angle between the interior stop and the sill. Then use the T-bevel to draw the same angle on a board. Finally, place a protractor on the board to find the angle's value in degrees. If you were cutting this angle, say on a table saw, you could simply transfer the angle to the workpiece using the locked T-bevel.

step, the putty tends to peel away from the glass as you smooth it.

Smooth the putty by wiping it firmly with the putty knife held at a diagonal angle. The precise angle depends on the depth and width of the rabbet. One corner of the putty knife contacts the glass to slice off excess putty as you work, while the edge of the blade rides against the top of the rabbet. To keep putty from being visible on the interior, hold the corner of the putty knife directly opposite the edge of the muntin.

After wiping all four sides and clearing off the excess putty, clean up the corners. Draw the knife away from each corner to form a neat 45-degree crease. After a few days the putty will skin over, at which point you should paint it to seal in the oils that keep it pliable. Use an oil-based primer followed by an oil-based or latex top coat.

Replacing Double-Hung Sashes and Tracks

It's possible to upgrade old, drafty double-hung windows without sacrificing their historical appearance. By replacing the old wooden tracks with vinyl tracks, you'll get smoother operation and less air infiltration. If you choose a *tilt-type* jamb liner, the new sashes tilt in for easy cleaning.

Jamb liner kits consisting of a pair of vinyl tracks and wood replacement sashes allow you to retain exterior and interior moldings while increasing your home's energy efficiency. The sashes can be made with the same muntin configuration as the originals, but with insulating glass instead of single-pane glass. This provides better weatherstripping than the originals and gives you the opportunity to fill the weight pockets with insulation.

Glazing: correct vs. incorrect

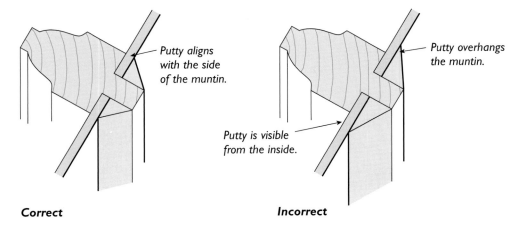

Putty aligns with the side of the muntin.

Putty overhangs the muntin.

Putty is visible from the inside.

Correct

Incorrect

> "The standard sill angle for replacement sashes is 14 degrees; a discrepancy of one or two degrees can be absorbed by the lower sash's weatherstripping."

WHAT CAN GO WRONG

Making Oversize Glass Fit

You can make a slightly oversize pane of glass fit by paring the sides of the sash rabbet with a sharp chisel. Alternatively, you can wet sand a little bit off the glass. Use a sheet of coarse silicone-carbide sandpaper wrapped around a block of wood, with water as a lubricant. Support the edge of the glass well to avoid breakage.

Measuring for a jamb liner kit

Measure the distance between the jambs to find the width. Make sure you measure carefully at the top, bottom, and middle, and go with the narrowest dimension that gives you the most leeway. Shimming the jamb liner inward is easier than trimming a sash that's too wide.

The height is measured from the head jamb to where the outside of the lower sash meets the sill. This is tricky because measuring further in or out on the sloped sill affects the overall dimension. The third item you'll need to specify is the slope angle of the sill. The standard sill angle for replacement sashes is 14 degrees; a discrepancy of one or two degrees can be absorbed by the lower sash's weatherstripping.

Installing a tilt-type jamb liner kit

First remove the interior stops, the parting beads, and the old sashes. Discard the parting beads, but try to save the interior stops for reuse. Now is the time to insulate the weight pockets. Then nail

Measuring sashes

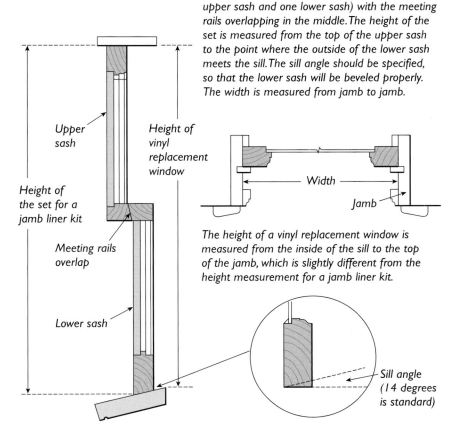

Jamb liner sashes are measured as a set (one upper sash and one lower sash) with the meeting rails overlapping in the middle. The height of the set is measured from the top of the upper sash to the point where the outside of the lower sash meets the sill. The sill angle should be specified, so that the lower sash will be beveled properly. The width is measured from jamb to jamb.

The height of a vinyl replacement window is measured from the inside of the sill to the top of the jamb, which is slightly different from the height measurement for a jamb liner kit.

Sill angle (14 degrees is standard)

Metal attachment clips are nailed to the existing jamb to secure the new jamb liner. The clips on each side must align vertically and opposing clips must be equidistant from each other.

New jamb liners snap in place over the clips.

Shopping for Vinyl Windows

Whether you're shopping for vinyl replacement windows or complete vinyl windows for new construction, here are a few tips to help you make an educated choice:

- Look for thick-walled *extrusions* (frame members). Try flexing a wide window in the showroom to see if it bends easily.
- Check for metal reinforcement. Metal strengthens extrusions but reduces thermal efficiency somewhat.
- Look for heat-welded corners, which are superior to mechanically fastened ones.
- Test the hardware. If it looks delicate or flimsy, it may soon wear out.
- Look for the American Architectural Manufacturer's Association (AAMA) certification label.
- Ask how long the manufacturer has been in business. Local fabricators come and go, but some have become regional leaders with excellent track records.

an attachment clip to the top, middle, and bottom of each jamb. Align the clips vertically with a straightedge, shimming them if necessary. Also make sure that the distance between opposing clips is consistent. Then snap the jamb liners in place over the clips. Press the replacement parting beads into the head jamb with the weatherstripping facing outward. The jamb liner is now complete.

As with a traditional double-hung windows, the new top sash is installed first, followed by the bottom sash. Spring-loaded carriers that slide up and down inside the jamb liners carry the sashes. To install the sashes, first pull the carriers about three-quarters of the way down from the top of the window and lock them

there temporarily with a screwdriver. Then tilt the bottom of the sash into the opening. The metal tabs on the sides of the sash should extend into the grooves in the jamb liners. Flip the sash upward and snap it over the ribs on the jamb liner. It helps if you compress the jamb liner with one hand as you press the sash with the other hand.

After snapping the sash into place, lower it onto the carriers. The metal tabs will automatically engage the carriers and release them, at which point the sashes will be counterbalanced. Now you can reinstall the interior stops, but check them to make sure they don't interfere with tilting the sashes. If they do, you'll have to rip them down slightly.

A spring-loaded carrier is locked temporarily at mid-height. Metal tabs on the sashes will ride up and down in these carriers.

> "The typical vinyl replacement window has a vinyl frame that fits within an existing wooden frame … a quicker and neater solution than replacing the entire window and frame."

TAKE YOUR PICK

Insulating Weight Pockets

If pocket covers are present, remove them and fish the weights out of the pockets. Remove the rope pulleys, as well. Now you can stuff strips of fiberglass insulation into the pocket from both ends. You could also pour in vermiculite or blow in cellulose. When the pockets are full, replace the pocket covers and tape over the pulley holes with duct tape. If no pocket covers are present, you can try insulating through the pulley hole alone, or you can gain access by removing the interior casings.

Installing nontilt jamb liner kits

Nontilt jamb liners and sashes fit together as a unit that slides straight into the opening. An extra pair of hands is helpful to keep the unit bundled together during insertion. Once the interior stops are installed, the jamb liners are held captive, so you need just two nails to hold them in place. Drive one nail at the top of the lower sash channel and the other nail at the bottom of the upper sash channel.

Nontilt jamb liners accommodate old sashes as well as new ones, though you may need to remove some paint to get the sashes to fit properly in the new tracks. Some routing on the edges of the sashes may be required, as well.

The upper sash is tipped into the opening. When both tabs have engaged their respective carriers, the sash will be flipped up to its normal position.

The installer depresses the jamb liner with his thumb to squeeze in the top of the sash. When he releases the pressure on the jamb liner, the sash is captured in the track.

Installing Vinyl Replacement Windows

The term *vinyl replacement window* is confusing. On one hand, you can tear out an old window down to the rough opening and replace it with a new vinyl window complete with a sill and exterior trim. The replacement procedure is basically the same as for a wooden window. However, the typical vinyl replacement window has a vinyl frame that fits within an existing wooden frame. This is a quicker and neater solution than replacing the entire window and frame.

Measuring and Specifying

As with a jamb liner kit, the width of a vinyl replacement unit is measured between the existing side jambs. However, the height is measured

---

TOOLS AND MATERIALS

Size Flexibility: Jamb Liner Kits vs. Vinyl Replacements

Vinyl replacement windows are typically made to order by local fabricators and offer excellent size flexibility. Units can typically be ordered in any ⅛-in. increment of width and any ¼-in. increment of height. In contrast, standard wood jamb liner kits jump by 4-in. increments of width and height. If your old window is a standard size, you can probably find a jamb liner kit to replace it. If it's an oddball size, you're in trouble, because trimming a wooden window permits only minor fitting adjustments.

IN DETAIL

Adjusting the Action of Vinyl Replacements

A pair of jack screws located at mid-height on each side adjusts the up and down action of the sashes. If the fit is too tight, back off the screws. If the fit is too sloppy, drive the screws forward to push against the old jamb. You may need to tilt the sashes inward to access the jack screws. In that case, pull the release clips at the upper corners of each sash to permit tilting.

from the *inside* of the sill to the top jamb, which is slightly different from the height measurement for a jamb liner kit (see drawing, p. 177). Vinyl replacement windows have a square bottom, so if the height measurement isn't taken at the high point of the sill, the unit won't fit. A snap-in filler strip conceals the gap between the square bottom of the new unit and the old sloped sill.

Installation

The hardware used for attaching and adjusting vinyl replacement windows varies from one

Measure between existing side jambs to determine the width of the vinyl replacements.

Set the unit on the floor to snap in the filler strips. Then trim the filler to the right width with tin snips.

> "Vinyl replacement windows have a square bottom, so if the height measurement isn't taken at the high point of the sill, the unit won't fit."

WHAT CAN GO WRONG

Check the Diagonals

When measuring for a vinyl replacement, check the diagonals of the existing wooden frame. If the frame is racked, you will need to make an extra deduction in the height.

TRADE SECRET

B e sure to cut the tip of a caulk tube cleanly with a sharp utility knife. A rough-cut tip leaves a messy bead that's hard to control.

manufacturer to the next. Read the manufacturer's instructions before you tackle the job yourself. Carefully remove the interior stops from the old window and save them for reuse. Then remove the old sashes, parting beads, and sash pulleys. Test the fit of the new unit in the opening and measure the gap between the old sill and the bottom of the replacement frame. Remove the unit, lay it on the floor, snap in the filler strip, and trim the strip to the correct width with snips.

Apply a bead of caulk to the back of the old blind stop along the sides and top of the opening. Then set the unit in place. Place the bottom of the unit in the opening first to clear the old stool. Lock the unit to square it up and then drive one screw at each corner through the jambs, shimming them if necessary. The two upper screws are located in the inner-sash channels, and the two lower screws are located in the outer-sash channels. To complete the installation, caulk lightly between the vinyl jamb and the wooden jamb on the inside, then reinstall the interior stop. Finally, caulk around the unit on the outside.

A bead of caulk is applied along the top and sides of the opening.

The unit is placed bottom first.

IN DETAIL
Lacquer Thinner for Putty Removal

You can soften putty by mopping it with lacquer thinner. Lay the sash flat, so that the thinner can eat its way under the putty. After five or ten minutes, the putty will break off in large chunks. Unfortunately, this method is practical only if you happen to be removing the entire sash at the same time you're reglazing it—for instance, if you're replacing sash ropes. It won't work with a vertical sash, because the thinner will run off too easily. Lacquer thinner is highly flammable so *never* use it with a heat gun.

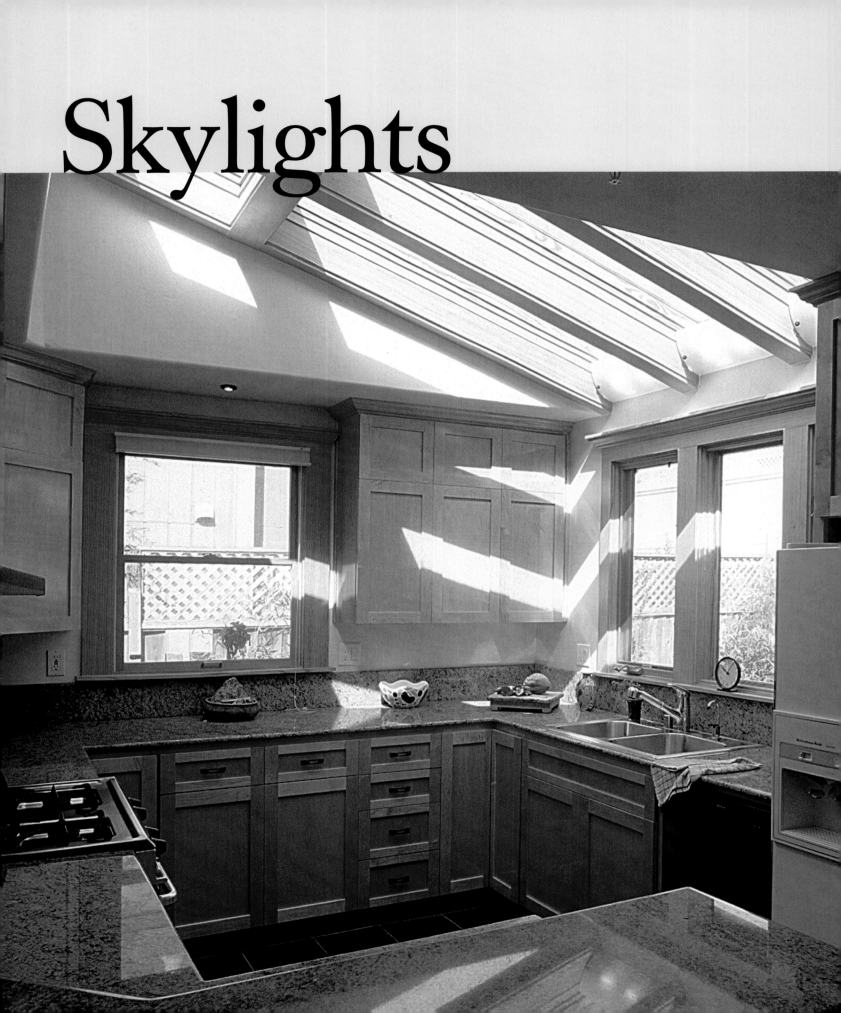

Skylights

CHAPTER TWELVE

Skylights can work magic, transforming a dark kitchen or a dusty attic into a bright, airy space. They're great for ventilating steamy bathrooms, and versatile enough to go in both flat and cathedral ceilings. Skylights have a downside, however. They foster intense solar gain in summer and lose more heat in the winter than a comparably sized conventional window. Perhaps their biggest liability is their potential for leaks. Skylights are less forgiving of faulty installation than windows, but installing them properly is not difficult. The trickiest part of the job is the flashing, which we'll explore as I walk you through a common installation in an asphalt-shingle roof. Finally, we'll take a look at installing skylights in less common roofing materials, such as metal and tile.

Choosing a Skylight

Back in the 1970s, most skylights were either homemade affairs or low-tech solutions. Remember those plastic bubble skylights? Then the energy crunch sparked interest in solar design, and manufacturers began developing sophisticated skylights that were truly watertight and energy efficient. Today, you can select from a wide range of models and accessories.

Operating types

There are two broad classes of skylights. *Fixed* skylights, as their name implies, don't open. They bring in light but not air. *Venting* skylights, which do open, are very effective for siphoning off hot air and steam, but their cost typically runs about 70% more than fixed units of the same size.

These Blefa tilt-turn skylights can be operated in a top-hinged mode (left) or a tilt mode (right). The tilt mode permits easy cleaning of the outside glass surface.

The Roto roof door provides unobstructed egress capability. This installation's special flashing kit features a lead apron that conforms to the roof tiles.

Venting skylights are available in three different operating types. The simplest type is a *top-hinged* skylight, and the sash opens like an awning window. This arrangement lets the screen stay in place at all times, or you can remove the screen in winter for greater clarity. *Tilt-turn* models have sophisticated operating hardware that allows them to function in two modes. In one mode, the sash hinges at the top like a simple top-hinged unit; in the other mode, the sash rotates to allow cleaning from the inside. To rotate the sash, the screen must be removed. In addition to easy cleaning, large tilt-turn skylights can satisfy code require-

> *"Large skylights should be approached with caution, not just because they're energy losers, but also because they require serious structural modifications."*

IN DETAIL

Standard Spacing for Rafters and Trusses

Stock skylight sizes are coordinated with the standard spacing of roof rafters and roof trusses. Trusses are typically spaced 24 in. on center (o.c.), while rafters are more often spaced 16 in. o.c. The resulting standard bay widths (after deducting 1½ in. for the thickness of the rafter or truss) are 22½ in. for 24-in. o.c. spacing and 14½ in. for 16-in. o.c. spacing. A double-bay spacing is either 46½ in. for 24-in. o.c. trusses or 30½ in. for 16-in. o.c. rafters. To simplify framing, R.O. widths for skylights usually correspond to these figures.

ments for emergency egress. The third operating type, called a *roof door,* is hinged at the side. This type, made by Roto (800-787-7099), is especially well suited for emergency egress, because the opening is completely unobstructed when the "door" is open.

Choosing the right size and orientation

Large skylights should be approached with caution, not just because they're energy losers, but also because they require serious structural modifications. Their large rough openings require headers at the top and bottom to transfer the weight of the roof to the neighboring uncut rafters, which also have to be doubled to carry the additional load. Beefing up rafters isn't too difficult in new construction, but it's tough in a remodel.

The easiest skylights to frame are units that fit between regularly spaced rafters or trusses. You can achieve greater width and still keep your framing simple by placing these narrow units side by side, with rafters remaining between them. Another alternative is to use a wide skylight with the rafters simply left in place. There's no conflict between the skylight's frame and the rafters, because the frame sits on top of the roof. The intervening rafters can be left exposed or wrapped with drywall or trim.

To prevent excessive solar gain, skylights should be sized at no more than 5% to 15% of the room's floor area. The orientation is important, too. North-facing skylights provide diffuse

Exposed rafters fly through the space below a wide skylight. This arrangement makes headers and beefed-up side rafters unnecessary.

light, while south-facing skylights admit strong light that creates shadows. Avoid a western exposure, because it will really cook the interior on summer afternoons.

Flashing

Some skylights have interchangeable flashing kits, so that you can order the type of flashing best suited to your roofing material. Other skylights come with only one type of flashing. To make an intelligent decision, you need to understand the difference between *continuous side flashing* and *step flashing.* The flashing components at the top and bottom of the skylight (called the *head flashing* and the *apron* respectively) are similar in both systems, but the side flashing is different.

TAKE YOUR PICK

Shading Options

Each skylight manufacturer has its own system for shading, so it's best to compare them in the showroom to find what you prefer. Translucent fabric shades merely reduce light, and venetian blinds can shade completely. Pella blinds are unique because they operate between the panes of the insulating glass, which protects them from dust and damage.

According to Code

The higher a skylight is situated, the more illumination and ventilation it provides. On the other hand, a low skylight is easier to operate by hand or by pole and may provide a better view. If you're planning for a skylight to provide emergency egress, your local building code will specify a height limit above the floor.

IN DETAIL

Skylight Finishes

Most stock skylights are clad with aluminum that is finished in basic brown, but some manufacturers offer a wider choice of colors that can be specially ordered. You can even have a skylight custom-painted at the factory—for a hefty price. Another way to modify its appearance is to order mill-finished (unpainted) aluminum or copper as the cladding and flashing material.

Roto skylights are available in a variety of colors. These "sweet-sixteen" units fit between standard 16-in. on center rafters. Mullion flashing is used to join the units side to side.

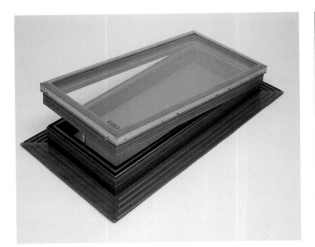

This copper-clad skylight by Sun-Tek® Skylights has continuous side flashing. Ribs in the side flashing keep water from wandering sideways.

Continuous side flashing

Skylights with continuous side flashing have an uninterrupted fin running down each side, with the roofing material laid over it. The problem with this system is that water tends to spread out as it runs down along the skylight (the lower the pitch of the roof, the wider the spread). Water that spreads out far enough can work its way under the edge of continuous side flashing, causing a leak. Due to this tendency, I prefer to use step flashing whenever possible, even though it's more time consuming to install than continuous flashing.

Step flashing

Step flashing consists of small, overlapping squares of metal or plastic bent into an *L* shape. These steps are woven into succeeding courses of roof shingles as the shingles are laid, and the upturned

This cutaway view of a Velux® skylight shows step flashing fitted between the wooden curb and the asphalt shingles.

portion of each step flashing fits tightly against the wooden frame (or *curb*) of the skylight. Water is shed to the exterior every few inches (at every shingle course), so it never gets a chance to wander very far under the roofing. Step flashing relies on gravity, a more powerful and durable force than any sealant.

Step flashing doesn't work on a low-pitch membrane roof where everything, including the skylight flashing, is adhered with some type of sealant. It also doesn't work on a sloped metal roof, because metal roof panels overlap vertically

> "Water that spreads out far enough can work its way under the edge of continuous side flashing, causing a leak."

IN DETAIL

Sealing Continuous Side Flashing

There are two strategies to prevent leakage in continuous side flashing. First, continuous side flashing can be ribbed or folded up along the outside edge to repel seepage. Second, sealant can be applied between the roofing material and the flashing. Unfortunately, a folded-up edge creates a slight bump in the roofing and sealant can fail over time.

IN DETAIL

Solar Heat Gain Coefficient

The solar heat gain coefficient (SHGC) is a rating of the amount of heat a window or skylight adds to an interior. A higher SHGC is an asset in cold climates but a liability in hot ones. Solar gain is measured on a scale of 0 to 1. A higher decimal indicates more solar gain. Suggested ratings are: Northern U.S., .55 or above; temperate climates, .40 to .55; Southern U.S., .40 or below.

Framing and Finishing a Skylight Opening

Framing a skylight opening in a new roof is easy. I usually leave out the rafters where a skylight will be located when I'm framing the regularly spaced full-length rafters for a new roof. The first thing I do is establish the elevation (the up and down location) of the skylight and draw the profile of the headers on the sides of the rafters.

The orientation of the headers greatly affects the amount of light that reaches the room. The top header is typically set perpendicular to the roof, while the bottom header is set vertically. The resulting splayed opening lets in more light and provides more clearance for removing a screen. A vertically set header needs to be cut

Step flashing needs careful subflashing.

rather than horizontally. Special flashing kits are available for these conditions (see Installing a Special Skylight, p. 196). Finally, step flashing leaves gaps that air can penetrate and must be carefully subflashed with roofing felt.

Glazing

In general, the same glazing options available for windows apply to skylights. However, since skylights are more directly exposed to the sun, you should pay special attention to the solar heat gain coefficient (SHGC) if you live in a hot climate. Good UV blockage is also essential to protect household fabrics, so always opt for low-e glass.

(see Installing a Special Skylight, p. 196)

Two methods can be used to set a vertical header between sloping rafters. The top and bottom edges of the header can be beveled (top) or the two halves of the header can be offset (bottom). Offsetting is quicker, but beveling provides better drywall support.

IN DETAIL

Low-e Coatings

Low-e coatings are invisible films applied to insulated glass (IG) units to reflect heat while admitting visible light. Make sure you get the correct type for your area. For cold climates, the low-e coating reflects heat back to the inside; in hot climates, it reflects the heat of sunlight to the outside.

TRADE SECRET

The lower wall of a lightwell meets the skylight curb at an oblique angle, making it difficult to determine the precise base of the skylight opening. To provide a margin of error, add 1 in. to the bottom of the R.O. You can then pack the opening later with shims, using a scrap of ½-in. plywood as a gauge to simulate the drywall.

A workman uses a scrap of ½-in. plywood to simulate drywall. This tells him how much to pack the oversize opening with shims.

A bottom cripple is fitted between a vertical skylight header and the bottom of the roof.

from wider stock than that for the rafters and its top and bottom edges need to be beveled. Or you can simply stagger the two halves of the doubled header. When you tack the headers in position between the rafters, make sure they're level and pull diagonal measurements to make sure the opening is square. Then nail off the headers and double the rafters on each side of the skylight.

Depending on the skylight's size and position in the opening, you may have to add jack rafters between the top and bottom headers to make the opening narrower. Then add any necessary cripple rafters from the top header to the ridge and from the bottom header to the plate.

Framing a lightwell

A lightwell conveys light from a skylight to a flat ceiling. To maximize light, the front and back of the lightwell are oriented the same as the skylight headers—the upper side runs perpendicular to the roof and the lower side runs vertically. The lateral sides of the lightwell can be splayed, as well, but this greatly complicates the framing. The opening in a flat ceiling requires double joists on each side and doubled headers, as well. Code may require joist hangers for all of the connections.

You can frame the sides of a lightwell with studs or use ¾-in. CD plywood to back up the drywall. Studs make it easier to install fiberglass insulation on the sides of the lightwell, but plywood is quicker and easier to install. If you opt for plywood, use the pieces as templates for the drywall.

Installing a Lightwell and Skylight in Existing Construction

Locate the lightwell's approximate location on the ceiling and set up a dust screen around the work area. To support the ceiling during surgery, go to the attic and nail 2×4 *strongbacks* across the tops of the joists. Position the strongbacks about 1 ft. back from the ends of the opening, with their ends resting on the nearest uncut ceiling joists.

Locate the skylight in relation to the lightwell. If there's plenty of headroom in the attic, you can do this before cutting through the ceiling. If the attic is low, remove some ceiling drywall first so

IN DETAIL
Doubling the Rafters

Doubling the rafters *after* installing the headers lets you nail through the rafters into the headers. This is easier than toenailing a header to a previously doubled rafter. For extra insurance, use framing clips to reinforce the rafter-header connection.

TRADE SECRET

Joist hangers can cause ugly bumps in ceiling drywall. To raise them out of the way, notch the undersides of the headers slightly with a jigsaw to make the hangers flush with the bottom of the joists.

you can work from the room below. Cut the drywall several inches inside the proposed layout, in case you need to make adjustments later.

Use a framing square to project the sloping upper wall of the lightwell perpendicular to the roof, and use a plumb bob or level to lay out the vertical lower wall. With the locations of the lightwell and skylight firmly established, you can now trim back the ceiling drywall and cut out the intervening sections of ceiling joist. Cut the joists 3⅛ in. back from the edges of the opening, so that the new double 2× headers are flush with the edge of the opening.

Drive nails up through the roof at the opening's corners. Then remove all the roof shingles within 1 ft. of the layout. Finally, cut out the roof sheathing from above with a circular saw before reframing the roof. If you're unsure about the precise location of the skylight, cut a

Locating a Skylight

Outline the approximate location of the skylight on the ceiling with painter's tape, which won't damage drywall. Skylights in cathedral ceilings can be located easily enough, but when the skylight is above a flat ceiling, you'll need to locate the lightwell first. Remember that the lightwell's opening is longer than the skylight's because the lightwell has a sloped end.

Make a rough estimation of the lightwell's length by drawing a cross section of the attic and the skylight to scale. Try to locate the skylight so that it falls between existing ceiling joists and rafters. If not, at least try to line up one side of the new opening with some existing framing. You can position the front-to-back location of the lightwell according to your preference, as long as the elevation of the skylight in the roof is negotiable up or down.

Watch out for obstructions. In the case of a cathedral ceiling, there's no way to see behind the drywall, so use a sensor to detect the presence of wires. If wires are present, seriously consider shifting the skylight's location. If the ceiling is flat, drive nails at the corners of the proposed lightwell for reference, and then go up in the attic to look for problems. Wires are fairly easy to reroute in an attic, but ducts and pipes are more troublesome. Be aware that rerouting may cause building-code problems.

Installing a lightwell

The locations of the lightwell and the skylight are coordinated from below after partially removing the ceiling drywall. When the layout is complete, the ceiling joist to be cut is supported by strongbacks, while the rafter to be cut is supported by struts. Headers are installed after cutting the necessary joists and rafters. Then the ceiling drywall is trimmed back and the roof sheathing is removed.

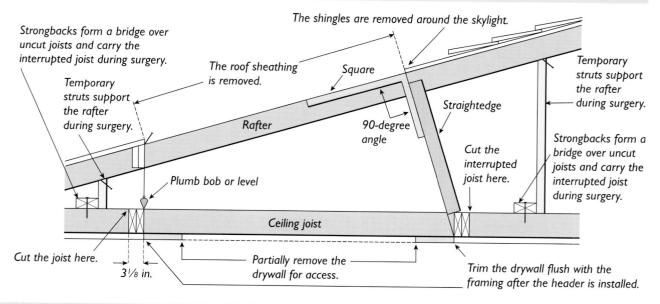

Strongbacks form a bridge over uncut joists and carry the interrupted joist during surgery.

The shingles are removed around the skylight.

The roof sheathing is removed.

Square

Temporary struts support the rafter during surgery.

Temporary struts support the rafter during surgery.

Rafter

90-degree angle

Straightedge

Cut the interrupted joist here.

Strongbacks form a bridge over uncut joists and carry the interrupted joist during surgery.

Plumb bob or level

Ceiling joist

Cut the joist here.

3⅛ in.

Partially remove the drywall for access.

Trim the drywall flush with the framing after the header is installed.

Roof Hips and Valleys

Don't locate a skylight on a hip or valley in the roof. Hip and valley rafters are usually visible in the attic, but when one roof is built on top of another, the valley is visible only from outside. Check from outside to make sure this isn't the case. If a hip or valley is present, you'll have to relocate the skylight.

TRADE SECRET

Some carpenters prefer to frame the skylight opening before cutting through the roof, but I like to open the roof first for light and air.

IN DETAIL
Installing Skylights Between Trusses

Installing skylights in a new trussed roof is not a problem. The truss fabricator furnishes special short trusses to fill in above and below the skylight, and the side trusses are beefed up to carry the extra load. However, adding a skylight to an existing trussed roof is another matter. You can't take a chunk out of a truss the way you can with a rafter, because the rest of the truss will be adversely affected. Your only option is to use a skylight that just fits into a standard bay (space) between trusses. For more light, you can place multiple skylights in a row, with the trusses in between.

A truss roof can be engineered to accept a wide skylight. Here, trusses have been doubled at the sides of the opening. A short tail truss below the opening is carried on a header.

"If you're unsure about the precise location of the skylight, cut a 'breather hole' first, and then trim back the remaining sheathing after the opening is framed."

Removing Asphalt Shingles

Asphalt shingles that are fairly new are flexible enough to bend upward. If you can lift the shingle enough, use a cat's paw or a flat bar to pull the nails in the course below. Old asphalt shingles, however, are too brittle to lift, so you'll need a shingle ripper. This tool has a long, flat tongue with notches in the end. Slide the tongue up under the shingle, hook it on the nail, and then beat down on the tool's handle to yank the nail out. A shingle ripper also works well for naturally rigid shingles, such as wood and slate.

Start removing shingles at the top and work your way down. The first course is the toughest, because the nails are hidden underneath the course above. After the uppermost course is removed, the nails in each succeeding course are exposed, making them easy to pull.

Asphalt shingles that are fairly new can be bent upward, allowing you to pull nails with a cat's paw.

Old asphalt shingles are too brittle to bend, so a shingle ripper is slipped underneath.

Part of an existing rafter is removed to make room for a skylight. A reciprocating saw is used to make the cut.

A header is reinforced with joist hangers where it connects the adjoining rafters.

"breather hole" first, and then trim back the remaining sheathing after the opening is framed.

Support the rafters with temporary struts to the ceiling joists below, then cut out the necessary sections. Install the new headers, check them for square and level, and add the joist hangers.

Next, double the full-length rafters flanking the opening. These rafters need to be cut about 1 ft. shorter than the originals to maneuver them into place, but they still do their job of reinforcing the existing rafters. If you need to reduce the width of the opening, add jack rafters between the headers.

Skylight curbs are grooved on their lower edges to receive the finish materials of drywall or plywood. This skylight is unusual because it's connected to the roof with metal straps instead of brackets.

A jack rafter is fitted between the top and bottom headers and a 2x4 is used to lever the jack rafter into position for nailing. A portion of the existing rafter that was removed has been recycled as the jack rafter.

"Make sure you have the right flashing kit for the model you're installing."

Interior finishing

Skylight curbs are grooved on their inside edge, and drywall or other finishing material fits into these grooves at the top of the lightwell (see bottom left photo, p. 191). A typical treatment for the bottom of the lightwell where it meets the ceiling is spackled corner bead, but if you've added a skylight to an existing ceiling, this means repainting the entire ceiling. An alternative is to use wood trim, which is quicker and neater to install. I've found that a quick-setting joint compound (such as Durabond 90) is better for corners and joints than slower drying drywall mud, because it lets me finish the job in a single day.

Installing a Skylight in an Asphalt-Shingle Roof

Installing and flashing a factory-built skylight in an asphalt-shingle roof is pretty straightforward. Asphalt shingles are flexible, easy to cut, and uniform in thickness. If everything overlaps correctly, there shouldn't be any problems. Make sure you have the right flashing kit for the model you're installing.

A Velux skylight surrounded by its "armor" before installation. From left to right: apron, bottom curb cap, side curb cap, step flashing, head flashing extension, head flashing, and sash hood.

Prepping the unit

After carefully unpacking the unit and removing the screen for safe keeping, lay it face up on a couple of 2×4s. Remove the sash hood and the top and bottom curb caps, laying them next to the unit. Spread out the parts from the flashing kit and rehearse the sequence in which everything goes together.

Next, prepare the mounting clips. Velux clips adjust up and down, thereby raising or lowering the curb relative to the roof surface. The correct height depends on the type of roofing used, with thick roofing requiring a higher curb. The goal is to have the top of the curb elevated just above the tops of the flashing.

A helper tweaks the unit from side to side with a prybar as the author reads a level. When the unit is level and centered in the opening, the mounting clips are screwed permanently to the roof.

Mounting the curb

Install a scaffold on the roof about 2 ft. below the skylight location. Use a scaffold plank at least 8 ft. long, so that you'll have enough working room. If the roof is too steep to walk on, lay a ladder alongside the opening with its feet planted firmly against the scaffold board.

Have an assistant hand you the skylight from inside and help you center it over the opening. Then screw the mounting clips to the roof, using only the clips' oblong holes. Your helper then fine-tunes the location from side to side with a prybar, while you make sure that the top and bottom are level. When everything is just right, drive the remaining screws.

Underlayment

At this point, you've installed shingles as high as the scaffold. Now it's time to prep the skylight with 30-lb. builder's felt. The felt, called

Underlayment

Felt underlayment prevents air leakage between the flashings and provides back-up moisture protection. Each of the four pieces of underlayment is folded against the curb and slit, so that the overhanging ends will lay flat.

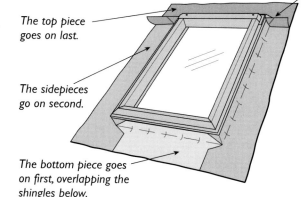

The top piece goes on last.

The sidepieces go on second.

The bottom piece goes on first, overlapping the shingles below.

Slits allow the overhanging ends to lay flat.

The ear is trimmed flush with the top of the curb and adhered with roof cement.

underlayment, prevents air leakage through the step flashing and also provides back-up water protection.

Lay the first piece with its bottom edge just overlapping the shingles and its top edge folded up

Roof Brackets

Roof brackets are triangular scaffold supports that have a flat tongue extending from the top. This tongue can be slipped under a shingle and nailed to the roof. To make the bracket easy to remove, the tongue has slots or tear-drop-shaped holes for nails, rather than plain holes. Instead of pulling the nails when the job is done, you simply hammer the bracket upward until the holes or slots clear the nail heads and the bracket pops off. The nails, which are left in the roof, are covered by shingles, so they won't leak.

Brackets *must* be nailed to rafters or trusses, not just to roof sheathing. I use 10d

common nails or 16d sinkers. Locating rafters under the shingles is easier if you've already driven nails up through the roof at the skylight location. Then you can find other rafters according to the rafter spacing.

Sometimes, a rafter falls close to the end of a shingle tab, and nailing there could cause a leak. In that case, simply drop down to the shingle course below. The offset between the shingle courses means that the tab below straddles the rafter.

IN DETAIL
Not All Mounting Clips Are Adjustable

Andersen mounting clips are not adjustable by height. They simply fold out and are secured with a single nail. This makes the clips easy to prepare, but if the roofing is extra thick, the tops of the flashing may need to be trimmed. In addition to the clips, Andersen fixed skylights have another feature that makes them easy to install. The sash is shipped unattached to the curb; after the curb is installed, the sash simply snaps over it. The unit is much easier to handle and center in the opening without the glass.

TRADE SECRET

When I'm fastening flashing and shingles with roof cement, I'm careful not to use big blobs of sealant, which can make water back up. Instead, I use roof cement that comes in a caulk tube to apply a neat "dot" of cement as a hidden fastener.

> "These full-width flanking shingles lay over the apron; the filler shingles below the skylight in the same course tuck under the apron."

against the skylight (see drawing, p. 193). Slit the resulting fold at the corners of the curb and lay the overhanging portions flat. Next, crease the sidepieces into position, make diagonal slits at all four corners of the curb, and fold the resulting triangular ears around the corners. Trim the ears just below the top edge of the curb and secure them with a dab of roof cement. Finally, install the top piece of underlayment so it reaches a few inches below the top of the skylight. The top piece's ears are likewise folded, trimmed, and cemented.

Installing the apron

After completing the underlayment, lay shingles up to the skylight, notching the last course to fit around the curb. Install the apron over the shingles, nailing the apron to the curb—*not* to the roof—with a single nail on each side. The neatest condition occurs when the bottom edge of the apron flashing aligns with a *butt line* (the lower edge of a shingle course). This is pretty easy to coordinate in a retrofit, because the shingles are already laid, but it rarely works out that way in new construction, unless you reconcile the elevation of the rough opening with the future shingles before framing the opening. That gets complicated.

When the apron *doesn't* align with a butt line, crosscut the first shingle tab that abuts the skylight on each side ¼ in. shy of the curb. These full-width flanking shingles lay *over* the apron; the filler shingles below the skylight in the same course tuck *under* the apron. This arrangement looks better than leaving the lower corners of the apron sticking out past the sides of the skylight

The apron is the first flashing to be installed. It wraps around the lower corners of the curb and laps over the roofing below.

(see drawing, facing page). To make sure that you don't nail through the apron when you're nailing the full-width shingles on top, use a small dab of roof cement. In fact, do this wherever a shingle is fastened over the flashing.

Step flashing

After the apron is installed, install shingles on both sides of the skylight, weaving step flashings between the shingles and the curb as you go. The shingles cover the flat portions of the step flashing, except for a ¼-in. gap alongside the curb to provide good drainage. Nail the upturned sides of the step flashing where they overlap the curb. Place the nails high enough, so that the curb caps cover them well. Trim the standing portion of the lowermost step flashing where it extends below the curb. Similarly, trim the standing portion of the uppermost step flashing flush with the top of the curb. In both cases, the flat portions remain uncut.

WHAT CAN GO WRONG
When Water Doesn't Drain into the Gutter

Water that strikes the head flashing just above the sash is supposed to drain into an extruded gutter on top of the curb. This may not happen, however, if extra-thick shingles push the head flashing up too high. To address this problem, Velux provides an extension that slips inside the head flashing. The extension isn't necessary, however, with regular asphalt shingles.

Flashing/shingle alignment

The neatest appearance is achieved by locating the skylight so the apron aligns with a shingle course (left). As an alternative, the shingle tabs in line with the curb are slit vertically (right), with one portion overlapping the apron and the other portion tucking under.

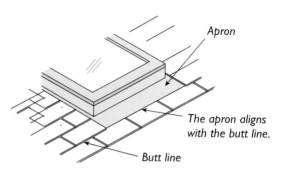

Apron

The apron aligns with the butt line.

Butt line

This part of the tab goes over the apron and is fastened with a dab of roof cement.

A nail under the apron holds the shingle.

The apron doesn't align with the butt line.

This part of the tab goes under the apron.

Head flashing

The head flashing wraps around the top of the curb and laps over the shingles flanking the skylight. Adhere the vertical edges of the head flashing to the felt underlayment with a bead of roof cement for extra protection against a backup. Then, lay a strip of felt above the head flashing with a sealed 1-in. overlap.

It's important to leave a wide expanse of bare flashing above the skylight between the curb and the shingles. This exposed strip of smooth metal helps flush away leaves and other debris, thus preventing a backup (pine needles can be particularly bad in this regard). The gap should be 2½ in. to 4 in. wide, with lower roof pitches requiring the larger gap. When the ¼-in. gap along the sides of the skylight between the curb and the shingles reaches the head flashing, enlarge it to ¾ in. This eases the bottleneck that occurs as runoff is diverted around the upper corners of the skylight.

Step flashing is nailed to the curb two at a time where they overlap; the nails are placed high enough to be covered by the side curb caps.

Part of the head flashing is left exposed, so that debris can be flushed away more easily by rain. Shingles that cover the ends of the head flashing are installed ¾ in. away from the curb, so that water can readily pass around the corner.

Unfortunately, exposed flashing can mar the sleek, distinct look of metal roofs. For that reason, professional roofers often make their own head and apron flashing from the same metal used for the roof. They also turn up the roof pan along the sides of the skylight. Aesthetically, this is the best solution, but there's a caveat: It creates an unavoidable Achilles' heel at the corners where the metal is cut to wrap around the curb. If the roofing metal is copper, terne, or galvanized, solder these vulnerable points.

"To flash a skylight in a metal roof, you can use the roof metal itself instead of a kit."

Installing a Special Skylight

Asphalt-shingle roofs are common everywhere, but tile, slate, and metal are also popular in some regions. When dealing with these less common roofing materials, you have two options: Hire a professional or do the job yourself with a special flashing kit. Roofers often make their own custom flashing—especially for metal roofs—and the results typically look better than factory flashing. For those with less experience, however, a factory flashing kit is the safest way to go.

Flashing tile roofs

Flashing kits for roofing tile include an exposed lead apron. The flexible apron conforms to the high, irregular profile of the tiles, so that rain can't blow underneath. Continuous side flashing is used instead of step flashing. Both the side flashing and the head flashing have an intermediate standing rib and a turned-up edge, thus creating a double barrier against water infiltration.

Although this type of flashing is commonly referred to as *tile flashing,* it's also used for other high-profile roofing materials, such as corrugated roofing, thick wooden shakes, and thick slates. Wooden shingles and thin slates are flashed with an ordinary step flashing kit.

Flashing metal roofs

The flashing kits sold for metal roofs are similar to tile flashing. A flexible apron laps over the ribs or standing seams below the skylight, but the side flashing has a channel into which the roof metal fits. The channel can receive only the flat portion of the roof metal, not a rib or a standing seam. Therefore, the side flashing has an extension, so that the flashing/roof metal interface can be shifted laterally to avoid a rib or a standing seam.

To flash a skylight in a metal roof, you can use the roof metal itself instead of a kit. The tricky part is sealing the corners of the head flashing. Copper can be soldered, but caulking is the only way to seal site-flashed corners made of prefinished steel. Manufactured flashing kits, on the other hand, have wraparound corners that are compression-sealed under factory conditions. Fortunately, there are now a number of high-performance caulks engineered specifically for metal. Check with the manufacturer of your roofing for a recommendation.

WHAT CAN GO WRONG

Don't Believe Everything You Read

Regardless of what the label says, the regular silicone caulk available at your local hardware store isn't adequate for sealing flashing on metal roofs. Use a sealant recommended by the roofing manufacturer.

Flashing for tile roofs has an exposed lead apron that can be molded to the tiles. The head and side flashing have ribs to block water that blows under the tiles. This type of flashing can be used with other high-profile roofing materials, such as corrugated metal or thick wooden shakes.

A flashing kit for metal roofs features an exposed apron and side flashing. An alternative is to use the roof metal itself as flashing.

Flashing multiple skylights

When skylights are installed side by side, U-shaped *mullion flashing* is used between the units. You can make this easily enough on a metal brake, but the manufacturer can also supply it. When ordering a mullion flashing, be sure to specify its width, because the rafters separating the skylights may be single or double.

When skylights are stacked vertically, it's best to use an H-flashing (or *transom flashing*) supplied by the manufacturer. This has wraparound corners, so it's difficult to make on site. Mullion or transom flashing may affect the R.O. dimensions, so check the framing specifications with your dealer.

Skylights on Shallow and Steep Roofs

An incline flashing kit raises a skylight in a low-pitch roof, so that water will drain off properly. The flashing comes in three pieces (top) and the skylight is installed over it (bottom).

Most off-the-shelf skylights are engineered for a minimum roof pitch of 4-in-12, which means the roof rises 4 ft. for every 12 ft. of building width. This corresponds to the minimum suggested pitch for asphalt shingles. If your roof has a somewhat shallower pitch (between 2-in-12 and 4-in-12), you can buy a special *incline flashing* that raises the skylight to the appropriate pitch. Incline flashing is adhered to low-pitch roofing materials, such as tar-and-gravel or rubber membrane roofing. (A word of caution: Incline flashing may alter the skylight's R.O.) Roofs between horizontal and 2-in-12 need extra-wide flashing built into the skylight unit.

There is also an upper limit to the acceptable pitch for off-the-shelf skylights. Such steep roofs are rare in residential construction, but if you plan on, say, installing a skylight in a mansard roof, you should investigate the manufacturer's recommendations. Typically, the manufacturer recommends using a *water deflector,* or wide Z-flashing similar to window head flashing.

Interior Trim

CHAPTER THIRTEEN

A doorway's personality comes as much from its trim as from the door itself, and the same holds true for windows. For instance, nothing says "1950s ranch" as clearly as the presence of clamshell casing on doors and windows. Greek Revival homes are marked by austere, dignified woodwork, whereas Victorian trim is a riotous mix of bull's eye corner blocks and heavy moldings.

Simple or ornate, installing interior trim is much the same for both doors and windows. Window trim usually terminates at the stool rather than at the floor, and has an apron that fits under the window stool. But otherwise, doors and windows are treated similarly. In this chapter, we'll learn how to install jamb extensions and trim out a typical window and door. For those who want a different look, try some of the trim options I suggest at the end of this chapter.

1 Installing Jamb Extensions, p. 200

2 Installing Door Trim, p. 204

3 Installing Window Trim, p. 207

4 Alternative Trim Styles, p. 212

Installing Jamb Extensions

Depending on the thickness of your wall, *jamb extensions* (filler strips that bring a jamb out flush with the plane of the wall) may or may not be required. Usually, door and window jambs come in standard widths to accommodate standard wall thicknesses. When the thickness of a wall strays from the ordinary, however, jamb extensions make up the difference.

Jamb extensions aren't often required for interior doors in new construction, because there aren't many variables with which to contend. Most walls are 2×4 construction with drywall on both sides, so a standard 4⁹⁄₁₆-in. jamb works fine (the extra ¹⁄₁₆ in. is for gaps and/or warped studs). In remodeling work, however, jamb extensions are a fact of life due to such factors as plaster walls and old, roughsawn 2×4 studs that actually measure 2 in. by 4 in. rather than the 1½ in. by 3½ in. dimensions of modern studs. Myriad other variables add up to a free-for-all of wall thicknesses.

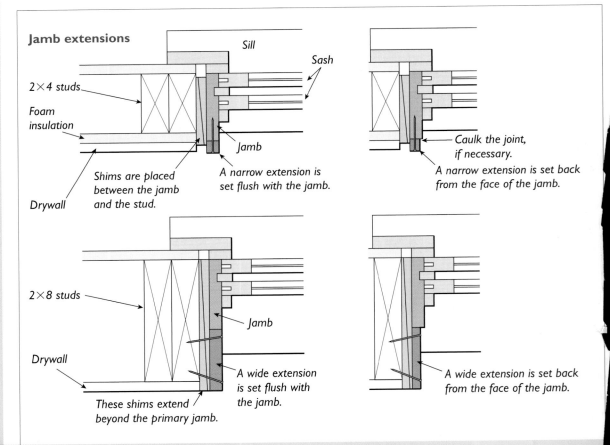

Jamb extensions

- 2×4 studs
- Foam insulation
- Drywall
- Sill
- Sash
- Jamb
- Shims are placed between the jamb and the stud.
- A narrow extension is set flush with the jamb.
- Caulk the joint, if necessary.
- A narrow extension is set back from the face of the jamb.
- 2×8 studs
- Drywall
- Jamb
- A wide extension is set flush with the jamb.
- These shims extend beyond the primary jamb.
- A wide extension is set back from the face of the jamb.

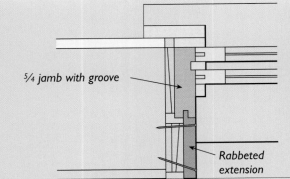

⁵⁄₄ jamb with groove

Rabbeted extension

Jamb extensions can be applied in different ways, depending on field conditions. A narrow extension can be nailed directly to the jamb (top left). Reducing the thickness of a narrow extension produces a setback that obscures the joint (top right). Wide jamb extensions are nailed through shims and into the studs (center left). Wide extensions can be set back, as well (center right). Rabbeted extensions fit into a groove in the primary jamb (bottom).

> *"In remodeling work, however, jamb extensions are a fact of life due to such factors as plaster walls and old, roughsawn 2×4 studs."*

Extension types

Jamb extensions can be *square edged* or *rabbeted*. As its name implies, a square-edged jamb extension has a simple rectangular cross section. Jamb extensions made on site are usually of this type. Rabbeted jamb extensions have an L-shaped profile and are typically supplied by the door or window manufacturer. The projecting tongue slips into a groove milled in the edge of the primary jamb. This aligns the face of the jamb extension perfectly with the unit's primary jamb, thereby making installation easier.

Jamb extensions can be installed in one of two ways, depending on their width (see drawing, facing page). Narrow extensions up to 1½ in. wide can simply be glued and nailed to the edge

Jamb extensions: Which side of the door?

Jamb extensions should be mounted on the edge of the jamb that's opposite the hinge (left). The door can then fold back against the wall. When extensions are mounted on the same side as the hinge, the swing of the door is restricted (right).

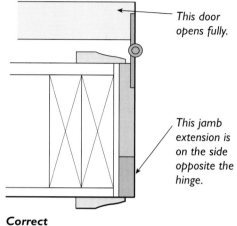
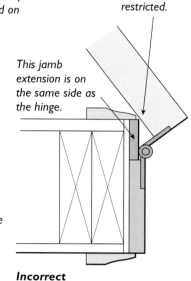

This door's motion is restricted.

This door opens fully.

This jamb extension is on the same side as the hinge.

This jamb extension is on the side opposite the hinge.

Correct   **Incorrect**

A set of wide jamb extensions is added to a window. The extensions will be face-nailed to the shims at the top and bottom of the opening. You can add the shims after the window is installed or you can simply leave an overhang on the shims that are used to wedge the window in place.

of the primary jamb. Size the nails to be twice the width of the extension. Shorter nails won't hold well, while longer nails are apt to wander and poke through the face of the primary jamb, especially in coarse-grained woods, such as fir. Extensions that are wider than ¾ in. should be predrilled to make nailing easier and more accurate. The pilot hole should be just a hair smaller than the diameter of the finish nails you're using.

If you have jamb extensions that are wider than 1½ in., it's best to face nail them to the jack studs and header, nailing through the same shims that wedge the primary jamb in place. When you initially shim the door or window unit, remember to leave your shims sticking out past the edge of the primary jamb to receive extensions later.

TRADE SECRET

f the trim will be painted, then it is safe to glue the joints. However, if the work will be stained or coated with a clear finish, skip the glue, because it can cause finishing problems later. You may not see dried glue on raw wood, but it shows up after staining as a light-colored smear or spot. The spot occurs because the glue seals the pores of the wood and thus prevents stain from penetrating. The only remedy is deep scraping and sanding followed by restaining.

Jamb Extension on the Hinge Side

The one case where an extension on the hinge edge may be considered is for an in-swing exterior door or casement window that already has the exterior casing and sill attached. You can't extend the outside edge of the jamb without rebuilding the entire unit, so you can use an interior jamb extension as a compromise. It should be set back as much as possible from the face of the jamb to allow the door to swing past 90 degrees. This is a less-than-satisfactory fix, so it's critical that the jamb width be specified correctly when ordering in-swing exterior doors and casements.

Thin Jamb Extensions Can Split

A reduced-thickness jamb extension is even more likely to split than a standard-thickness jamb extension, so be sure to predrill.

> "If the dimensions vary by more than ⅛ in., then you'll have to taper the cuts to conform to the wall."

Jamb extensions can be mounted flush with the primary jamb or set back slightly, like a casing. Flush joints will be almost invisible if the mating edges are planed perfectly straight (more on that below). If you don't have planing equipment, a setback, or "reveal," will effectively obscure the joint. To produce a setback the jamb extensions may need to be reduced in thickness, which you can do by *resawing* them (ripping them on edge) with a table saw.

When adding extensions to door jambs, the extension should go on the edge of the jamb that's opposite the hinges. This will leave the barrel of the hinge where it belongs—sticking out past the wall. That way, the door can fold back against the wall without binding on the casing. If an extension is added to the hinge edge of the

Jamb extensions with a consistent width can be ripped on a table saw.

jamb, the barrel of the hinge will be recessed in the opening and the door will open only partway (see drawing, p. 201).

Out-swing exterior doors and windows are always set flush with the outside, and jamb extensions (if necessary) are applied on the inside. Many window manufacturers don't even try to match a standard wall thickness with their window jambs. Instead, the unit comes with a narrow primary jamb and the necessary extensions to fit either a 2×4 or a 2×6 wall.

Measuring and cutting jamb extensions

To measure the width of your jamb extensions, hold a long straightedge that spans the width of the door or window opening against the wall.

To measure the required width of jamb extensions, hold a straightedge against the wall surface. Check the dimension at several locations, because it may vary.

Sometimes, jamb extensions must vary in width to conform to uneven walls. You can get around this to some extent by letting the casing lay less than flat, but the more you do this, the worse your miters will fit and the more obvious the discrepancy will be. Also, gaps will appear, either between the casing and the jamb or between the casing and the drywall. When the difference in width between both ends of the jamb extension exceeds ⅛ in., it should be tapered to match the discrepancy. This tapered cut is best done with a bandsaw or a jigsaw.

A mini-jointer is used to plane a jamb extension so it will fit tightly against the primary jamb.

A power plane is used to quickly reduce a jamb extension to the required width.

doesn't already have a smooth factory edge can be *jointed* (planed straight) on one edge before being ripped. The best tool for this is a *jointer*. If you're comfortable with hand tools, you can also use a long handplane (#06 or #07) to joint the edge. After jointing, run the clean edge against the table saw's fence. When installed, the jointed edge will fit tightly against the primary jamb without a gap.

The ripped edge of the extension faces the room. The edge will show slightly where the casing is set back from the jamb. To smooth it, set the table saw's fence to rip the extension about 1/16 in. *heavy,* or extra-wide, and then plane the extension to the final dimension. Planing can be done before the extension is installed or *in situ* with a block plane or power planer. Planing after installation is time-consuming, but it's the most accurate way to conform a jamb extension to an undulating wall surface.

Measure the gap between the unit and the straightedge in several locations—at the top, middle, and bottom at least—because it may vary.

Jamb extensions are usually ripped to width on a table saw. If the required dimension is consistent, set a fence to rip all of the extensions to the same width. If the dimensions vary by more than 1/8 in., then you'll have to taper the cuts to conform to the wall. Jamb extension stock that

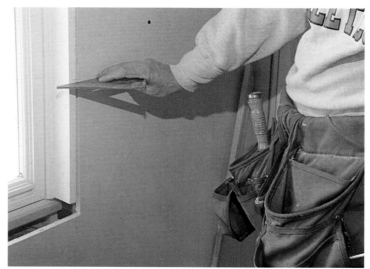

A carpenter uses his speed square to see if a jamb is flush with the drywall.

SAFETY FIRST

A workpiece that inadvertently twists against a spinning table saw blade will be hurled back at the operator. It can cause injury, amputation, or even death. If kickback occurs, your hand may very likely be dragged across the spinning blade. To minimize the risks associated with kickback, always use a fence when ripping lumber. Never cut freehand. Never reach beyond the blade! Use a push stick to guide the workpiece. Always stand with your body to one side of the line of cut and never behind the workpiece, so that if there is kickback, you won't get hit. To protect your face, wear a full face shield—not just goggles.

TRADE SECRET

When a door or window frame is out of square, the casings must be mitered at slightly more than 45 degrees at one corner and slightly less than 45 degrees at the other. On some miter saws, swinging the turntable *slightly* away from 45 degrees can be difficult, because the positive stops want to kick in. It may be easier to shim between the workpiece and the fence to change the cutting angle. The closer the shim is to the blade, the greater the deviation is from 45 degrees.

TRADE SECRET

If you're using air nailers, it's nice to have two set up with different nail lengths. If only one nailer is available, nail both edges of the casing with 2-in. brads or staples.

> "If the wall sticks out beyond the jamb, you can compensate a little by pulverizing the drywall with a hammer."

A block plane is used to trim back a jamb. If the plane is pressed firmly against the drywall, it will stop cutting when the jamb is flush with the wall.

Installing Door Trim

The Greek word for the assembly surrounding a door or window is *architrave*, but most folks just call it *trim*. The term *casing* refers specifically to a molding that bridges the gap between a wall and a jamb. Trim may consist of casing only, or it may incorporate additional elements, such as plinth blocks and cabinet heads. I'll discuss simple mitered casing here and we'll look at some fancier types of trim for doors and windows at the end of this chapter.

Mitered door casings

Simple door trim consists of two leg casings and one head casing. Start by square-cutting these pieces to a rough length—7-ft. lengths work perfectly for the legs of standard-height doors (order 7-ft. or 14-ft. lengths for these). Standard colonial casing is about 2¼ in. wide, so to estimate the rough length of a casing head, add 6 in. to the door's width (longer if you're using wider casing).

First, inspect the jamb (or jamb extension) to see if it's flush with the drywall. I do this by running the edge of my speed square around the opening (see photo, p. 203). If the wall sticks out beyond the jamb, you can compensate a little by pulverizing the drywall with a hammer. Draw a

The first piece to be mitered and installed is the head casing.

IN DETAIL

Casing Margins

Most door and window casing is set back slightly from the face of the jamb. On a door, this setback, or *margin*, provides clearance for the hinge barrel and looks neater than setting the casing and jamb flush. The margin is typically ⅛ in. to ¼ in., though a heavy hinge may require an even greater margin.

Experienced carpenters gauge their casing margins by eye. Beginners should scribe a line to guide them. You can use an adjustable square or a pair of *scribers* (a little compass), or make a simple wooden gauge block to scribe the margin.

Adjusting Miters for Jamb Width

A common problem is a jamb that isn't quite wide enough. This causes a gap at the inside corner of the miter, where the casings rotate to make contact with the recessed jamb. You can shave the offending miters with a sharp block plane, though some carpenters use a portable disc sander for fine-tuning miters. My favorite method is to adjust the fit with a chopsaw. Using shims, I simulate the prevailing field condition on the bed of my saw as I make the cut, placing a shim under the thick edge of each casing as I cut it. Now the joint will fit properly.

If the jamb sticks out too far, the long point of the miter will gape open. To solve the problem, slip a shim behind the joint and trim off the excess with a knife.

When the jamb is a little too wide, a gap will show at the outside corner. In that case, shim under the thin edge of each casing as you miter it. Another way to deal with a protruding jamb condition is to shim between the casing and the wall at the outside corner. Pin the corner with a couple of brads, cut off the excess shim with a utility knife, and caulk the gap between the casing and the wall.

A gap at the short point of a miter is usually caused by an inward rotation of the casing. The rotation occurs when the jamb doesn't quite reach to the face of the drywall. To solve the problem, shave the miter with a block plane. Another solution is to undercut the miter by propping up the thick edge of the casing when you miter it.

When marking a leg casing, cut the miter first. Then, stand the casing upside-down and mark it even with the top of the head. This is where the bottom of the casing will be square-cut.

✓ According to Code

Garages are required by code to have ⅝-in.-thick fire-code drywall rather than the standard ½-in. drywall. If you forgot to order a special jamb, you'll have to add a ⅛-in.-thick jamb extension to make the standard jamb flush with the drywall on both sides.

TOOLS AND MATERIALS

Finish Nailers

A pneumatic finish nailer really speeds up trim work, and the nail hole it produces is smaller than the hole left by a hand-driven nail. Finish nailers shoot either 15-gauge or 16-gauge nails, with 15-gauge being slightly larger.

Some nailers have a magazine (nail track) that's oriented perpendicular to the head of the tool. However, I prefer an angled magazine, which lets me reach into tight corners. Another nice feature is a rubber tip that cushions the wood against recoil. Nailers without this feature sometimes leave dents in the work surface.

The angled magazine on this nailer lets the nose reach into tight corners. A rubber tip prevents dents caused by recoil.

> "The underside of the stool can be rabbeted or flat, depending on how it mates with the sill."

pencil line on the wall representing the outside edge of the casing, so that you don't pulverize beyond that point. If the jamb sticks out more than ⅛ in. beyond the drywall, use a block plane to trim it back. By keeping the rear portion of the block plane's sole pressed firmly against the drywall, the blade will stop cutting when the jamb and the wall are flush.

Miter and install the head casing first. If you're right-handed, miter the left side of the head, holding it in place over the door and ticking off the short point of the other miter. Be sure to add the casing *margin* (the setback of the casing from the face of the jamb) when marking the length of the head. Then, cut the second miter and install the head.

One way to measure the casing's leg length is to stand the legs in position and mark the top of

A sharp block plane is effective for adjusting miters.

the head casing, which is the long point of the miter on the leg. It's a little easier, however, to miter the legs before cutting them to length. Then stand them upside-down and mark the top of the head, which is where you will square-cut

Bullnose Metal for a Trimless Look

The revival of adobe-inspired architecture in the western U.S. has led to the development of trimless door and window treatments. When stucco is used on the outside of a house, the edges of the jamb are plowed with a wide groove. A continuous key is formed when the stucco oozes into this groove. For inside work, bullnose metal is slipped into a narrow kerf sawn in the edge of the jamb. Drywall fits under the bullnose metal and joint compound is applied to simulate the look of a door or window opening in an adobe wall.

The jambs used with these methods are called no-mold jambs. They differ from ordinary jambs not just because of their grooved edges, but also because of their width. While conventional jambs span the total wall thickness, no-mold jambs stop flush with the framing on the interior and are flush with the underside of the stucco on the exterior.

Bullnose metal is slipped into a kerf in the edge of a jamb. The metal will be spackled with joint compound for an adobe look.

the bottom of the leg. It's visually easier to cut square through a given point than to miter through a given point.

Nail the outside edge of the casing with 6d finish nails and nail the inside edge with 4d finish nails. Stay back from the ends about 3 in. to avoid splitting. Drive your nails to within ⅛ in. of the surface, and don't set them until everything is aligned—you may have to pull one or two to make an adjustment.

Unless the wall and the jamb are perfectly flush, there's usually some fussing required to make miters fit tightly. For paint-grade work, you can fill up to ¹⁄₁₆-in. gaps with caulk or spackle, though this makes for a muddy-looking joint. Also, caulk shrinks and spackle cracks and eventually falls out. Therefore, it's better to shave the casing with a block plane for a proper fit.

Installing Window Trim

Window trim is basically the same as door trim, except that most windows feature a *stool*. Often this piece is mistakenly referred to as a sill, but that term is more correctly applied to the heavy member that forms the base of the window unit and slopes toward the exterior. Leg casings butt into the top of the stool, while the stool extends beyond the sides of the casing and is supported underneath by an *apron*.

The front edge of a stool usually features a *bullnose* (half-round) profile or an *ogee* (double-curved) profile. The underside of the stool can be

Stool Profiles

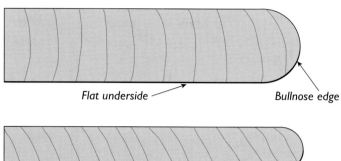

Flat underside — Bullnose edge

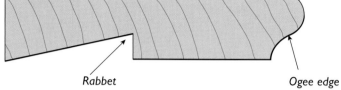

Rabbet — Ogee edge

Window trim

The first trim member to go on a window is the stool. The stool sits on top of the sill, which is the bottom of the window frame. An apron goes under the stool, and leg casings stand on the stool.

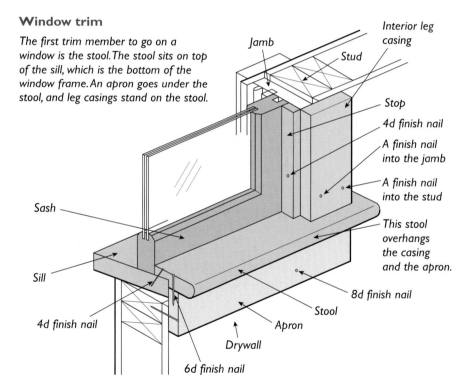

Jamb • Stud • Interior leg casing • Stop • 4d finish nail • A finish nail into the jamb • A finish nail into the stud • This stool overhangs the casing and the apron. • 8d finish nail • Stool • Apron • Sash • Sill • 4d finish nail • Drywall • 6d finish nail

Modern vs. Old-Fashioned Double-Hung Windows

Modern double-hung windows are different than their predecessors in several ways. For one thing, the sashes are thicker to accommodate insulating glass instead of single-pane glass. This reduces the width of the little shelf along the inside of the sill where the stool sits. In addition to being narrower, the little shelf is leveled off in most modern double-hung windows, so a flat stool is used instead of a rabbeted stool. Water that seeps between a modern sill and a flat stool is just as likely to run inside as outside, so apply a bead of caulk under the stool when you install it.

TOOLS AND MATERIALS

Nails for Fastening Stools

I use 4d finish nails for ¾-in.-thick flat stools and 6ds for flat stools made of 5/4 stock. For a rabbeted stool, I use 4ds in the sill and 6ds in the apron.

> "Installing a flat double-hung stool is similar to installing a rabbeted stool, except that the stool's overall width isn't governed by the location of the rabbet."

Trimming a double-hung stool

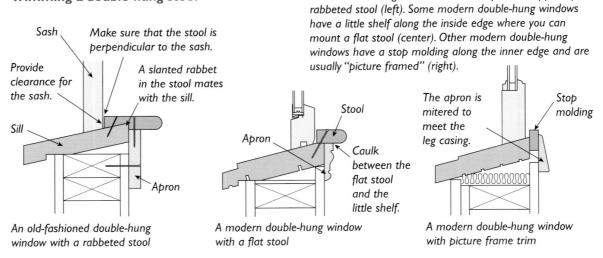

Older double-hung windows have a sloped sill capped by a rabbeted stool (left). Some modern double-hung windows have a little shelf along the inside edge where you can mount a flat stool (center). Other modern double-hung windows have a stop molding along the inner edge and are usually "picture framed" (right).

Sash — Make sure that the stool is perpendicular to the sash.

Provide clearance for the sash.

A slanted rabbet in the stool mates with the sill.

Sill

Apron

An old-fashioned double-hung window with a rabbeted stool

Stool

Apron

Caulk between the flat stool and the little shelf.

A modern double-hung window with a flat stool

The apron is mitered to meet the leg casing.

Stop molding

A modern double-hung window with picture frame trim

rabbeted or *flat,* depending on how it mates with the sill on which the stool is mounted. In general, rabbeted stools are used on old double-hung windows and flat stools are used on casements and newer double-hung windows. The rear edge of a double-hung stool fits against the sash, while the rear edge of a casement stool fits against the interior edge of the sill. When talking about stool installation here, I'm referring to both casements and double-hung windows. See the sidebars for more information on the particularities of each window.

Measuring and cutting the stool

First, determine the stool's overall length and width. The length of the stool is the distance from the outside of one casing to the outside of the other casing, plus an overhang on each end. Since the casings haven't been installed yet at this point, use a scrap of casing stock to mark their eventual location on the drywall. The amount of overhang on the ends of the stool should roughly equal the distance that the front edge of the stool extends past the face of the casing (see drawing, p. 207).

The front-to-back width of the stool is determined by adding the following: 1) The distance from the double-hung sash or casement sill to the plane of the interior wall; 2) the thickness of the apron; and 3) an overhang that's visually pleasing (typically ¾ in. to 1¼ in.). The width of an off-the-shelf stool fits standard windows and walls.

After cutting the stool to length, notch it to fit inside the window opening, leaving *horns* on

A stool is notched to fit within a rough opening. First mark the width of the notch (left), then the depth of the notch (right).

both ends to receive the bottoms of the casing legs. Hold the stool centered in front of the opening and mark sides of the opening. Next, tilt the stool into the opening and mark the face of the wall. Square in from these two marks to lay out the notch, and then cut out the notch with a handsaw or jigsaw.

Installing a stool on a double-hung window

Old-fashioned double-hung windows have a sill whose top is sloped all the way to the inside edge. The stool for this type of window has a slanted rabbet to complement the slant of the sill. Modern double-hung windows have a flat stool instead of a rabbeted stool. In either case, apply a bead of caulk under the stool when you install it to prevent water from seeping inside.

To install a rabbeted stool, measure the width of the little shelf between the lower sash and the inside edge of the sill. Then, rip the stool so that the width of the rabbet equals the width of the shelf. Plane an additional ¹⁄₁₆ in. off the sawn edge. This smoothes the edge and provides clearance between the stool and the sash so the sash can close easily. Finally, notch the ends to create horns.

Installing a flat double-hung stool is similar to installing a rabbeted stool, except that the stool's overall width isn't governed by the location of the rabbet. Instead, find the width of a flat stool by adding the exposed width of the sill, the thickness of the apron, and at least ¾ in. of overhang.

Installing a stool on a casement

Usually, the inside of a casement sill has a square edge, and the back edge of the stool butts into it. If the wall is much deeper than the window unit, a few inches of rough sill is left exposed, so that the stool can be nailed to it. Some packing may be required to elevate the stool to the right height.

On the other hand, if the sill terminates flush with the inside of the wall (or close to it), there won't be a ledge on which to nail the stool. In that case, nail through the edge of the stool into the edge of the sill. Predrill the stool to avoid splitting and to keep the nail from wandering off course. Reinforce the joint with glue, being extra careful to avoid glue squeeze-out if the work will be stained. In some situations, biscuits can be used to attach casement stools.

Trimming a square-edged casement sill

When the width of a casement sill equals the depth of the rough opening (left), the stool is edge-nailed to the sill or subsill. When the rough opening is deeper than the width of the sill (right), the stool is top-nailed to the exposed rough sill.

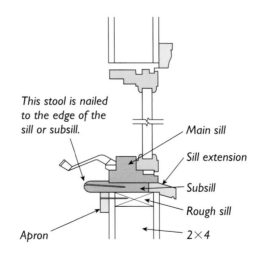

This stool is nailed to the edge of the sill or subsill.

Main sill
Sill extension
Subsill
Rough sill
Apron
2×4

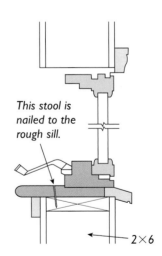

This stool is nailed to the rough sill.

2×6

N DETAIL

Picture Framing

Windows can be trimmed without an overhanging stool, a technique called *picture framing*. The stool is flush with the wall, just like a jamb, and casing runs around all four sides of the opening. Stationary picture windows and accent windows are sometimes trimmed this way, especially when they're located so high that people are unlikely to use the stool for display purposes.

Casing wraps around all four sides of these gable windows for a picture frame look. No stool is used.

TRADE SECRET

A window stool needs to be supported in a level position by the top edge of the apron below. Push the apron tightly against the underside of the stool as you nail it. If you need even more pressure, jam a stick between the floor and the apron, gently tapping the bottom toward the wall to raise the apron into position. Use a piece of scrap wood as a cushion between the stick and the apron to prevent damage.

Push the apron up tight against the stool as you nail it. Otherwise, the stool may eventually sag forward.

"Simple flat casings for a curved window aren't hard to make."

Trimming a grooved-edge sill

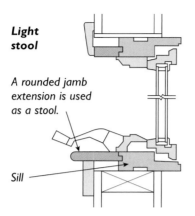

Andersen casements have a grooved-edge sill that can be finished in different ways. A rabbeted jamb extension can be rounded to create a ¾-in.-thick stool (left). Heavier stock can be milled with a tongue to fit the sill's groove (center). A picture frame look is achieved by treating the bottom of the window with casing, just like the sides and top (right).

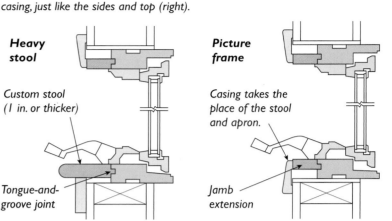

Light stool — A rounded jamb extension is used as a stool. / Sill

Heavy stool — Custom stool (1 in. or thicker) / Tongue-and-groove joint

Picture frame — Casing takes the place of the stool and apron. / Jamb extension

Andersen casement windows have a grooved sill instead of a square-edged sill. To make a stool for this type of window, use a wide piece of Andersen jamb extension, which is carried as a stock item by some lumberyards. The jamb extension is rabbeted to produce a tongue that fits into the groove in the sill. Rip the jamb extension to the width you need and round its edge with a router. Unfortunately, this jamb extension is only ¾ in. thick, which looks a little skimpy for a stool. I prefer to make a custom stool of 5/4 stock, which means I have to rabbet both sides to produce a tongue (see drawing, above).

If the sill isn't as wide as the wall, the stool will need to be notched. Drive a nail through each horn into the jack stud to help keep the stool from tipping downward. The top edge of the apron also keeps the stool level. Space the nails about 10 in. on center.

Cutting an apron

The apron supports the stool both structurally and aesthetically. Aprons are usually made of the same stock as the casing, though a narrow piece may look better. A narrow apron, when combined with the thickness of the stool, approximates the width of the casing to create a balanced look.

The ends of both the stool and the apron are *returned*, meaning they're profiled the same as the front edge. Some carpenters do this by mitering tiny pieces on the ends. I think that's overkill, and cutting small pieces on a power saw can be dangerous. I prefer to form returns directly on the stool with a router, block plane, or sander. Then, use a coping saw to return the ends of the apron. The profile of the apron return cuts should approximate the cross section of the apron itself, though you can deviate quite a bit without spoiling the effect. Just don't chop the ends of the apron at an angle—that looks terrible.

SAFETY FIRST

Cutting small pieces with a power saw is extremely dangerous. If you can't cut a small piece from a larger piece, consider switching to a handsaw.

WHAT CAN GO WRONG

When Short-Grained Casing Breaks

The pointy ends of curved casings are said to be *short-grained*. This means the grain of the wood cuts diagonally across the width of the piece. Short-grained ends break off easily, especially when they're being machined. Make segments for curved casings extra-long, so that you can trim off the broken ends.

Interior finishing for round-top windows

Casings for round-top windows are made specifically for each window—the wider the window, the gentler the curve. Some manufacturers offer interior trim for their windows, but you can also make your own trim. While those with more expertise (and tools) may elect to make molded casings, simple flat casings for a curved window aren't hard to make.

The end of an apron is profiled with a coping saw. The end profile should match the cross section of the apron.

First, establish the inside radius of the window jamb. Add ⅛ in. to find the *inside radius* of the casing, so that the casing will have a slight *reveal,* or setback. Then, add the desired width of the trim to the casing's inside radius to find the *outside radius.* Use a trammel rod to lay out the casing on a sheet of plywood or cardboard.

Divide the entire casing into segments that are narrow enough to be cut from the boards you have available. In general, the larger the window, the greater the number of segments required. I usually divide a half-circle into thirds. Cut out one of the segments with a bandsaw or jigsaw, sand the edges smooth, and use it as a pattern to lay out the rest of the pieces for the casing. As a final touch, you can mold the edges of the casing with a router bit.

Finding the radius of a springline casing

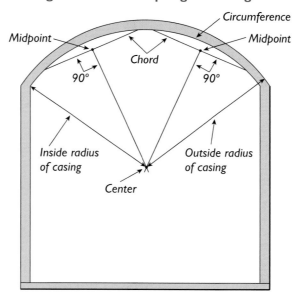

N DETAIL

Geometry for Circular-Curved Windows

o find the radius of a circular curve when its circumference is known, draw two hords, or lines that cut off center across a circle, through the curve. Then, draw nes perpendicular to each chord through the midpoint of the chord. The lines ill cross at the circle's center. This is useful for finding the radius of a springline indow, so that a trammel rod can be made to cut the sheathing and trim.

TRADE SECRET

The practice of specifying a board's thickness by quarters derives from the thickness of the board when it is first sawn at the sawmill. Drying and planing reduces the board to its actual, or *net,* thickness. A nominal 4/4 board is actually ¾ in. thick.

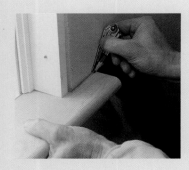

Scribing Stool Horns

Window jambs often protrude slightly past the drywall, which prevents the stool horns from fitting tightly against the wall. The solution is to scribe the horns to the wall. First, measure from the edge of the jamb to the sash or casement sill. In theory, this is the width of the notch in the stool; however, cut the notch ¼ in. less. Hold the stool in position, with an even ¼-in. gap between the stool and the sash or casement sill. Set your scribers to ¼ in. and scribe the back edges of the horns parallel with the drywall. After cutting, the entire stool will slide ¼ in. further into the opening, making a tight joint at the horns and at the sash or casement sill.

> "A nice feature of edge-mounted backband is that it can be scribed to fit a wavy wall surface."

Alternative Trim Styles

While there's nothing wrong with trimming out your doors and windows with standard one-piece casing, there are some fancier alternatives.

Built-Up Mitered Trim

It's not difficult to mill a beaded edge onto a flat board with a router, shaper, or molding cutter-head mounted on a table saw. After mitering and installing the beaded casing, you can then apply a *backband* to its outer perimeter. This can be either a molded backband on the face of the casing or a square backband around the edges. The latter requires a transitional molding bedded between the backband and the casing. A nice feature of edge-mounted backband is that it can be scribed to fit a wavy wall surface.

Cabinet-head trim

This style of trim is well suited to late 19th- and early 20th-century styles, including Victorian, neoclassical, and prairie. It features a wide head-piece supported by square-cut legs. The inspiration for this scheme derives from the columns and entablature of classical Greek architecture.

From the carpenter's point of view, this casing style is convenient because it doesn't have wide miters that require a lot of fussing. There are more pieces involved, of course, but with a chopsaw and nailer, you can move along rapidly. If many of the doors and windows are the same size, you can even mass-produce the pieces beforehand.

Cut and install the legs first, then nail the fillet

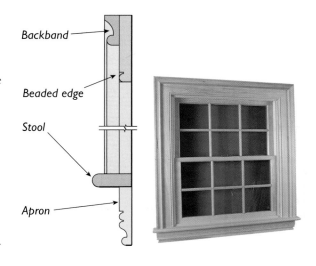

Backband

Beaded edge

Stool

Apron

Built-up mitered trim is a step up from ordinary casing. A mitered flat casing is enhanced with a beaded edge and a backband.

to the tops of the legs. If you can't find fillet molding at your lumberyard, you can make it easily enough with a router. Use a round-over bit with a cutting radius half the thickness of the fillet. The fillet extends past the legs and its ends are returned. You can do this by mitering small pieces at the ends, but it's easier to simply round the end grain of the fillet with a router or a block plane. A stationary sander also works well.

Cut and install the head. Its length is the distance from the outside of one casing to the outside of the other casing. Nail the fillet to the bottom edge of the head and nail a cornice to the top of the head. Sometimes the cornice is plain and sometimes it's wrapped with a mitered *bed molding*. It's a good idea to mock up the head detail initially to make sure you have the correct proportions and the right overhangs on the cornice and fillet.

TRADE SECRET

Smooth the edges of a curved casing after sawing. The best way to produce a graceful curve without any lumps is to use the offcuts from the sawing process as sanding blocks. Save blocks for both the inside and the outside curves. Start with very coarse paper, such as 36 grit, and don't step down to a finer grit paper until all the waviness has been removed from the curve. Waviness is most apparent if you eyeball the casing from one end. Sanding with a block cuts the high spots before the dips, while freehand sanding only smoothes the entire wavy edge.

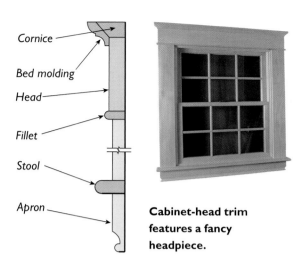

Cornice
Bed molding
Head
Fillet
Stool
Apron

Cabinet-head trim features a fancy headpiece.

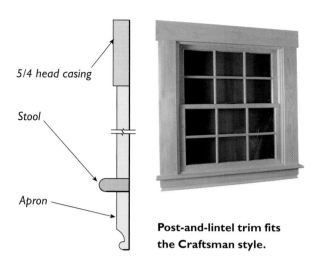

5/4 head casing
Stool
Apron

Post-and-lintel trim fits the Craftsman style.

Post-and-lintel trim

A simplified cousin of cabinet-head trim is *post-and-lintel* trim. It features square-cut legs and a head without a fillet or cornice. Its only ornamentation is a slight projection of the head past the legs. The name *post-and-lintel* derives from its suggestion of heavy timber framing. Because of its no-nonsense personality, post-and-lintel trim is friendly to Craftsman-style bungalows.

Plinth blocks and corner blocks

Old styles of door trim often incorporate *plinth blocks.* These are located at floor level where the baseboard and leg casing intersect. Plinth blocks are typically made of 1⅛-in.-thick 5/4 stock, which allows the plinth to stand proud of the adjoining base and casing. The casings are typically made of ¾-in.-thick 4/4 stock.

Corner blocks are similar to plinth blocks, except they are located at the top of the door

rather than at the bottom. They usually feature a circular routing of some sort, known as a *bull's eye* or *rosette.* The casings used with corner blocks are usually symmetrical in profile, unlike mitered casings, which are usually thicker on the outside than on the inside. Corner blocks can be used on windows, as well.

Plinth blocks are used at the intersection of the door trim and baseboard. The plinth block should be made of heavy stock so it will stand proud of the adjoining trim.

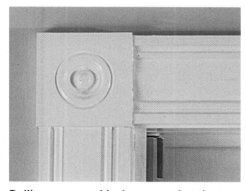

Bull's eye corner blocks are used at the top of a door or window where the leg casings intersect the head casing. Casings used with corner blocks are usually symmetrical in profile.

WHAT CAN GO WRONG

Damage from Trim Nails

Some types of double-hung windows have a balance mechanism housed inside the head jamb. Nails used to fasten the casing to the edges of the jamb may pierce the balance or sash cords if they're too long. Be sure to check the installation instructions. Sometimes, a special decal is attached to the window to indicate where it is safe to nail into the jamb.

IN DETAIL

Casing for Elliptical Windows

To make a flat casing for an elliptical window, tack a piece of plywood against the inside of the window and trace around the inside of the jamb. Cut out the inside curve, then use a compass set to the desired width of trim to draw an outside curve parallel to the inside curve. This requires some trial and error to obtain a *fair* (smooth) curve. After cutting the outside curve, use the plywood as a template to lay out and cut the boards for the casing.

Index